Grace

Michele Guinness

Grace

The Remarkable Life of
Grace Grattan Guinness

HODDER

First published in Great Britain in 2016 by Hodder & Stoughton
An Hachette UK company

This paperback edition first published in 2017

1

Copyright © Michele Guinness, 2016
Photographs © Michele Guinness

A CIP catalogue record for this title is available from the British Library

ISBN 978 1 444 75341 7
eBook ISBN 978 1 444 75340 0

Typeset in Sabon MT by Hewer Text UK Ltd, Edinburgh
Printed and bound in the UK by Clays Ltd, St Ives plc

Hodder & Stoughton policy is to use papers that are natural, renewable
and recyclable products and made from wood grown in sustainable
forests. The logging and manufacturing processes are expected to
conform to the environmental regulations of the country of origin.

Hodder & Stoughton Ltd
Carmelite House
50 Victoria Embankment
London
EC4Y 0DZ

www.hodderfaith.com

For Peter, a partner in every sense for over forty years

Contents

Family Trees   ix

Introduction   1

Prologue   5

PART ONE

The Memoirs 1858–1903   9

1858–65   11

1866–87   20

1887–90   33

1890–93   44

1893–99   50

1899–1903   64

PART TWO

The Letters 1903–10   81

Our Short Courtship   83

Our Long Honeymoon   102

Our Last Years Together   131

PART THREE

The Diaries 1910–63   153

    1910–13   *I Am Alone*   155

    1914–18   *We Are At War*   168

    1919–37   *I Am My Own Woman*   190

    February–April 1939   *My Trip To Egypt*   257

    1939–45   *We Are At War Once More*   272

    1946–54   *My Nomadic And Transitory Life*   303

    1955–63   *The Lady Of Bathampton Manor*   351

Epilogue   379

Notes   381

Acknowledgements   385

The Hurditch Line

Charles Russell Hurditch = Mary Holmes

- Beatrice
- Lillie = Harry Harte
- Percy = Daisy Kopper
- Gertrude = Revd William Evill
- Philip = Hester Bevan
- Ruth = Revd Arthur Fisher

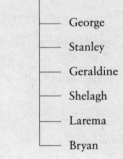

  - George
  - Stanley
  - Geraldine
  - Shelagh
  - Larema
  - Bryan

- Grace = Henry Grattan Guinness DD, FRAC, FRGC

  - John
  - Paul

The Guinness Line (1)

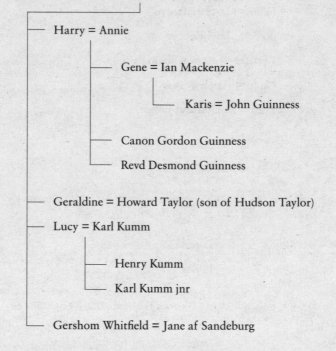

Henry Grattan Guinness = Fanny (d. 1900)

— Harry = Annie

—— Gene = Ian Mackenzie

—— Karis = John Guinness

—— Canon Gordon Guinness

—— Revd Desmond Guinness

— Geraldine = Howard Taylor (son of Hudson Taylor)

— Lucy = Karl Kumm

—— Henry Kumm

—— Karl Kumm jnr

— Gershom Whitfield = Jane af Sandeburg

The Guinness Line (2)

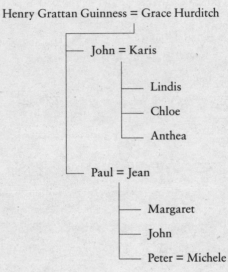

Henry Grattan Guinness = Grace Hurditch

— John = Karis

— Lindis

— Chloe

— Anthea

— Paul = Jean

— Margaret

— John

— Peter = Michele

The Guinness Line (3)

Revd Wyndham Guinness = Dora
(Henry Grattan Guinness' brother)

— Revd Percy Wyndham Guinness (Wyn),
DSO, MC, OBE

— Flora Guinness

Introduction

We were staying with my parents-in-law in the lovely, whitewashed villa on Ibiza, that on their retirement they had had built into a steep hillside high up over San Antonio Bay, commanding some of the most magnificent views on the island. From the dining terrace we looked out over miles of pine forests sweeping down to the sea, which curved and dipped around countless rocky inlets and bays. Over dinner one day my father-in-law happened to say, almost in passing with a dismissive wave of the hand, that a trunk in his study cupboard was 'full of bits and pieces' – poems, letters, the detritus his mother had collected over the years. He wasn't exactly sure what was in there. He had always been more interested in the memorabilia of his famous father, who had died when he was only two years old.

The view across the bay suddenly lost its thrall and I rushed to the top of the house as soon as the meal was over, heaved the large, antique trunk out of the study cupboard and prized it open. I could hardly believe my eyes. It was stuffed to the brim with papers, withered with age. There were letters dating back over a hundred years, in packs tied up with ribbons, newspaper cuttings from as early as 1815, volumes of poetry, postcards, journals, diaries and notebooks – a collection of memories and musings from childhood to old age, as if she knew that one day someone would recognise their importance. Whether she ever thought her story would be written is another matter. And it nearly wasn't.

We took the contents of the trunk home to the UK and stored them in the loft. Sad to say, work and motherhood drove them from my mind, and it was only when I was writing my biography of the

Guinness family* that I dipped into them again, concerned primarily to look for nuggets about Grace's husband, Henry Grattan Guinness – I was struck then by her wit and vivacity, her wry and entertaining comments about her childhood, romance and marriage, and her extraordinary forthrightness for an Edwardian lady. I took a handful of her letters to her sister, Ruth, and wove them into a docudrama for Radio 4, broadcast as *A Wedding of Considerable Interest*, with Joss Ackland taking the part of Henry.

As remiss as my father-in-law, I had still never read the diaries of her later life. Not until we began to clear out our loft in preparation for Peter's retirement did I decide I really ought to read them properly before they were destroyed. I found myself entranced, totally caught up in Grace's life and times.

In many ways she was very ordinary, the seventh child of a comfortable, middle-class Victorian family with maids and a nanny. She made an unusual marriage, had two children, was widowed and went out to work in order to keep them. She was also a well-read social commentator on her times – times that encompassed five monarchs, two world wars, the introduction of motor transport, electricity and the telephone, the discovery of antibiotics and the invention of vaccination. Hers was a life strewn seemingly at random with encounters with famous people.

So in some ways she was also an extraordinary woman, ahead of her time for an Edwardian lady, a rebel against the constraints of her narrow religious upbringing, unconventional in her choice of husband, defiant of a society that frowned on a well-bred single mother going out to work, a businesswoman who ran her own private hotel, and an early feminist who believed in birth control. She worked in fact until she was well beyond the age of seventy, read *The Times* every day and at least one book a week, and could comment in an erudite manner on politics, science, philosophy, theology, music and literature.

* *The Guinness Legend* (first published by Hodder & Stoughton, 1989, republished in paperback in 1990 as *The Guinness Spirit*)

Introduction

This is a fictionalised work, strongly based on fact. The childhood account is hers, as are the letters to Ruth. I also have the letters Henry wrote to her during their honeymoon world tour, but have had to imagine hers to him, and her feelings at their separation at such a time. Her later diaries were filled with reviews and critiques of all she read and then later heard on the wireless, far too many to include. On the other hand, she would go for months, even years, without writing in them. Then again, she went back over her diaries, sometimes years later, adding notes in the margins, at the top, or at the foot of the page. This made the thread of her life hard to follow, so I have had to fill in some of the gaps, using information gleaned from the remaining members of the family, who still remember her vividly. Inevitably, there are some informed guesses, some quantum leaps, some chronological conundrums. The Prologue itself is my fabrication, of course, based on what I know of her last years in Bath – but I rather think she would have liked it.

It has been both a challenge and immensely enjoyable to try to get inside Grace's head and speak with her voice. I was fortunate enough to come across *Grandmother's Tracks* by Margaret Fisher,[*] her recent memoirs of her grandmother, Ruth, who was Grace's gifted, free-spirited sister. The two women were exceptionally close and appear to have encouraged one another in breaking some of the taboos of their generation.

Was Grace as true to herself in her journals and diaries as she might have been? Not always. At times, certainly in the account of her childhood, she is writing for the public. She remembered only too well the stir caused by the huge bestseller and now classic *Father and Son*,[†] a rather vindictive critique of a rigid evangelical childhood. Grace loved her family enough to want to avoid subjecting them to that kind of censure and disparagement. Equally she is wonderfully tongue-in-cheek at times.

[*] Lulu.com, 2010
[†] Edmund Gosse Heinemann, 1907

In her private letters, however, particularly those that describe her love for Henry, she is extraordinarily frank, almost risqué for a young woman of her time, determined that there should be no doubt about her enjoyment of their full marital relationship. Later, on their extraordinarily extended honeymoon, alone and in a strange environment with a new baby, it is abundantly clear that she didn't find the loneliness easy when she was without Henry. But her awe at her own privileged position, as she saw it, and her pride at being married to such a man, prevented her from being as honest about her difficulties as she might have been. Money was manifestly an object of worry, but we have to read between the lines to get a full sense of this. On these occasions I have tried to put myself into her shoes, to express the thoughts that may not have gone into her letters to Henry.

As she grows older, though her diaries are never less than honest and she never minces her words – especially in her letters to the press and public bodies – she is nonetheless more reluctant to put her emotions on show, and I have had to make an educated guess at times as to what she truly felt or thought. Out of respect for Grace and her family, some things must remain hidden, because that is what she would have wanted. But this in no way detracts from the story of a life that was in many ways unpretentious and unnoticed, yet unique in the setting of the age in which it was lived.

Prologue

1963

I always wanted to be the lady of the manor, and now, finally, I am. So – welcome to my stately home. Let me show you around Bathampton Manor, a rather lovely Grade II-listed country house, once in the ownership of Ralph Allen, to whom the inhabitants of Bath are indebted for the promotion of its local stone and for many of its finer buildings, not to mention the reforms he brought to our beloved postal service.

The manor is set in a beautiful countryside position, close to the Kennet and Avon Canal, St Nicholas Church and several local hostelries, although I tend not to frequent those. A sheltered patio has been added to one side of the house and a large sunny Garden Room on the other, but in general care has been taken to preserve many original features. My particular preference is the grand hall-cum-library, with its lovely colonnades, floor-to-ceiling bookshelves and comfortable leather settees arranged around a roaring fire – the epitome of congenial grace, elegance and style. This is the restrained opulence to which I have always aspired, I reflect contentedly, as I sit here in the morning, *The Times* on my lap, to be perused as and when it takes my fancy. My glasses and a lace handkerchief are in the handbag that hangs over the back of my armchair. I never go anywhere without my beloved handbag – a relic from the last war. It held my gas mask. 'Waste not, want not,' my mother always said. It is a rather intriguing accessory, and people do stare. It is polished until I can almost see my reflection in its shiny, soft brown surface that feels like satin beneath my fingertips, and it still gives off that satisfying leather smell.

My bedroom is at the top of the house, looking out over the long gravel drive and carefully maintained, landscaped gardens with their ancient choice trees, providing a benevolent, swaying shelter for the walkways, interspersed with benches that provide a rest for my tired old bones when I galvanise myself into a brisk constitutional. I never tire of looking out, and I can time my watch by the fast steam train from Bristol to London which flashes past in miniature on the far side of the estate, against a backdrop of the distant, damp and misty hills. A cat's cradle of electric cables somewhat obscures the view, which is rather annoying. I commented on it to my daughter-in-law, Jean: 'Those nylons are an absolute pain.' She found this hilariously funny. 'I think you mean pylons, Mother,' she said sweetly. The correct words escape me all the time these days. Whatever the word, I suppose we can't put a halt to progress.

My clothes, believe it or not – and I for one do find it hard to believe – fit into one large wardrobe, but then I rarely entertain these days, and one rather chic little black number for musical evenings suffices for my needs. On top of this useful wardrobe I keep a box labelled 'Brown Paper', full of bundles of brown paper tied up with string, as remembering the birthdays of my children and grandchildren with suitable presents is one of my biggest responsibilities. (If you think me abstemious, one of my neighbours keeps a box on top of her wardrobe labelled 'Useful Pieces of String', which are basically too small to be of any use at all.)

My hair is still long, past my shoulders, and pure white. Every morning one of the maids brushes it until it stands out from my head with what they call 'the static' (probably caused by those dratted pylons), then they twirl it and pile it onto my head in the top knot I have always worn. I think they would rather like me to have it cut because the little wisps refuse all their attempts at pinning, and by the end of the day there is more hair out of the bun than in it. But Henry always said my hair was my crowning glory, so I will keep it as he liked it. I prefer blouses with ruffles around the neck – mine is unattractively scraggy these days – so that I can always wear the beautiful cameo he gave me. The staff are faultless, perfectly trained, but of course, as far as they are concerned, I am simply a rather dotty elderly lady who was never young and never really had a life – I just appeared one day from nowhere, exactly as I am now.

But oh, I had a life, and what a life! So, although the staff claim not to be terribly interested in what they refer to as 'the olden days', on a quiet afternoon when there is little to stave off their restless yawns, one of them might urge me to share my memories. 'Mrs Guinness, how does that poem go again, the one your husband wrote to you on your engagement, about death never parting true lovers? It's so romantic.'

I need no encouragement. They gather around my chair, sit or stand open-mouthed and listen silently as I recite Henry's poems and tell the story of an extraordinary passion between a young woman and a man old enough to be her grandfather – from the moment I was moved to sit on his knee, to his last breath some seven years later. 'The secret,' I say, 'is not to resent the fact that love was found so late, but to be thankful it was found at all. And such a love! Enough to last a lifetime. But once experienced, hard, so very hard, to live without.' And the tears threaten again, always so near the surface, even now, over fifty years later. 'You should write about it,' they say. 'It would make a wonderful book.'

I have written about it all, about my incredibly rich little life: so many precious memories committed to diaries, letters and journals, and stored in a large, wooden public-school-style trunk under my bed. Perhaps one or other of my dear children or grandchildren may find them an interesting record – of a rarefied childhood in old Queen Victoria's reign, of a surprising marriage to a major celebrity from a prestigious family who swept me up into his worldwide travels, of a young widow left with two young children to support at a time when there were so few working opportunities available to women, of two cataclysmic world wars in which I played a not insignificant part, of a lonely bedsit existence, and now, at last, in these so-called 'swinging sixties', promotion from impecunious companion to lady of the manor at last.

On the other hand, upon my demise all these scribbles and paraphernalia may simply be consigned to the dustbin. If so, what does it matter? It is not the record of the times, but the living of the life that counts. And that is all we bequeath to the next generations.

Part One

The Memoirs 1858–1903

1858–65

My parents were born in the great religious revival of 1858. In point of fact this was their Second Birth, but it was of such unparalleled importance in their lives that their actual birthdays, by comparison, were of no significance, and we children might have been forgiven for imagining that they had simply leapt into existence, fully adult, in that fervid moment, had it not been for the list of dates in the family Bible and the small collection of miniatures and daguerreotypes scattered over the walls of our home. As I study my ancestors now, I wonder how far our history influences what we become. Was it perhaps the Huguenot strain in my father's blood that inclined him towards the extremer forms of Protestant belief? Or was it simply in his nature?

This religious revival, like a number of enthusiasms before and since, had its origins in America. Thence it swept through Ireland, England, Wales and Scotland, until around 1862 it was continually blazing into life, turning every town it touched upside down. Theatres, music and concert halls, any buildings capable of seating an audience, were daily filled with people, some of them waiting from early morning to get places at an evening service. No echelon of society escaped the infection. From Almack's social club that met in Willis's rooms in St James's, to the West End drawing rooms where the upper classes met to see and be seen, all were soon buzzing with concern about the eternal welfare of souls. 'Gospel field days' were held at country seats; factories hushed their machines while the workers gave themselves to prayer. Clergy and ministers barely had the stamina to cope with the demand of the people, or with services lasting from three to four hours, often ending in harrowing scenes – men and women

falling to the floor groaning under conviction of their wrongdo-
ing, then shouting with praise as they proclaimed themselves
delivered from the bondage of Satan. Market places were thronged
with eager crowds hanging onto every word of such famous revivalist preachers as Charles Haddon Spurgeon, William Booth of
the Salvation Army and his wife, Catherine, and the firm favourite – a handsome, long-haired youth called Henry Grattan
Guinness who distinguished himself by preaching abstinence on
the steps of his grandfather's Dublin brewery, and brought out
thousands in Ireland, including the local elite of judges, MPs,
university professors and even the Lord Lieutenant, to hear him.
According to the newspapers, each announcement that he was to
preach put the entire population on the move. In Aberdare, an
audience of ten thousand responded to his invitation to come
forward in repentance, mobbing the platform, which collapsed
under the pressure. Guinness himself was dragged to safety with
a minor leg injury, to the relief of my parents, who were much
disconcerted by the near loss of this brightest star in their
firmament.

As I study the social history of the time, conditions, it seems,
were singularly favourable to such a movement. Europe was a
political cauldron, seething and bubbling with uncertainty. The
ambitions of Imperial Russia hung like a dark and brooding
cloud on the horizon, while all the energies and resources of the
British Empire were sorely tried. The philosophies of the day
were sceptical and materialistic and had nothing to offer a
depressed world. The church seemed half-paralysed by the shock
of its first encounter with modern science. Only here and there
was an individual such as William Wilberforce or Lord
Shaftesbury stirred to protest against the evils of sweated labour,
ignorance, dirt and slums. And such men found themselves
nearly powerless against the inertia of indifference. Something
explosive seemed necessary to divert the thoughts of the middle
classes from their growing prosperity and complacent accumu-
lation of wealth.

And it came – and was so much more than merely the enjoyment of stirring preaching. Keen young men and women started night schools where working people were taught to read and write, where factory girls learned to sew and cook; street urchins and hooligans were gathered into clubs where they were given instruction in trades and hobbies. All this ten years before the first Education Act, with its technical schools and evening classes.

The work of the revivalists was not without opposition from certain pillars of the established church. The intrusion of laymen into church services was bitterly resented by some, as were the clergy who dared to preach in 'unconsecrated' buildings like music halls or, heaven forbid, public houses. Women (the daring of it!) began to follow the lead of Catherine Booth and the American Phoebe Palmer and preach at revival meetings – though not without long heart-searching and much anguished prayer about its propriety. There was an outcry against such licence, of course, amid quotations from the Fathers and St Paul. But the broader-minded soon came to see that resistance to such compelling sincerity was in vain.

In the middle of these exciting events, my father, Charles Hurditch, aged twenty and newly reborn, came to London from his home in Devonshire, where he had trained as a perfumer, and plunged instead into a flood tide of spiritual endeavour. He became involved in the services at the Stafford Rooms off the Edgware Road, one of the centres of the newly formed YMCA,* and such were his gifts as a speaker that he soon received invitations to become a candidate for the ministry from the Wesleyans, the Primitive Methodists and a small society of evangelical churches known as the Countess of Huntingdon's Connexion. But the truth is, he was a born freelance. No one denomination could have held him for long. Instead, he accepted the secretaryship of the Stafford Rooms, which gave him the freedom and contacts he needed for the evangelistic work he felt called to do.

* Young Men's Christian Association

Charles Hurditch

It also gained him an introduction to fifteen-year-old Mary, daughter of a well-known professional cricketer, William Holmes, who assisted my father at his meetings. How often Charles and Mary saw each other over the next three and a half years is not known, nor under what constraints and with what secret hopes, longings and fears their passion grew. But in 1864 he finally wrote to her, saying:

> *After patiently waiting for guidance, I have arrived at the conclusion that I ought at no distant period marry. But I feel I want a helpmeet in the work whereunto my dear Lord has called me, not for my sake alone, but also for the sake of Christ and precious souls. Now, having carefully observed your character and deportment for some time, I am induced to place before you the following enquiries, and to ask your careful consideration of them and your frank judgment:*

> *1. Can you entertain for me sufficient affection as to lead to your consent to become my wife?*
>
> *2. Do you long to become a soul-winner for Jesus?*
>
> *3. Could you share the afflictions of one who may be called to suffer for Christ's sake?*
>
> *If your answer is yes to each of the above, what shall hinder our entering upon an engagement to that end?*

What young woman could refuse such a romantic proposal? My poor, dear father – so deeply spiritual on the face of it, but the record in his journal tells a rather different story. He delivered the letter, then went back to his rooms where he could pace the floor in private:

> I must be calm and prepared to receive either 'yea' or 'nay'. At last I fall soundly asleep, in perfect peace. Until morning dawns. It is noon before a note, the note, is finally placed in my pocket. I hastily conclude the meeting then hasten to my private rooms in Tichborne Street. Another moment finds me with the unsealed letter. 'My dear Mr ... I ...' Enough! Enough! And thus the most anxious and most peaceful week of my life passed away after witnessing tears of affection and prayers breathed from my very inmost soul for a united eternity of bliss.

They were married at Marylebone Parish Church on May 11th, 1865, but there was no honeymoon. Nothing was allowed to interrupt my father's work. In fact, life continued just as it had before, except that Mary moved into 164 Alexandra Road, St John's Wood, just a few doors down from her father. She was only nineteen when she bore her first child, my eldest sister, Beatrice.

It was one of my father's most fervent beliefs that the whole of life could be, and ought to be, maintained by faith alone. Faith, he thought, was not only capable of removing mountains, but also of supplying the smallest material necessities for every day, and on that principle he eventually brought into being seven children and a vast organisation of religious and philanthropic work. My mother, fortunately, shared this belief with him, and although it is a consolation to think that her private income was at least sufficient to cover their household expenses, the result of his eager philanthropies meant the turning of her life into one continuous act of self-denial, while the strain on my father's health would ultimately cost him his life.

*

By the time of his marriage my father was in fact no longer a communicant member of the Church of England, and would rather have married in his new spiritual home, the Plymouth Brethren, were they not seen as a sect and denied a licence for weddings. 'The Peebs', as they were referred to, were a group of religious reactionaries who broke away from the established church because they felt it had become as immersed in rites, ceremonies and formalism as rigid as the Pharisaism Christ deplored. They denounced the inconsistency of a Christian continually calling himself a miserable sinner and in need of a priest's absolution. 'We are saints,' they asserted, 'saved by grace . . . holy and unblamable.' (But woe betide a brother who fell from that grace and was found to be a miserable sinner after all!)

The Peebs were sometimes referred to as 'The Peculiar People', based on a verse in the New Testament, 'But ye are a chosen generation, a royal priesthood, an holy nation, a peculiar people . . .' The word 'peculiar' did not then have the connotation of oddity it acquired in later years – but turned out to be strangely apt nonetheless.

By the time my father joined them, their own camp was already divided into opposing forces of Exclusive and Open Brethren, depending on how rigidly they expected their followers to adhere to their doctrine of separation from 'the world'. But there were many subdivisions even within the two groupings, under the influence of men whose sole qualification for leadership seemed to me to be an indebtedness to the principle of the survival of the fittest.[1]

Having been born into Brethrenism, it is of some consolation to me to recall that our lot was cast among the Open variety, though exactly how apposite that term was in reality is difficult to gauge. My father was often censured for inviting evangelical Anglican clergymen and other ordained ministers who were not regarded as sufficiently 'sound' in their theology to co-operate in his work and preach at his mission halls and conferences. Some said, 'Our dear Brother is going off the lines.' His platform was decried as becoming 'broad enough to accommodate an apostate'.

And so he resigned the secretaryship of the Stafford Rooms, a position which had become too narrowly confined for his liking, and started on his independent philanthropic and evangelistic work, gathering around himself a large band of loyal and dedicated workers, both rich and poor. In addition to building or purchasing halls across London, in the provinces and in some of the coastal towns, he regularly rented St James's Piccadilly, the Oxford, Metropolitan and Marylebone music halls, and the Hammersmith 'Temple of Varieties'. He even contemplated purchasing St George's Hall on Regent Street as a strategic centre for 'making a distinct attack on the kingdom of Satan in London', but was advised that renting it for this purpose might be more prudent.

Meanwhile, Henry Grattan Guinness had opened Harley College in Bow – the first so-called 'faith' Bible Training Institute. Here eager young men with a calling to follow missionaries such as C.T. Studd to Africa or Hudson Taylor to China could train at minimal charge. Unable to afford the fees of the established, academic theological institutions, they depended entirely on God and the Guinnesses to put food on their plates and a shelter over their heads. Such was the demand for places that a generous benefactor also gave Henry a property in Derbyshire that became Cliff College, where the syllabus included the rudiments of subsistence farming – vital for any would-be missionary.

My father approached Guinness with a view to providing the students with practical preaching experience during the summer months, and this was the start of a happy collaboration between the two men. Groups of twos and threes, equipped either with a special 'Bible carriage' or just a tent, were sent to preach in the market places and on village greens. With their own hands they built permanent mission halls in those villages deemed to be 'hotbeds of ritualism' – often to the dismay of the local vicar, whom they regarded as the demon of ritualism himself, but who in many instances was too advanced in years to put up much of a fight against such overwhelming odds.

Editorial work occupied most of my father's night hours. He published in succession five magazines, changing their character and style according to the needs of the day. Thirteen million tracts were issued from his office in sixteen years – he was the editor of them all. He compiled two hymn books and was himself the composer of thirty of the hymns – these reached a circulation of over half a million.

Unemployment was as acute then as it has ever been and he could never see want and suffering without making some effort to alleviate it. The immediate needs of starving families would be met by the opening of soup kitchens and the distribution of coal and food tickets. He would try to find employment for the men, if not in connection with his own properties, then by enlisting the help of large building contractors and others. I can remember one terrible winter when misery and poverty abounded and woeful, hungry-looking men roamed the streets, their only meal of the day the midnight suppers of roast meats and pickles, bread and butter, cakes and fruit that my father provided not only for them, but for busmen, cabmen, postmen, policemen and lamplighters – any one of the 'poor souls' out on the streets in those unsociable hours.

No challenge ever appeared to faze him. 'Launch out into the deep' was one of his favourite mottos, which not infrequently launched him out of his depth!

'There is a danger of running in front of the Lord,' his most generous patron, Lord Radstock, once wrote to him. 'I believe it is not faith but presumption when we undertake to spend what the Lord has not given us.' But characteristically, his wealthy aristocratic friend gave him £100 and saved the day all the same.

Into this life and circle seething with religious activities, we seven children were thrown, sinners by nature and therefore kicking against the restrictions of the religious world in which we lived.

Bee, the eldest, born in 1866, loving and amenable when the mood took her, but given to a wilfulness that in my parents' eldest child was a source of great surprise and concern to them; Lillie, a year younger, more biddable, but inclined to be a crosspatch, ever in Bee's shadow and resentful of it; then came Percy, with the boundless energy of a puppy dog, a source of constant entertainment and amusement, the instigator of our pranks and inheritor of our maternal grandfather's flair for cricket; followed by Gertrude, sweet-natured and pretty with her golden ringlets, the family pet, which disposed her to vanity and the taking for granted of opportunities denied the rest of us. We youngest three were close companions – Phil, born in 1873, was a frail child, inclined to pick up every infection and left with a heart weakness after diptheria, yet characterised by a cheery nature that carried him over the rocky shoals on which many a barque might have foundered; and Ruth, only a year older than I, had a brain that filled that high forehead of hers and more than made up for her lack of looks, wise beyond her years. We all, even the older ones, looked to Ruth for the final say on any enigma.

I was the youngest, born on December 2nd, 1876, the year in which Alexander Graham Bell made the first ever telephone call. Queen Victoria had been on the throne for six months short of forty years, a widow for the past fifteen of them; and my husband-to-be was in his forty-second year.

Of our father we saw little and knew less; his time and energy were wholly given to religious and social work – work in which my mother shared so far as she was able to combine it with her duty to the consequences of perpetual child-bearing. But their lives and letters testify to their devoted love for us. My father never left home without carrying in the pocket of his tailcoat a concertina-like morocco-leather case containing our portraits.

The most vivid personality of my childhood memories is that of our old nanny, Nurse Tye, who devoted her entire life to our service. We came after only the dear Queen (and her own offspring) in her affections. A large coloured print of the royal family adorned our nursery walls; there must have been at least forty persons in that group, and our nanny knew the intimate history of each and every one.

But for her, indeed, our family might have lost one of its own. It happened in the summertime, when my father's heart was stirred with pity for the children of the slums, whom he would send in their hundreds in two-horse brakes for a day in the country. We usually accompanied them on these expeditions, though our nurse did not entirely approve of my parents' democratic ways and would contrive to keep us apart under pretext of the fear of infection.

It was on one such occasion, at Bushy Park, when we were picnicking under the shade of the chestnut trees, that my sister Ruth, aged five, wandered off to gather wild flowers and was snatched up by passing gypsies, smuggled into their caravan – and away they went.

Our nurse, startled by the screams of a child, at once noticed that one of her flock was missing. She saw the retreating cavalcade and realised what had happened. Seizing her large umbrella, she gave chase and, empowered with the superhuman strength that comes in moments of acute danger, hit out to right and left, fought her way into the retreating caravan, grabbed the child and returned to the terrified little group under the trees, where she collapsed in a fit of violent hysteria.

In spite of her outstanding heroism, however, I still have a resentment of the foolish terrors she implanted in us – namely of cows, policemen and the devil. She once inflicted a totally unmerited punishment on me that involved sitting on a chair in the corner of the nursery over a mouse hole. We had been taught to pray over the most insignificant happenings in our lives, so I put up a fervent petition that the mice might be kept below so long as my punishment lasted. Their non-appearance considerably strengthened my faith, and may have prevented a lifelong mouse complex.

I sometimes wonder, when I read modern psychologists on the repressions and inhibitions from which we Victorians are supposed to suffer, whether their perception of us is entirely true. I think of those nursery days – the clash of temperaments, the salutary though sometimes heartless correction of personal idiosyncrasies, the outspoken criticisms, the give and take and smash and grab, the intimate confidences and loyalties that have stood the test of a lifetime – and I don't think they did us any serious harm. It is true that some unwholesome ideas were disseminated which took years to eradicate, and perhaps there was too much insistence on unquestioning obedience, but we seven survived relatively sound in mind, redeemed in no small way by those unregenerate propensities of ours.

One criticism may certainly be made of our Victorian nanny: her inviolable rule was that we ate everything that was set before us. My special antipathy was to macaroni, and this led to a serious nursery revolt. We knew on which day of the week this milky pudding would arrive, and laid our plans accordingly. At a given signal from my eldest brother Percy, we rushed from the table armed with spoons and forks, and launched an attack on the under-nurse as she entered with the loathsome dish. Its contents were flung in all directions and shouts of delight greeted my brother's achievement in making the glutinous matter adhere to the ceiling.

I must tell of another outrage we perpetrated one Boat Race Day. We had unanimously voted that year in favour of the

Cambridge Light Blues, for the wholly illogical reason that our father was antagonistic to the Oxford Tractarian Movement, it being too 'Roman' for his liking. This resulted in zealous persecution of our under-nurse, whose High Church proclivities led her to back the Dark Blues. She wore what, building on our precocious apocalyptic knowledge, we thought of as 'The Mark of the Beast' in the form of a badge in her mob cap, which we forcefully removed by means of a broom that we successfully manipulated from our vantage point on the landing as she ascended the stairs.

My mother's arrival on the scene was the occasion for this maid to give one month's notice. It is regrettable that the visits of our beautiful mother to the nursery should be associated in my mind with the painful consequences that followed these outbreaks of original sin in us. Though I think on this occasion we were animated by inquisitional zeal and sadly misjudged.

*

Sambo – a remnant of pre-Wilberforce days, and a convert of one of our missions – looms large in my childhood memories. His black face had no terrors for us children, for it was overspread with a beaming smile and enhanced by gleaming white teeth. He would clean our nursery windows to the accompaniment of Negro spirituals sung in a rich melodious voice that held us spellbound and brought tears to Nanny's eyes. Then he would edge up to her and slip an arm round her waist: 'Dawn't you cry, Honey . . . promise you'll marry me someday.' At which point she'd give him a slap and send him packing.

When the time came for us to go on our summer holidays to my father's family home in Devonshire, Sambo, with beads of perspiration dropping from his face, would swing aloft the luggage onto the roof of the two-horse omnibus that was to take us to Paddington Station. The dome-shaped linen basket with its black oilcloth cover – almost as big as a bathing machine – would fall with a thunderous noise onto the roof, followed by the luncheon baskets, the bath, the perambulator and innumerable trunks whose contents had occupied our mother, nurse and sewing maid for many weeks: bathing dresses made of heavy naval serge (which enveloped us from the neck to the ankles), decorated with three tiers of white flannel braid, sailor suits and fishermen's jerseys, cotton socks and sun bonnets.

We travelled by Pullman car in 'The Flying Dutchman' to Barnstaple, where the railway ended and a four-horse coach was waiting to take us to Ilfracombe. As we drove through the villages, the guard raised his long brass trumpet and gave a thrilling blast that we referred to as 'the Last Trumpet', and brought children running out from the lanes and meadows; mothers came to the doors of the cream-washed cottages and old men waved their caps in welcome.

*

Before leaving our nursery days, I must give a brief description of my maternal grandfather, the former professional cricketer, for he was uniquely peculiar, even in our circle of peculiar people. He is associated in my mind with but two great passions: reading the Bible, and watching cricket from the grandstand at Lords. We children would often accompany him to Lords, and his eccentric behaviour would mark him out for observation – not infrequently to our embarrassment. With astonishing facility he could pass from the most technical discussion of the play of the great W.G. Grace into complete abstraction and communion with his Lord. Whether between cricket overs or at the tea interval, or equally when travelling in trains and omnibuses, his lips would be seen moving in prayer, and when he opened his eyes to meet, perhaps, the questioning gaze of those whose attention he had so unwittingly drawn to himself, he would explain that he had been enjoying 'precious crumbs from the Lord'. Any sympathetic response on the part of the public would only encourage further confidences, and on one occasion he told an omnibus full of passengers that he had 'twenty-five grandchildren – all on the Lord's side', whereupon a gentleman enquired of his neighbour, 'What Bill is before the House of Lords that the old man's grandchildren are backing?'

Grandfather Holmes would spend hours writing long addresses in preparation for his Sunday morning ministrations to the saints in his own, or our, local Brethren Assembly, and he contributed Bible outlines to my father's periodicals. These would be set out as mathematical formulae, and the number seven was given as the key to unlocking their mysteries. It may sound strange, and my older siblings certainly found it amusing, but in later years that number would turn out to have a profound significance for me.

Saturday afternoons were reserved for long walks with my grandfather and he would take us to a little shop that bordered on Fortune Green. Corn bins and trusses of hay covered most of the floor space, but on the shelves were rows of glass jars filled with eight-a-penny sugar balls in most attractive colours. At the sound of our voices, a rotund old lady in mob cap and white apron over a black alpaca dress would waddle in from a back parlour and lift down the jars – tipping in an extra ball – and away we went with bulging cheeks, through the buttercup fields, past the old farmhouse and a herd of cows and on to the Hampstead ponds, where our retriever, or collie, or St Bernard – whichever we might have at the time – would plunge in for the sticks we had gathered from under the elm and oak trees that adorned the countryside around the Hampstead of our childhood days.

How we loved Christmas Day in their home – happily exempt from the Brethren's usual ban on all 'worldly frivolities', because for some reason it wasn't regarded as a 'religious' festival and therefore its celebrations escaped being labelled pagan or popish as they otherwise might. I remember the towering Christmas tree, dripping with tin-foil balls, the crackling log fires, the table elegantly decorated with shining silver and cut glass, the sumptuous fare, the decanters of red and golden 'wines' – of which we were only permitted the orange variety – and the somewhat lugubrious speeches of the uncles, which had a lachrymose effect on the aunts and reacted on the excited nerves (or overloaded stomachs) of some of the grandchildren, who would be led howling from the room by their respective nurses. Then the silence of the afternoon rest, followed by hilarious games, when slippers were concealed beneath the frills of lace petticoats, or snatched from under velveteen knickerbockers. Some person unknown would appear as Father Christmas and distribute the presents, and when at last the tree stood stark and grim in its nudity, my maiden aunt would go to the piano and, with a loud pedal heavily pressed, would roll out a sequence of rippling chords – waltzes, polkas and mazurkas – and to our surprise and delight our grandparents would lead off in a cotillion, 'just to show the young people how we danced in the good old days'.

And my father would slip away with his pockets full of newly minted shillings, carrying a large Gladstone bag bulging with fruit and sweets. He would call on poor old lonely people and visit an orphanage or two in the neighbourhood, where his coming would be hailed with delight.

*

Among other social enjoyments of those days were the Bank Holiday conferences. Their success was, I think, in no small measure due to the fact that they offered a solution to the problem – potentially perplexing for the gentleman's family in non-motoring times – as to how to employ the day. They were traditionally recognised as the servants' fiesta, with the family remaining at home feeling smugly virtuous for allowing their entire domestic staff to be off duty, save a few old retainers long past the enjoyment of merry-go-rounds, Aunt Sallies and coconut shies.

This was all changed in Brethren circles. Houses were closed down while the entire family, including the servants – some of whom, I doubt not, sighed for the lost pleasures of Egypt – would repair to the meeting places, which had laid on their own rather holier delights. One such, established by my father, played host to over a thousand people.

Looking back I cannot honestly say I can give any account of their spiritual portent. To me they assumed the character of a delightful indoor picnic with miles of tables covered in unbleached linen cloths adorned with pink spirea, endless rows of pink-bordered Delft teacups and saucers on which were inscribed the words 'Jesus Only' in a circle of pink. There were plates piled high with bread and butter and penny buns, the buttering of which had occupied all the morning hours of my mother and other sainted women. There was the high table, at which we were privileged to sit with the speakers – who on platform heights above us had seemed such awesome persons, but who were now benevolence and fun personified.

I was fascinated by an eyeglass that continually jumped from its precarious holding in the twinkling eye of General Sir Robert Phayre, and the long pointed nanny-goat beard of Dr McKilliam, that waggled as he ate and talked. I would watch the ferret-like eyes of a notorious gaol-bird whom the revival had transformed into a popular preacher – which sparkled with humour or glinted with steel as he regaled us with stories of his prison life – and I would wait for the loud click that followed the opening and shutting of his large mouth, accompanied by the hissing sound of indrawn breath between clenched teeth.

There was also a burly American evangelist – or rather, I think perhaps he was an itinerant Englishman who had imported the American accent – whom I remember introducing, in a voice calculated to raise the dead, the hymn, 'Oh for a Thousand Tongues to Sing my Great Redeemer's Praise', and I wondered what he would have looked like if his wish had been granted. Lord Congleton was there – a long, lean, graceful-figured man with a face of popular melancholy who, to judge from his correspondence with my father, was arbiter-in-chief in the Brethren's quarrels; the Earl of Shaftesbury, who had pondered on the cruelties inflicted on the little boys who were made to climb and clean

London's foul chimneys, and from which, by his offices in Parliament, he managed to get them all released; Sir Robert Anderson of Scotland Yard, who knocked down his biblical opponents like ninepins; and the aesthetic-looking young Campbell-Morgan, with high cheekbones and an abnormally high forehead, from which long hair was thrown back, who appeared at conference with a red rose in his buttonhole. This was considered worldly by the Brethren and my father had it blocked out when reproducing his photograph, thereby incurring his displeasure. Of this young preacher my father prophesied great things. And he was not mistaken. Years later I stood in a queue of hundreds in Westminster waiting to hear him preach. I noticed that the touch of colour, so dear to him in his youth, had now been replaced by the scarlet of a DD* hood.

The May Bank Holiday conference was always held at the new Mildmay Conference Hall, built by the late Revd William Pennefather, vicar of St Jude's, Mildmay Park in Islington. Hortatory addresses were given, if fine, under the enormous, ancient mulberry tree standing in lovely grounds, where deaconesses in trailing grey dresses and white lawn caps glided among the guests and friends, or served strawberry cream teas in the marquees. If the weather was inclement we children joined the masses pushing their way into an auditorium so vast it left us wide-eyed and overawed.

As well as having the largest auditorium in the area, the Mildmay Mission, dedicated to enabling the local populace to find gainful employment, provided a men's and women's night school, sewing classes for widows, a lads' institute, a servants' training home, and a newly built, large modern hospital of fifty beds, all run by their 'deaconesses', the first female ministers and nurses in the country and the protégées of William Pennefather's wife, Catherine. Young women of 'consistent Christian character, with a reasonable education' were taught cookery, sewing,

* Doctor of Divinity

housekeeping, book-keeping, biblical knowledge, singing, and nursing care. The Mildmay deaconesses had had a formative influence on Florence Nightingale, the 'Lady with the Lamp' herself, whose nurses were now matrons at many of the London hospitals. Even so, preaching and caring for undesirables were not considered suitable occupations for young ladies and earned the deaconesses a great deal of scorn. I admired them enormously, and entertained dreams of joining them – dreams which I kept to myself, as I wasn't sure my parents' zeal would stretch that far.

Nonetheless, to my father, Anglican or not, the Pennefathers were paragons of missionary-minded endeavour, and he had been suitably flattered to receive an invitation to join them, and William and Catherine Booth, Dr Tom Barnado, Henry and Fanny Guinness, and other church leaders committed to alleviating the miseries of the poverty-stricken East End, at the Earl of Shaftesbury's famous monthly 'tea parties'. Shaftesbury needed first-hand examples to inform and inspire his own representations in Parliament. They needed him to pass on any particular needs for pecuniary assistance to his wealthy associates.

Once the May holiday had passed, July and the week of the Keswick Convention drew nearer, and we children could barely control our excitement. For the previous ten years, since 1875, for a brief season that tiny town nestling in the heart of the Cumberland mountains had been overrun with more than ten thousand persons, intent on one purpose and filled with one aspiration – to feast on the teachings of famous preachers from all over the world, to be transported to new heights and depths of faith, to indulge in the luxury of a week away from the trials and temptations of their earthly lives in a heavenly holiday with the saints. Controversy went unheard, denominational differences were forgotten, race, colour and creed all blended into one, as, in the words of its founder, the Revd Hartford-Battersby, 'We were taken out of ourselves, and led, step by step, to such a consecration to God, as in the ordinary times of a religious life, hardly seemed possible.'

There were old friends to meet and new ones to make, wonderful walks around Derwentwater or up Skiddaw with its breathtaking views across the fells, unusual hotel fare, Kendal mint cake and Grasmere gingerbread. And then the stirring youth rallies, admonishing young people to 'throw our lives away for Jesus', a sentiment to which we readily concurred, with little understanding of how to throw away what we hadn't yet had.

A deep quiet pervaded the vast crowds as they poured like so many ants out of every hotel, guesthouse and tent, and made their way expectantly to the big top for the massed morning and evening services. It was truly thrilling to hear the deafening sound of all those people rise to their feet to sing together, in voices that shook the marquee and resonated in the very depths of our souls.

> *Not a surge of worry,*
> *Not a shade of care,*
> *Not a blast of hurry,*
> *Touch the spirit there.*
>
> *Stayed upon Jehovah,*
> *Hearts are fully blessed;*
> *Finding as he promised*
> *Perfect peace and rest.*

In the blink of an eye, or so it seemed, this taste of heaven, so long awaited, was over and the little Lakeside town settled back into its tranquillity. The hordes departed, promising to stay in touch, leaving the perfect peace and rest behind, as we returned to the hurry, worry and care of our mundane lives, though with our hearts fully blessed. And a profound sense of anticlimax.

In the months between Keswicks the mass missionary conventions at the Exeter Hall provided us with a taste of the same heady mix of entertainment and spiritual challenge. I remember being most bemused on one occasion to see Lord Kinnaird, a Scottish peer, occupying the chair, wearing brown trousers with a black frock coat. A fashion *faux pas* if ever there was one. Was this something to do with his fame on the football pitch, I whispered to Phil, the younger of my two elder brothers. Phil leaned across and said, 'Lords, Gracie, can wear anything they want, you know.'

Oh, the excitement as the missionaries rose to speak – perhaps one who had barely escaped with his life from a cannibal feast, or was the sole survivor of a party of pioneers, all of whose companions had succumbed to deadly African fevers. And then there were the new recruits, who would rise and tell us how the Call had come to them. Our enthusiasm would reach such a pitch that it seemed as if the roof would be lifted as we sang our final hymn, then filed out onto The Strand – into a world which seemed so unreal and impersonal in contrast. It was as if we were still treading the golden streets of our Exeter Hall paradise and were unable to adapt our exalted selves to the prosaic procedure of going home in a lumbering two-horse omnibus, so we often begged our brother to allow us to walk through Leicester Square, Piccadilly and Regent Street.

'Is it *really* true, Phil, that it's not safe to be in the West End after dark?'

'Yes, my dears, not even in twos; take my arm and on no account must you look at anyone.'

So we rushed along, past the hordes of painted and overdressed women, pushing our way and being pushed by the crowds that now began to pour out of the music halls and theatres; it seemed as if we were escaping the judgement of Sodom and Gomorrah.

At Marble Arch we would mount an omnibus and with the spirit of adventure still strong within us, would ride on top, a most unladylike procedure in those days – huddling up close to our brother on the knife-board seats for warmth. Arriving home after midnight, we would find our parents sat around the supper table discussing the delights of the meeting – sometimes with the Earl of Shaftesbury or Lord Radstock, occasionally with the speakers themselves, such as the famous, larger-than-life American evangelists Moody and Sankey, whose presence would stun us into silence as we ravenously consumed the remainder of the cold roast beef and apple tart.

It was at one such meeting, listening to an exceedingly pretty young woman called Geraldine Guinness describing how she could no longer resist the certainty that she must go to save the lost in China, that my twelve-year-old sister Ruth, to whom I was the closest in sentiment as well as age, decided that she too was called to be a missionary. I was too young to have any idea of the implications of such a decision. Nor did I know then to what extent Geraldine Guinness's path would one day cross with mine.

Thus the excitement of conferences and conventions tempered my opinion of the religious austerities of those days, as well as affording me excellent fodder for the observations that would inspire my character impersonations – of which more anon.

Worship normally reserved for the Almighty was extended only to one other – our beloved Queen. From infancy we had never been allowed to miss an opportunity of seeing her. Amid hustling and jostling, we had been driven, pushed or carried to vantage ground in the parks to see her pass in procession, and great was our enthusiasm when she turned her head and inclined – as we verily believed – towards our family circle. Though it must be said, her appearances had been fairly rare since the death of Prince Albert in 1861, and for me she was almost a mythical figure, a character in a storybook.

On June 20th 1887, when I was ten, Victoria celebrated her Golden Jubilee. Though there was little I didn't know about her, this was the first time I actually remember seeing her. We waited as a family with Mother and Nurse Tye, both of them in a state of extreme nervous excitement, as the Queen processed through London to Westminster Abbey as Empress of India, escorted by the Colonial Indian Cavalry. My impression was of a thousand gorgeous colours of race, costume, uniform, festoons, bunting, flowers and full-budded trees mingling in a kaleidoscope of pageant glory, into the midst of which came the golden coach bearing our Queen. As she appeared we cheered, waved, rose and curtsied, laughed with a sheer exuberance of joy and wondered why our mother's eyes were filled with tears. Nurse Tye was so overcome that she was forced to sit down for a while on a park bench, as she was in no fit state to escort us back to the tram.

*

To return to the subject of our leisure activities, our reading and amusements were strictly circumscribed, though it was possible we were spared much that was worthless in both. Books of fiction were rigorously eschewed, but we had access to unlimited versions of the Bible – all richly bound, books of travel – mostly missionary ones, which, however, were thrilling enough in the days of Livingstone, Carey, Paton, Burns and Mackay, and some of the poets, including Longfellow, Whittier, Wordsworth, Tennyson and Keble – though we were warned of the dangers of the High Church teaching in Keble's *Christian Year*. (Frankly, I had no desire to tackle such a ponderous volume anyway.) I am thankful to record that the works of Shakespeare, taboo in some households, were not banned. Indeed, I attribute much of my father's eloquence in preaching to his intimate knowledge and love of Shakespeare's plays. On one occasion, we visited friends in the country who lived in an old-fashioned rambling house with an entrance hall adjoining a big dining room, the ceiling of which was upheld by a double row of supporting pillars, an ideal setting for charades. One day we decided to attempt *As You Like It*. The dining room was converted into a veritable Forest of Arden, and the entrance hall formed one of the rooms of the palace. It was just as Rosalind and Celia were planning flight ('Now go we in content / To liberty, and not to banishment . . .') that our hostess appeared, 'shocked and pained', she declared, 'by these worldly theatricals'. In vain did her son explain that it was only Shakespeare. We were told to remove our Babylonish garments and to repair to the study, where a circular letter from some part of the mission field was duly read to a very subdued group of young people.

In the musical world we were allowed greater liberty, though our parents had qualms about the singing of an oratorio when 'sacred words were sung by unconverted lips'. Their love of music finally prevailed over this misgiving, but opera, with all its unbridled lust and passion, remained forbidden to us. As did the Henley Regatta – a great favourite with my school friends, but a danger to vulnerable young minds, for reasons I couldn't quite fathom.

Thus, for all forms of amusement, we children were almost entirely dependent on our own resources, which, however, made for originality and the development of any artistic gifts we might possess. Our entertainments usually took the form of representations of the religious ceremonies with which we were familiar. Baptism by immersion was the most popular.

Watching total immersion baptisms was one of the high points of church life. The church's baptistry was sunk into the floor of a raised platform, with steps leading down into the water as at a swimming pool. The women candidates were attired in mob caps and long white gowns, which had an embarrassing way of blowing up like balloons as they stepped into the water. The men wore black alpaca garments like a priest's cassock, which somehow managed to stay in place. The baptising elder placed his right arm around their shoulders and, taking their folded hands with his left one, lowered the body backwards into the water. This solemn moment was unfortunately often marred by the hysteria of some of the female candidates, so the congregation was encouraged to burst into hymn-singing on cue to drown out the noise of any embarrassing distractions.

We children recreated our baptistry by means of sheets suspended from a four-poster bedstead, into which we were plunged by an 'elder' who stood precariously poised on a bedside table. I must confess that somewhat unholy mirth, rather than hymn-singing, accompanied the proceedings when occasionally elder and candidate fell in and suffered 'total immersion' together.

My contribution to our entertainments usually took the form of the impersonation of the revivalist preachers, or those of our mission hall congregation, whose peculiarities I had observed during Sunday services. My repertoire enlarged as I grew older, for in the shop windows my attention had been attracted by the photographs of the leading actors and actresses of the day. My 'quick changes' included the characterisation of persons as widely diverse as Henry Irving, Ellen Terry, May Yöhe, Mabel Love, Edna May, Apollyon of *Pilgrim's Progress*, Neptune, Britannia,

Greek goddesses (duly draped in the style approved by the Popes of the Middle Ages), and the leading lights of the Plymouth Brethren.

So the limitations imposed on the 'Saints' in accordance with the Brethren's code of conduct in no way deprived us as a family of the *joie de vivre* which is the prerogative of youth. We lived in a whirl of social and religious activity, for our parents kept open house. Sundays, far from being the gloomy days usually associated with that epoch, were especially bright and cheerful once we returned from the statutory 'Breaking of Bread' – and even that provided a certain amount of entertainment.

To commemorate 'The Lord's Supper' the Brethren would assemble in a room or hall, and sit within a roped-off portion. We children were permitted to sit in this inner circle, as both our parents, our maiden aunt and our nurse were among the bona fide Breakers of Bread, so, had we sat beyond the pale, there would have been no one answerable for our conduct. I used to look with perplexed interest – not unmixed with envy – on those who sat on the other side of the rope; it was not a satisfactory explanation to be told that they were not 'in fellowship'. Among them was my eldest brother, Percy, but my other brother, Philip, sat with us, perched up on hymn books as a precautionary measure against cane-chair markings on the seat of his velvet knickerbockers.

Services usually lasted for about two hours and were conducted in turn by anyone who felt led to speak. My father, when present, and my grandfather, in my father's absence, were always amongst the 'led' ones. I was vaguely aware that my father put things over well, judging by the rapt attention of his audience and appreciative comments afterwards about 'a feast of fat things, wine on the lees well-refined'. But my grandfather's one invariable theme was the Song of Solomon. He would expound it with rapturous delight; tears would flow down his venerable white beard as he described the lover's search for his lost bride, and his face would beam with joy when she was found.

Other expositions of Scripture would be given by some of our local tradesmen, but their remarks, it would seem, were not always profitable and on such occasions my grandfather would cut them off with a terse, 'Now, dear brother, I think we'll sing a hymn,' and he'd give my mother the sign to lead off. Thanks to her trained voice and musical ear, the singing did not suffer through lack of any musical accompaniment.

As we reached the age of adolescence we felt led to seek admission in our own right to the inner circle of the Plymouth Brethren, which was by means of adult baptism. The desire to partake of this rite was usually a spontaneous one, with no preparatory instruction. All that was required was that we should submit to an interview by the elders at a fellowship meeting and satisfy them that there were manifestations of divine grace in us.

The customs of the sect were paramount, so we children were in turn duly interrogated and approved for baptism by the elders; not lightly did we submit to the ordeal of total immersion in the presence of such a large audience, but as we were to some extent privileged persons, we thought ourselves within our rights to stipulate that none but our father should baptise us. And we got our way.

As the youngest member of our family, I was the last to be baptised. Until my fourteenth year I had expressed no desire for this sacrament and had evidently given no signs of the change of heart which was the necessary preliminary so as to encourage others to urge it on me. But it was in response to my mother's promptings one Sunday evening after she had been reading *The Pilgrim's Progress* to me that I decided I should like the burden of my sins to be rolled away. Biblical instruction at home with my mother usually involved the wanderings of the Children of Israel in the wilderness, or the sufferings of the Egyptians under the plagues. I confess that the Old Testament stories had a great fascination for me, which may have been partly due to my mother's gifts as a raconteuse. I can hear her now, speaking in the tones of an angry Pharaoh, or the suppliant voice of Moses, emulating the rebellious spirit of the stiff-necked generation of Israelites. The dramatic element made a strong appeal to me. But it wasn't as powerful as *The Pilgrim's Progress*.

My baptism once accomplished, I could now sit inside the rope in good faith, and 'break bread', an expression that so puzzled one of my school friends that she asked her vicar for an explanation, which led to a distinct cooling in our friendship. Being a 'peculiar people' had its drawbacks.

On Sunday afternoons the lonely young businessmen my father had come into contact with in his earlier work at the Stafford Rooms would assemble around our tea table, a little awed in the presence of my mother, who sat behind a massive tea urn, teapot, cream jug, sugar bowl and basins mounted on a beadwork stand, quite happy to be sheltered behind this barricade of silver since she was both shy and reserved and never lost her habit of blushing (something which delighted my father). In the centre of the tea table there stood a silver wickerwork basket with a semicircular handle, containing a large Dundee cake covered with white-sugared almonds. There would inevitably come a moment, for which I, as a little girl, seen but not heard, would expectantly wait, when some shy young man was asked to pass the cake. He would clutch the handle nervously, the basket would overbalance and the cake would crash down onto the surrounding dishes – the embarrassed young man's blushes vying in intensity with those of my mother, while my father invariably opined, 'Tut, tut, that basket must *not* be used.' It continued to appear weekly for the next forty years.

Tea would close with the singing of the hymn 'Praise the Saviour, Ye who Know Him', and Phil and I would struggle to suppress our giggles as everyone got inextricably tongue-tied with the verbs when we came to the verse:

> *Then we shall be where we would be*
> *Then we shall be what we should be*
> *Things which are not now nor could be*
> *Then shall be our own.*

After this, we would repair to the local mission hall where a thousand or more people were assembled for a stirring, dramatic service, wholly devoted to 'The Unsaved'. The message of those days could be summed up in the first few lines of a long poem written by my father:

> *A single soul! A single soul!*
>
> *Who can its value tell?*
> *Yet, oh my God! what myriads*
>
> *Sport on the brink of hell.*
> *How rapidly they slide along*
>
> *The slippery incline,*
> *To where a single ray of hope*
>
> *Can never, never shine . . .*

Family friends would be the guests at Sunday suppers. When my father was away on his evangelistic tours, and my mother was taking the waters at Harrogate, and we were left in the care of some poor, unsuspecting aunt, practical jokes would convulse us all with laughter. Mince pies would be served, some containing pieces of brown paper; or soap skilfully disguised as peaches would be offered to the maiden aunt; china danced on the table by air pressure from beneath; a tumbler filled with water and placed on the top of the door awaiting the arrival of a latecomer would inadvertently fall on the parlourmaid's head, while hysterical screams would be uttered by my aunt as a clockwork mouse whirred across the floor.

When my parents were at home musical evenings were the order of the day, the hostess's family and guests expected to contribute to the success of the evening. Invitation cards bore the words *Please bring your music*, and though our amateur efforts rarely reached high artistic level, everyone did their best. We all took music lessons irrespective of any natural ability or inclination.

In our family circle, Bee was the accompanist on the piano or organ. Percy made our flesh creep with his dramatic recitals of *Eugene Aram* and other tragedies. He also played the banjo and sang duets with Lillie ('O, That We Two Were Maying', 'Excelsior' and 'No Sir!'). Lillie sang in a high soprano – 'Roaming In The Gloaming' and 'Trespassing', with rather more sentimentality than my mother approved. Gertrude and a troupe of girlfriends played on mandolins draped with multicoloured ribbons. Father would listen entranced as Ruth rendered Mascagani's *Intermezzo* on the violin, and Mother would wipe her eyes with a Honiton-lace handkerchief when Phil sang 'The Better Land'. I recited tragic and comic prose and poetry, but reserved my character impersonations and Albert Chevalier's barrow-boy songs for those evenings when our parents were at the Brethren's prayer and fellowship meetings.

Hypnotism and planchette were the other forms of entertainment that at one time had our serious consideration, and then, without the knowledge of our parents, became a major source of amusement. A fascination for 'the other world' – ghosts, spirits and the psychic – was very much in vogue, thanks to the writings of such as Sir Arthur Conan Doyle. We children were of course aware that these interests were regarded by the Brethren as a dangerous intrusion into a forbidden world, but that intrigued us all the more and made us determined to try them out.

Bee had been staying with friends in Yorkshire where one of the sons of the house, a medical student, was absorbed in the new and fascinating subject of hypnotism, with its revelations of the surprising complexities of the human personality. He and Bee, together with a self-styled medium called Madame Aesculapius, tried out various experiments. When Bee came back to London she hypnotised our housemaid (with her consent) and our tabby cat (without it). Family members were reluctant to submit their will to what was seen as her control, and only permitted localised experiments such as the stiffening of an arm or hand. Bee could also induce self-hypnotism, and while in this state was seen by my grandfather who rushed from the room in horror, exclaiming, 'Of the devil, of the devil . . .'

One day, when we were playing planchette, that curious little heart-shaped piece of wood on wheels spun out such amazing stories, and with such rapidity under Bee's touch, that she could scarcely keep pace with its peregrinations. When asked by what power it worked, it promptly wrote, 'The devil' (the scapegoat of all unknown phenomena in our home).

Our interest in hypnotism waned and passed from genuine to sham performances that were so cleverly counterfeited by Phil as to cause both panic and protest amongst those who considered them seriously hazardous. So they were promptly banned. After that, our only legalised form of entertainment was our reproduction of Maskelyne and Cook, the popular magicians who called themselves 'Royal Illusionists and Anti-Spiritualists'. Their aim was to unmask the charlatans who sold themselves as having genuine powers, while they explained to their audiences how their tricks were done. We became quite a convincing band of young tricksters.

*

Homeopathy, however, far from joining the long list of the forbidden, seemed to go hand in hand with Brethrenism. Possibly their affinity lay in their break with tradition, and what has been said about one is true of the other, that both constituted 'the acme of individualism'.

Samuel Hahnemann, the founder of homeopathy, was born in Germany in 1755 and was the first doctor to use the virus of disease for remedial purposes, which eventually resulted in the wonderful modern practice of vaccination and inoculation.

All that was required for carrying out the treatment was a pharmacopoeia and the stock-in-trade, which consisted of a dozen or more small bottles filled with clear white or brown liquid, or infinitesimally small pills. In our family the administration of remedies was undertaken by my mother. They were kept in an attractive mahogany box which stood on our dining room side-board, fitted with oak shelves rising tier above tier, with holes, duly labelled, into which the bottles neatly fitted.

Some careless person would occasionally replace a bottle in the wrong hole, or fail to exercise the necessary patience to allow the minute doses to pass through the lip of the bottle. Bee was known on more than one occasion to have swallowed the entire contents of whatever bottle came to hand – nux vomica, belladonna, aconite or arsenicum. My mother would hastily look up the chapter in her pharmacopoeia dealing with poison antidotes, and Bee's faith in the value of both the overdose and the antidote would result in an instantaneous cure. When our ailments were too deep seated to respond to Mother's treatment, the compensation was an exciting journey into the city or the West End to visit the famous homeopathic physician of those days, Dr Joseph Kidd. 'Iodine Kidd' he was derisively called by his allopathic contemporaries – but those were the days long before the invaluable properties of iodine came to be recognised and universally used, as it was during the Great War and after. To see this renowned doctor it was necessary to make an appointment weeks in advance. Even then, we set out in the early hours of the morning as we still had to enter our names on the long waiting list for that day. On arrival at Hanover Square or Finsbury Circus, wherever the consultation was to take place, there would be huge queues of broughams, landaus and victorias which had brought patients from near and far.

We arrived on foot and were shown into a somewhat dismal waiting room, with chairs and sofas covered in black horsehair; large circular tables filled the centre of the room, on which were several morocco-bound Bibles and a few periodicals. Somewhat furtively, we young people would select *Punch*, while our mother became engrossed in *The Christian*. At last our names would be called by the butler, and with palpitating hearts we were ushered into the presence of the great man. One's first impulse on seeing him was to kneel and receive his blessing. But that would have pained a fellow Plymouth Brother.

In appearance he was exactly like a picture that hung in our morning room of Aaron as high priest. He had a long white beard, a serious face illumined with a benevolent expression, deep-set, penetrating eyes that seemed to take in at a glance the entire human viscera and its disorders, which led to a rapid diagnosis usually followed by the application of iodine. With a little green bottle in one hand and a brush in the other, he painted the patch that was responsible for the cough, or organ that was the seat of pain. Or he applied an iodine compress. Then he would fold the prescription and a suitable diet sheet, place them within a small envelope (one noticed the beauty of his shapely hands as he did this), and he would gather up the gold sovereign that had been placed on his desk and slip that, too, into the envelope – for no fee was ever accepted from those engaged in the Lord's work – and we would pass out from his presence with a sense of having received his benediction. Maybe he too was conscious that strength had gone out of him.

My two eldest sisters, Bee and Lillie, had been boarders at a school for young ladies situated in Upper Clapton. It was here that Bee's talent for music and painting were first recognised, and ardent masters begged my father to allow her to go for further study to the continental schools. But he was fearful that such gifts might prove a snare of the devil, or, worse, lead to the concert stage, so he refused his permission. Thus the only outlet for Bee's gifts was in painting landscapes and texts that adorned our home or the walls of the mission halls, and in composing and playing gospel hymns, to which tasks she would unstintingly give the best years of her life.

Percy was educated at St Paul's School, became a Middlesex County cricket player, and after a few years in the City announced his intention of going to the West Indies. He set out to make his fortune in the most optimistic of moods – as every enterprising young man does. His departure was one of my early sorrows, for I hero-worshipped him. He was always the most appreciative of the family audience of my character sketches and it was to his banjo that I first learned to express myself in 'rhythmical move-ment' – to which we did not dare give the name of dancing.

I suspect, as I reflect upon it now, that his departure may have been prompted by a desire for larger liberties. I recall a discussion between him and my father which centred around theatre-going, and the painful silence that followed Percy's final retort: 'Well, I saw Mr X at the Haymarket the other evening.' Mr X was a lead-ing light in the Brethren, and although I had no idea what the Haymarket was, I knew by my father's expression that this was a very serious charge. The association of the theatre with the infernal regions was not unusual in our movement. An elderly relative told us that on his first visit to London he was sorely tempted to go to a theatre, but was mercifully deterred by seeing a sign that pointed 'TO THE PIT'.

The business opportunity that opened up for Percy quickly led him onward to the United States, but he rarely wrote home, and when he did, it was to tell us of his many cricketing successes and his pleasure at introducing the Belmont Cricket Club of Philadelphia to the joys of soccer. My parents read and re-read his few letters, seeking some indication of interest in spiritual matters, but to their sorrow there was none, and certainly no mention of his having sought out 'Peculiar' fellowship.

The interaction of the ideas of our parents' generation with ours did, however, begin to modify some of their cherished yet rather more rigid attitudes. A new mental outlook led to the challenging of accepted traditions and this was first noticeable in our home furnishings. The oval walnut table, covered with a beautiful sample of my grandmother's crewelwork, that had stood in the centre of our drawing room was now removed to a corner, its polished surface laid bare; the cottage piano with its fluted red silk facing was exchanged for a Broadwood grand; an inlaid Sheraton cabinet ousted the marble-top chiffonier. Lustres gave place to modern Worcester; the crystal chandelier was replaced by one in lacquered brass; pictures went into limbo, including *The Battle of Trafalgar* and *The Death of Nelson*. Gustave Doré's *Christ Leaving the Praetorium* was the only one to survive. Maple and Co. successfully completed the transformation from the early Victorian to the nondescript mid-period; dull gold tapestry replaced the red velvet upholstery, and Roman satin draperies concealed the nakedness of white marble mantelpieces.

Our bedrooms also showed signs of our developing personalities. 'In Darkest Africa' – painted in large black and yellow letters on the door of Bee's room – was a veritable jungle. The floor was covered in leopard skins; the large mirror over the chimney-piece was transformed by means of her paint brush into an African swamp, with tall papyrus grasses half-concealing crocodiles and rhinoceroses. Elephant tusks, assagais and calabashes hung from the walls. There was a tripod and kettle, beneath which we would make a real fire. This room at once became the most popular rendezvous for the younger generation.

Our bookshelves were changing their contents with kaleido-scopic rapidity; novels were no longer concealed or read in the lavatories. I recall with awe watching Ruth's library grow. Where once there had been Jukes and Newton on the Prophets and C.H.M.* on Leviticus, were now Emerson, Martineau, Farrar and Drummond, and to these were added Ruskin, Carlyle, Tolstoy, Darwin and Aristotle.

Among my limited collection was a book, whose author I have forgotten, entitled *Making the Most of Life*. In late adolescence it made a deep impression on my plastic mind and led to the termi-nation of an amorous liaison with a medical student who had proposed a clandestine marriage, owing to my parents refusing their consent. It also led to my discontinuation of the lessons I had been taking with an eminent professor of elocution, whose high fees I had met by selling my much-prized bicycle, for despite the end of my romance, my secret longings for a stage career had somehow transmuted to that of a medical one. It's so often the fortuitous little events that change our destiny.

The changing opinions and wider outlook of the late Victorians in my sphere were largely due to the work of the pioneers of the Higher Education for Women movement. To these we owe unfeigned gratitude; but the movement's true influence on some of us is debatable. For my sister, Ruth, it was the royal road to achievement – the winning of prizes, the development of her liter-ary tastes, and doubtless the preparation for the extraordinary career that was to come. For me, it only led to the exposure of my crass stupidity – particularly with Euclidian deduction methods in mathematics. Often, during homework, a book would be

* Charles Henry Mackintosh

hurled at my head by Ruth, whose patience broke down under the strain of my inability ever to arrive at the *quod erat demonstrandum*.

It appeared to me that the famous Greek geometrician was an irritant to women's nerves. During the Euclid period the temper of our mathematics mistress was peppery to say the least, and I recall how she would harangue some helpless adolescent who was trying to design an isosceles triangle on the blackboard, with the promise that when she was married she would bring a lot more fools into the world.

Ruth and I were both educated as day pupils at Hampstead High School for Girls when Miss Benson was headmistress. 'Big Ben' we nicknamed her. She did not appreciate my inability to refrain from reproducing the peculiarities and eccentricities of the teaching staff, and I hovered on the brink of expulsion more than once. While my impressions increased my popularity with the pupils, they seriously diminished my prestige with the staff and I never rose beyond the Upper Fourth.

But as I look back I think we girls took our 'higher education' far too seriously. Every subject was approached in a pugnacious spirit and with unrelenting compulsion. The method of acquiring, for example, the German declension table inoculated me with such antipathy to that orderly and thorough race that a lifetime has not wholly cured me of it. To obtain exemption from any subject, a medical certificate on grounds of ill health was necessary. I successfully manipulated an exemption from Latin by calling on an octogenarian doctor, who, as I planned and hoped, instantly snorted, 'Latin! Latin for *women*? I've no patience with such newfangled notions.'

I was, however, an instinctive rebel and determined to try out some of the more attractive 'newfangled' delights before my parents and my better nature forced me to give them up. How could there be any real sacrifice in eschewing pleasures one had never known? Caught up in their work, battle-weary by then from dealing with long years of mutinous adolescence, from trying to protect their offspring from dangers physical and spiritual, real and imagined, my parents appeared blissfully unaware of their youngest child's indecorous habits – until, by an unfortunate coincidence, I was seen one day by one of my uncles with my professor of elocution, who had politely offered to escort me from his studio to Victoria Station at the close of the lesson. A report reached my father that his youngest daughter had been seen in the vicinity of the Army and Navy stores *in company with an actor*.

On another occasion, from his favoured position beside the driver on the front seat of a two-horse London omnibus, he looked down on a smart red-wheeled buggy with high-stepping mare, driven by what the busman informed him was 'the finest lady-whip of St John's Wood, sir' – only to recognise with profound shock his youngest daughter as the holder of the title. My favourite pastime was instantly banned, of course, but not before I had had the exhilarating pleasure of driving a four-in-hand – a beautifully polished, long-retired stagecoach harnessed to four magnificent thoroughbreds. This privilege was normally reserved for the select members of the four-in-hand club, of whom none was ever a woman, and I drew many surprised but admiring looks from the thousands of spectators who had turned out to cheer on the procession, not just on its usual route around Hyde Park but from London all the way out to Pinner.

Although my many breaches with 'Peculiar' protocol were a source of some anxiety to my parents, it was Bee, their firstborn, of marriageable age and giving very little indication of real belief, who bore the brunt of my parents' concerns and restrictions. They could only go so far in embracing the new world, as a letter to Bee in her twenty-fourth year indicates so clearly:

> *I dare not disguise from you, my darling firstborn, that I still fear you are far too much taken up with the lighter things of life, yea, its frivolities, than seeking to bear in mind its more serious purposes and responsibilities which should not be forgotten even amidst our rest and recreations. Certain I am*

that the seductive power of the world hath bewitched you from
the beauty and simplicity of a life in real fellowship with God,
and as sure as you live, if you seek your satisfaction in the
world and its delusive pleasures, you will not only find it a
sham and a lie, and utterly inadequate to fill the heart that God
alone can satisfy.

The particular 'seductive power' that had bewitched Bee was a good-looking young man with a fine tenor voice, a voice which was frequently to be heard singing solo parts in London's leading churches. But he had dared to take Bee to a performance of Gilbert and Sullivan. He was refused admittance to our house, all correspondence was forbidden and Bee was sent away to a mission centre in East London to serve the poor. Only to become further compromised there by the amorous advances of a missionary from the Congo, whose efforts to persuade her to accompany him back to that region were fortunately unavailing as he died there of tropical fever shortly after.

These prohibitions had a lasting effect on us. Years later, when they were both grown women, Ruth wrote to Bee, '. . . will you think me very wicked when I tell you that I want to hear Melba, Caruso, Tetrazzini and others, not on the concert platform, but in their right setting in opera?'

Being single young people in such an environment was never going to be easy. Our future horizons were somewhat limited, due to ideas and beliefs that enabled some, though not all, of us to thrive when we eventually forged our own way.

The pre-eminent subject of the religious teaching of those days was how the world as we knew it would come to an end. There were exceedingly diverse and various interpretations of the Bible, but the Plymouth Brethren held to the view that Armageddon, the final battle, would herald the moment when Christ would appear on the clouds, and all his own would fly up to meet him in the air – while the sinners left behind on earth were subjected to 'The Great Tribulation', whatever horrible disaster that entailed. It seemed to me not quite playing the game for the Brethren to escape the havoc and destruction of what was to come, but the older members fervently expected to be numbered amongst the 'raptured' ones. I once asked one of my aged relatives what would happen to her clothes as she rose into the skies, to which she replied, 'I expect, dear, that they will just fall to earth.' Thereafter I informed my mother that I rather fancied being raptured out of the bath so that I would fly up naked as the day on which I was born – a reflection that left her visibly shaken.

With much earnestness we young people freely engaged in discussing predestination and free will, original sin, eternal punishment, final perseverance and creationism. Ruth was generally recognised as our leader in matters theological. We would sit cross-legged on the massive brass bedstead which had replaced the four-poster bed of nursery days.

'How can you reconcile what it says in the Bible, that God created the world in six days, with the fact that it takes two thousand years for a stalagmite to rise one inch from the floor of a cave?' I would ask.

Ruth would look a little superior and say, 'But surely, you wouldn't go to the Bible for chronology, geology or even theology, come to that. It appears to me as a record of human gropings after truth, after God . . . We are not fair to the Bible if we take it all literally. The East writes in hieroglyphics and expresses itself in parables. Adam and Eve may be historical fact, or it may be everyman's tragedy.'

'Well, my dears,' Bee would say with a yawn, 'what does it all matter? Let's have some ginger beer and doughnuts.'

And Phil would add, 'These things don't trouble me; but I hope you girls won't let the pater know what you believe or don't believe, because it would be an awful blow to him if he knew of your heterodoxy.'

To have consulted my father on the spiritual difficulties that inevitably presented themselves to our growing minds would not only have been an affront to his orthodoxy, but also invited his censure; while to have sought help from the elders of our community might have lowered the prestige of my father, to whom they looked for guidance in matters of faith and doctrine. He and they were more infallible than the Pope, but the trouble with infallibility is that it allows no personal judgement and therefore demands the surrender of the right to investigate. So the conflict between faith and reason, science and revelation, tradition and experimental religion had to be fought entirely on our own; or else Ruth was deputed to consult some leading young theologian whom she usually found more amenable than the doctrines they discussed, and the conclusion reached was that three steps in any direction of research invariably led to a very pleasant experience of the unknowable.

But the belief in the imminent return of Christ led to an unprecedented effort on the part of the Christian church to evangelise the world. Hundreds rallied to the standard of the intrepid pioneer Hudson Taylor, who went with 'neither purse nor scrip' into the great empire of China. The lure of Livingstone's travels in Africa, and Henry Stanley's challenge for Christian teachers to respond to the request for education from the people around the great inland lakes, led to the rapid opening up and development of this hitherto unknown continent. Missionary, trader, government official, soldier and sailor went forth to make the rough places smooth, or the smooth places rough, according to their respective goals and ambitions.

And this meant that for the first time there was given to women an opportunity such as hitherto had only been possible to the exceptional, such as an Elizabeth Fry or a Florence Nightingale. The 'call to the mission field' may have been the echo of that natural longing for a life and expression freed from parental control, which, alas, many parents fail to recognise and respect.

*

And so the call came to Bee when she was twenty-eight. She and a female colleague were seen off by a crowd of family, friends and well-wishers who accompanied them to the train with loud tears and even louder hymn-singing that continued with much gusto as they steamed out of Victoria Station. They were bound for Africa – not the Africa of which Bee's room was the fantastic representation, but a civilised portion of that country where life was lived very much as it was in England, only under a tropical sun.

Their work, on arrival in Zanzibar, was to visit all incoming ships, to conduct services on board – when they could gain the permission of the captain – and to invite the men to visit the institute that catered for their welfare. The naive efforts of the missionary ladies evidently made an impression, as one of the government officials, a young lawyer, wrote to Bee of his resolve 'to lead a reformed life', if she consented to share it with him, with immediate effect. About the sincerity of this proposition my father had grave doubts, the burden of them being, 'I should die with sorrow if you were drawn back into the world after marriage . . .'

Too late. Bee, terrified of looming spinsterhood, held her ground. Our home became a seething mass of preparations for the coming wedding; the trousseau was ordered and wedding gifts dispatched to Africa. My mother sent her admonitions and wisdom to the bride. 'Be sure and be forbearing towards your future husband and always remember that he is the head.' An uncle wrote that he had 'some splendid cigars for missionaries on furlough', a letter my father dispatched instantly to the dustbin. Lillie, our second sister, who was also about to marry a solicitor, Harry Harte, struck a characteristic Lillie-ish note by moaning continuously about the strain on the family exchequer caused by our mother's jubilee, Ruth's coming-of-age and Bee's wedding clashing with her own, as if it were all done deliberately to thwart her. *She*, she added, though not in the least resentful, was 'satisfied with a humbler government official on an income of two hundred a year'. So why she should be the one required to make the sacrifices, as ever, she couldn't fathom.

How often an apparently insignificant event alters our destiny. Among dispatches received at a certain consulate was an order from the then Prime Minister, Lord Salisbury, that sent Bee's government official to Constantinople to conduct an important legal case. In view of this unexpected departure, he suggested their marriage take place immediately, but Bee could not consent to this. Her wedding dress, trousseau and presents were all on the high seas, and to be married without the regalia would have been like offering a lamb without the imposing ceremonials of the sacrifice.

And so the wedding was postponed – for always. There was no explanation, only a brief letter in which he said, 'I write in great sorrow to ask you to annul our engagement . . .' Desolate and humiliated, Bee returned immediately to the comfort and security of her family home, and never really managed to leave it again in order to become a fully fledged member of the adult world.

Many years later I had occasion one day to go into a room in our home that we called the box room. There, silhouetted against the window, stood Bee, her back towards me; before her was an open box, across which lay her wedding gown – yellowed with age and stained with the dead orange blossoms that lay among its folds.

*

Sister number three, Gertrude, had been adopted by my maternal grandfather, in the hope that her vivacious temperament would bring brightness into the home that was now overshadowed by the death of my grandmother. She became the petted niece of my maiden aunt and the constant companion of a jolly bachelor uncle, who gave her many amusing diversions and incursions into a world other than the mission halls. I was jealous and comforted myself with the self-righteous certainty that she would one day pay for her vanity and worldliness – until she sent us a letter that said something to the effect that, 'It is a big responsibility to stand between God and sinners.' All that frivolity – and yet her faith intact as well. It simply wasn't fair.

Phil, meanwhile, never strong, never fully recovered from the diphtheria he succumbed to in the epidemic of 1893, when over three thousand died, predominantly in London. We had watched helplessly as he developed all the classic symptoms – the terrifying false membrane that grows rapidly across the throat and threatens all the air passages, the bodily pain and paralysis. Only half of those who contracted the disease survived. Twice he hovered on the verge of suffocation, narrowly defeating the arch-enemy, Death, when the experts in Harley Street had retreated from the onslaught. I refused to move from his bedside, his self-appointed nurse, during what I considered to be the last watch, for he lay in a coma for three days and nights, only to be startled as he suddenly turned to me with a smile and said, 'Feeling so fit, little sister.' True, hundreds had prayed that his life might be spared; and who knows what life-giving forces were set in motion by their importunity? However, his heart muscles had been severely inflamed and the resulting myocarditis left him prone to bouts of extreme fatigue and difficulty in breathing.

The experience left me severely torn for some years between a noble, long-term desire to nurse and, courtesy of my gift of mimicry and looks, an irresistible pull to the bright lights. I was supposed to bear a strong resemblance to Miss Edna May, the American actress, popular in musical comedy, who was appearing in London in *The Belle of New York*. If I say so myself, she was a postcard beauty, her face displayed all over the town. Shopping in the West End one morning, I was suddenly overtaken with such violent toothache that I decided on an immediate visit to an American dentist, whose signboard caught my notice. On entering his room, he rushed towards me exclaiming, 'My dear Edna – what a surprise!' It was with considerable embarrassment I had to explain that, much as I might pass for her, I was not the Belle of New York.

This resemblance to the famous actress made my father doubly solicitous and watchful of any attention I received. When stories of my mimicry got abroad, and led to an offer being made to him by someone connected to *The Sketch* of an immediate opening on the stage, commencing with a salary of £50 a week – a small fortune – he replied, 'I would rather see her in her grave.'

Given my situation, neither of my professional ambitions was realistic, but of the two, I knew which was the more selfless calling and, of course, which stood the greater chance of success when put to my parents. I took a deep breath and told them I should like to train as a nurse, quickly adding, to mitigate their initial alarm, that it might make me more useful in the event of being called to the mission field – an argument guaranteed to throw all their objections into confusion. And so, with their reluctant permission, in 1895 I found myself at the London Hospital.

Two years later, at the Queen's Diamond Jubilee, a more subdued occasion than her Golden Jubilee, I served Her Majesty

Grace Hurditch

in the humble capacity of a Red Cross unit, and it so pleased my father that he took seats in a room at the Golden Cross Hotel in Trafalgar Square from which to admire the Queen – and his youngest daughter.

*

The following year my father awoke one morning to find himself the possessor of a strange legacy – the entire contents of a large house in our neighbourhood, where had lived a spinster of considerable means. They were left to him with the stipulation that they were to be used for some missionary purpose. Several coastal towns were visited in search of a suitable property for what he had in mind, and on the West Marina, St Leonards, a large, newly built, four-storey terraced house with large bay windows overlooking the sea was found. According to my father, Wilton House of Rest for Christian Workers was 'a place of recuperation and entertainment for those in need of such reviving as change of scene on the sea-shore provides', adding another branch to his manifold organisations – and providing his children with a delightful new holiday home. The charges, which varied according to the rooms, ranged from about ten to twenty-one shillings per week, with the additional advantage granted by the railway company of return tickets from London at a mere five shillings each.

His only sister, our Aunt Helen, became the honorary superintendent – a gracious, white-haired lady with corkscrew curls held in check by a white lace cap. She had up to that point conducted a small school for young ladies in her mother's home in Devonshire, in that generation teaching being the only acceptable outlet for the mental activities of unmarried daughters. I remember her with affectionate gratitude as supplying me with the biblical texts that had to be uttered alongside grace before meals. 'Bells and pillows' they were called, though I can't for the life of me think why. One morning she whispered in my ear, 'Go to the ant, thou sluggard, learn of her ways and be wise,' which I faithfully endeavoured to repeat saying, 'Go to the aunt, thou sluggard.'

She conducted morning and evening prayers with becoming humility when no man was available to officiate, and spent the rest of the day crocheting woollen shawls or discussing some portion of her annotated Bagster Bible[2] with her medical attendant, a dear brother, as she invariably called him, from the local Brethren fellowship.

My father would allow no printed rules or regulations to mar the home-like atmosphere. There was a comforting rather than comfortable solidity about the Victorian furnishings and a sense of richness in the massive gilt-framed pictures that hung on the walls, some of which had been bequeathed by an artist of repute, a fellow of the Royal Watercolour Society, whose chief merit according to my aunt was that he was in fellowship with the Brethren. Illuminated texts, the handiwork of the Mildmay deaconesses, adorned the walls of the bedrooms and lavatories, together with the poetical effusions of our family. Such was the demand for rooms that my father raised a further £3,000 to buy the large property next door, so that we could accommodate thirty visitors and staff.

His work was at its flood tide. He now had the active co-operation of most of his children. In any free time we had, Bee, Gertrude and I helped to run Wilton House, while Ruth was co-editor of the magazines and Phil installed as co-director of the missionary enterprise. Phil, who had been denied all the advantages of education in consequence of the medical prognostication that he would not survive to benefit by it, was blessed with a sunny, outgoing disposition that left him wholly undisturbed by life's whirlpools and undercurrents and always carried him through, thus defying any limitations his health might impose upon him. His sole equipment for life was Personality, with a capital P – that, and a remarkable ability at preaching. He was in great demand, though in the end was forced to confine his evangelistic campaigns to missions for men – a diplomatic decision, by reason of the embarrassing numbers of his women converts. In jocose mood one day, he had the audacity to display on the walls of his room some hundreds of unsolicited photographs, which he named 'A Dream of Fair Women'. My father was deeply grieved at such levity, but failed to find a reply to my brother's response that there was safety in numbers!

And then, suddenly, almost without our notice, at the end of the century the ebb-tide crept up on us. My father's correspondence indicated the coming change. 'The old landmarks are disappearing and soon there will be none to show us the way . . . The world gets lonely – in a crowd . . . I have lost by death over a thousand former friends and subscribers.'

A series of disruptions and divisions resulted in the diminishing prestige and influence of the Plymouth Brethren, closing the door for the wider opportunities of his ministry. But there were other, far more wide-reaching contributory causes to the downturn of his fortunes. In the realm of science, the findings of Hooker, Wallace, Spencer and Darwin, expressed with such overwhelming conviction in the latter's publication *On the Origin of Species*, were having a profound effect on national thought. So was the 'New Theology' with its critical undermining of the inspiration of the Bible. My father could make no compromise. Evolution and higher criticism were anathema to him. As was the rising tide of Anglo-Catholicism.

Yet despite his narrowing influence, he never lost his gift of oratory. Long before I could comprehend the subject matter of his discourses, I was fascinated by the beauty of the rhythm and harmony of his words. One particular address remains an abiding memory. It was in a tiny mission hall, less than a hundred present, and it was based on some words from Psalm 73: 'Until I went into the sanctuary . . . then I understood.' As I listened to him, it seemed as if I knew him as never before. The inevitable gulf fixed by the changing thought and outlook between one generation and another was bridged by that rare experience when a soul is laid bare and spirit calls to spirit. He led us into 'the secret place of the

Most High', where life's problems and perplexities, its joys and sorrows, were all resolved in one cataclysmic moment in time. At the cross. *Then I understood.*

*

'The call' finally came to Ruth in 1898. At twenty-four she had convinced herself that since Gertie and I had taken more than our fair share of the family good looks, leaving her with our maternal grandfather's somewhat prominent Roman nose, she must embrace a life of singleness and dedicate herself instead to the people of Africa. She had co-operated with Father in his campaigns and editorial work for five years. I used to go and hear her speak and was a merciless critic of her voice inflections and erratic gesticulations which had the effect of tilting her hat to one side, but I envied her familiarity with the Bible and her fluent exposition.

Reciprocally, she would attend the medical lectures I gave, but without criticism, assuring me that if I studied my Bible with the diligence I applied to my medical books, I should become as fluent on its themes as I was on the subject of anatomy and physiology. I was then giving enthusiastic, elementary lectures on these subjects to a long-suffering group of contemporaries, having been moved to compassion by their ignorance of the most rudimentary knowledge of the human body. Equipped with facsimile animal specimens of the human viscera which I had obtained from our local butcher, I would proceed to demonstrate the fascinating action of the valves of the heart by pouring water into the auricles and ventricles, and to show the working of the lungs, which I inflated by means of my bicycle pump; when suddenly there would be a thud, thud, thud, as one after another of my audience fainted away at these 'ghastly sights'.

I viewed the prospect of being parted from my sister with some dismay, convinced the shaky foundation of my faith would suffer from the lack of her support; while she confessed to being reluctant to give up her maternal vigilance over my congenital attraction to the world, the flesh and the devil.

But before she went off to the women's missionary college for six months we decided on a summer holiday together, a walking tour of Scotland. It was unheard of for girls to travel unchaperoned at that time, and our parents were greatly perturbed by the idea. We managed to overcome my father's objections by playing him at his own game, as his offspring had so skilfully learned to do. 'Does not a kind Providence watch our goings-out, comings-in, sitting-downs and our rising-ups wherever we are? Is Scotland outside of his omnipresence?'

We left Euston by a midnight train, duly equipped with knapsacks, walking sticks, a compass and our Post Office savings account, excited and resolved to enjoy ourselves at the minimum of cost. We were turned out onto Carlisle Station at five o'clock in the morning with an hour to wait. (Probably due to our own economy, because I cannot think there were no overnight through trains to Scotland in the late 1890s.)

Though it was springtime, the air was piercingly cold, the station abominably draughty and the restaurant foully stuffy, so we wandered out into the town, where there was no alternative choice for breakfast at that early hour between an hotel or an undistinctive Lockhart's coffee tavern. We opted for the latter and found ourselves in the company of a roomful of noisy chimney sweeps, which did not, however, diminish our enjoyment of a steaming hot bowl of coffee and a bannock at the cost of twopence.

We reached Perth at dusk and followed our resolve to stay in the simplest apartments or cottages so as to reserve the major portion of our limited funds for the closing days in Edinburgh. From Perth we set out on a 150-mile walking tour in fifteen days, which took us through scenes of wild grandeur and beauty.

At Pitlochry, the owner of the charming little flint cottage where we stayed became embarrassingly kind and attentive when she discovered we were the daughters of the London preacher who had conducted a mission in Glasgow alongside the famous

Charles Spurgeon at which she was 'convairted' in her youth. From then on the table was laden with bannocks and porridge; Scotch broth overflowed the bowls and all payment was refused.

From Pitlochry we continued northwards through the pass of Killiecrankie to Blair Atholl, across the Rannoch moors, beyond where the Highland railway had yet penetrated. In fact, there were engineers working on the line who took a bit of a fancy to two young women all alone in the world, and I had to employ my acting skills to save us from their unwanted company. They had followed us to a shanty-like hostel, miles from anywhere, where we were obliged to stay. Seated at the window of the sitting room, I took on the vacant, idiotic grin of a half-wit (of whom we had seen many as we passed through the villages), and my fatuous antics had the desired effect of sending them further afield for accommodation.

We climbed Ben Nevis one Sunday afternoon amid such startling beauty of scenery that we both burst into singing 'O Worship the King, All Glorious Above', when round the bend we came face to face with two staff officers from Sandhurst. They wished us good luck in the ascent, which they had made earlier in the morning, and we thought no more about it – until we subsequently met them so consistently that we began to suspect they were arranging their tour according to our plans rather than their own. It annoyed us intensely and made us determined to outwit them.

We were now at Oban, about to take the steamer for that wonderful day's journey through the Kyle of Bute, when we saw our pursuers come on board. We deftly dodged them, slipped up the gangway and climbed one of the surrounding hills overlooking the harbour. We lay low until the siren sounded and the paddle wheels were churning up the water, then we stood up and waved them a fond farewell with our handkerchiefs. But the adventure robbed us of one of our precious three days in Edinburgh, though perhaps it was just as well since our resources had been seriously depleted by an enforced stay in a de luxe hotel in Glencoe. We couldn't afford the restaurant, so dined on the hillside instead, on ham, bread and cheese which we had purchased at the village post office. In the early hours of the following morning the proprietor seemed astonished to see us set off on a fifteen-mile walk without having breakfasted; but doubtless the chambermaid would tell him later that cocoa had been made in our tooth jars with the hot water which Boots had supplied for our ablutions. What she couldn't know was our predicament when we discovered that our one and only pocket knife had been left on the hillside the previous evening, and we were forced to use our toothbrush handles instead for spreading the butter and potted meat on our morning rolls.

On our return to London we discovered a large map of Scotland which Father had ordered from Phillips, nailed to the study wall. He had followed our progress day by day with paper flags that he pinned to our various destinations. As we went north across wild stretches of moorland his anxieties increased to such an extent that he was desperate to recall us by telegraph – except the daily postcards we sent gave no forwarding address.

Ironically, one year later he similarly followed Ruth's 800-mile missionary tramp on foot and bicycle from Mombasa to her ultimate destination, the kingdom of Toro in British East Africa – but this time without the slightest misgiving.

1899–1903

In the winter of 1899–1900 the country was in sullen mood. The South African war was upon us and nobody really knew why. Public opinion tacitly agreed that war was inevitable, but that the preparations could have been better managed. The jagged state of the public's nerves was all too plainly revealed some months later when London went mad on Mafeking night, celebrating the lifting of the Boer siege of the British forces there.

The gloom had entered our home in Alexandra Road – but for very different reasons. Trunks, Gladstone bags, holdalls and other impediments cluttered up the hall and landings. 'Hold', 'Cabin' and 'Wanted on Voyage' labels lay scattered about the writing tables, insistently reminding us that the dreaded parting was at hand.

How could I bear to be separated from Ruth, who had shared all the fun and laughter, the doubts, difficulties, ambition, disappointments, heart-burnings and soul-longings that can encompass the first two decades of life? Would I ever see her again, or would we be parted forever by some deadly fever?

We gathered for the last time around the fire 'In Darkest Africa', which room now seemed a great waste of ugliness, its trophies and relics packed away, as Bee was travelling with Ruth for part of the way, to join the staff of a mission school in the Bombay Presidency. There was no laughing or mimicry that night, nor the singing of Negro spirituals. Guitar and violin lay silent in their zinc-lined cases. Ruth laughingly reminded me of our schooldays when she pitched books at my dull head, and now flung across the leopard skin that lay stretched between us a booklet on whose green pages I mechanically read *Dover–Calais: Calais–Dover. Paris Nord–Geneve*.

'What does this mean?' I asked.

'That you are coming with us as far as Paris, and after that you can visit the Swiss professor's family just as you've always wanted.' (This professor had been a guest in our house during a conference organised by the Palestine Exploration Society.)

'But what about Phil?' I could tell that despite his usual bravado he was trying to conceal his dismay at losing three of his sisters.

'Oh,' he said, 'I shall come with you as far as Dover.'

He subsequently wrote to us from the Lord Warden Hotel that his depression was so acute that he had decided to go to the local theatre and asked the waiter what was billed for that night. '*The Sorrow of Satan*, sir.' Phil went to bed instead.

In Paris we had the good fortune to stay with friends who had an apartment on the Champs-Élysées. My first impression – that this was the most beautiful city in the world – was confirmed the following day as our carriage rolled along the wide and gracious boulevards to the Place de la Concorde, the Bastille, La Madeleine, the Musée du Luxembourg, Le Panthéon, La Sainte Chapelle and Notre Dame, whose interior had an ethereal quality as the morning sun lit up its stained-glass windows. We had an unsatisfactory glance at some of the world's masterpieces in the Louvre, and that night the Paris–Marseilles express bore my sisters further and further away; thankfully, I did not know then that it would be ten years before I would see Ruth again.

I boarded the Geneva train. In the early morning hours I was awakened by the loud clanging of a bell. My eyes opened slowly, then widely on a magical, shining world. Snow everywhere. High mountains and deep valleys encircled us; the chalet railway station stood amongst a forest of statuesque, snow-laden fir trees. The bell went on clanging as the *chef de gare* plodded through the snow, calling out, '*Descendez, messieurs et mesdames, descendez s'il vous plait.*' And so we all got off, dishevelled, unwashed, bootlaces untied, gloves forgotten, coats and rugs dangling from our shoulders, and stood, ankle deep in snow, half-dazed with sleep and intoxicated with the sight.

The breakdown on the line caused by the excessive snow meant the train was four hours late into Geneva, and there was no one to meet me. The combination of saying goodbye to my sisters and travelling entirely alone to a strange destination had left me in a highly emotional state, and when the *fiacre* I took eventually drew up at the professor's house in the Bois du Buisson and he chided me for my lateness, I might well have fallen into his arms and burst into tears – but couldn't get near for his excessive corpulence.

The petty evidences of the acrimonious hatred of the English felt at that time are amongst my foremost recollections of those six months on the continent. In Paris, torrents of abuse were hurled at us by street urchins, who were several degrees more vulgar than their British counterparts. In restaurants and public buildings, odious comments were made in our hearing, with references to '*de roas bif*', and '*de plum pudin*", which we acknowledged with good humour, only to be rewarded with rude scowls. The illustrated papers were filled with scurrilous cartoons of our Queen, while Kruger, the Afrikaaner President of the Boers, was portrayed in a halo of saintly martyrdom.

In Switzerland my presence meant my hosts were subjected to a mild boycott, or else my name would be omitted from invitation cards. The one exception was the family of the gracious, highly-acclaimed pianist Paderewski, whose fame gave him more reason to be selective in his guests, yet who welcomed us openly into his cosmopolitan home at Morges. The delicate white façade of their chateau-like chalet, Riond-Bosson, rose up through the towering mountains like a stage setting for a fairy tale. The rooms were filled with the souvenirs the great concert pianist had brought home from his triumphal world travels, and in pride of place was his portrait by Burne-Jones. There were pianos in every room, so that he could play at any one of them whenever the mood took him, and an Aeolian organ in the large billiard room.

Sunday afternoons were spent wandering the grounds along the lake shore with the concert pianist's famous St Bernard dogs, or sitting in the salon listening to his records on the newly invented pianola. Madame Paderewski, meanwhile, raised poultry in a pagoda-like hen house with turrets and was always on the lookout for new breeds and new ideas. When he left on tour, Madame could never make up her mind whether to leave her hens and accompany him or not. Once she got as far as Paris, when a telegram informed her that the Polish servants as well as her poultry had run amok. She telegrammed back, '*Le bon Dieu vous garde, je pars pour les Etats-Unis.*' Off they went to the United States, where she opened a shop selling Polish dolls and never came back.

I went on long cycling tours round the shores of Lac Léman. I came to know the exact spot on the hillside where I could obtain the best view of the undulating silhouette of Mont Blanc and watch a dazzling white shroud slowly envelop the rose-crowned peaks as the sun went down. When all the peaks were lost to view in snow and mist, there were the hills with their vine-coloured slopes – the gnomish roots all curled up in winter's sleep after the bacchanalian feast of summer. I would cross the lake and explore the shores of Savoie, astonished at the contrasting conditions, the dilapidation of its villages and the poverty of the peasants, most of whom seemed afflicted with goitre and mental deficiency.

My Swiss hosts were scandalised by my solitary expeditions.

'Who should I be afraid of?' I asked. 'Surely not the simple peasant folk?'

'No, no, but there are Italians out there, *chère mademoiselle*.'

'Yes, I've seen gangs of them coming home from work, but I offer them a friendly *buona sera* and they seem very polite.'

This made their horror complete. They were on the point of telegraphing my parents to come and take me home when I promised to submit to their superior wisdom, seething inside at what seemed a ridiculous and wholly unnecessary curbing of my freedom.

*

I returned to London just in time for Mafeking Night in May, 1900. Phil took the gong from its stand in the hall and handed me the smaller one from our dining room sideboard. We jumped into the first available hansom cab and paid an exorbitant fare to be landed in the midst of a seething mass of excited humanity. As the theatres emptied, to prevent our being crushed, women were hoisted onto the men's shoulders and from this elevation we sang patriotic songs and choruses, joined by hilarious groups of people standing on the roofs of the cabs and carriages jammed in by the crowds. As the night deteriorated into drunken brawls, fights and theft, we made a swift exit.

The war still dragged on dismally and then, at the dawn of the new year, 1901, we lost our much beloved Queen. She had reigned for sixty-two years and most of the nation had known no other monarch. It was a most personal bereavement. We watched this last great Victorian pageant with bared heads above a wall of concentrated blackness, as a gun carriage with the Union Jack lying limply across a small coffin went slowly past, accompanied by an intense silence, broken only by the sound of muffled drums and stifled sobbing.

*

By now we children, one by one, had left the Plymouth Brethren and joined those sections of the church that were more satisfying to our intellectual needs, more sympathetic to our spiritual searchings, better suited to our differing temperaments.

Lillie chose to be a star in suburban nonconformity rather than a rushlight in the metropolis and joined the Congregationalists. Gertrude became an Anglican by reason of her marriage to William Evill, a clergyman and former school friend of Phil's, to whom our brother had explained confidentially that he would have no difficulty in securing ladies as church workers, but the chance of marrying a pretty one only came to vicars once in a lifetime. My mother was not thrilled by the match, fearing that her daughter was 'tending Romeward', the Roman Catholic Church and the suffragettes being her two pet hates. Gertrude's husband, however, remained firmly Anglican, an incumbent in the midst of a dense artisan population of London's hottest 'Reds', which caused him considerable anxiety when royalty visited the district.

My eldest, runaway brother, Percy, had, as we siblings suspected, decided to live outside organised Christianity altogether. He married an American woman, made his fortune as a businessman, and secured fame by putting California cricket on the map. He went on to play for New York and Philadelphia, and according to the rare newspaper cuttings he sent home, was regarded as the best wicket keeper New York had ever seen. His credo in work as well as in play was 'originality in all things'. The model batsman, said the newspapers, he combined timing and power, grace and aggression. Intrepid and confident, he made the game seem effortless, epitomising the ideals of the golden age of cricket when style was supreme – how you looked as important as how many runs you scored.

Phil continued in that happy state of being 'all things to all men' – a free churchman – while Bee remained unsure of what she wanted; certain, however, that it wasn't the church of her childhood. Ruth wrote to her, begging her not to discuss the matter with our parents, thereby upsetting them unnecessarily. She herself, for reasons of the heart, was about to be drawn into the Church of England. I followed her there several years later – but that's a story in itself, and I run on too fast.

*

In the spring of 1901, I persuaded my parents to let me move to a squalid part of London on the Bermondsey side of the Thames, often referred to in the newspapers as 'A Den of Thieves', as it had served for Charles Dickens' description of Fagin's bastion in *Oliver Twist*. I cannot claim the privilege of having heard a call to work in some of the lowest parts of London, nor was I seduced by the new fashion for what became known as 'slumming' – bored, well-to-do young things from the West End spending an evening gawping at the poor of Whitechapel or Shoreditch purely for entertainment. But the Mildmay Hospital, staffed largely by volunteers, most of whom were preparing for mission abroad, had urgent need of a fully trained home-visiting nurse, and I felt I could not turn down such a request.

Life in the East End offered undreamed-of rewards and rich experiences – if one was willing to pay the price. It involved, among other things, the loss of all social contact, for nobody paid afternoon calls there; nor was it safe to wear our own clothes and venture down the highways and byways, where even the police always went in twos and threes, and our only safety was our uniform. Only once, when returning from a summer holiday, did I inadvertently appear in mufti, to be instantly relieved of my gold half-hunter watch and chain concealed beneath my coat.

One dark night I appealed to two men who were standing on a street corner to escort me on my way to see a desperately sick child. Every moment counted and I could not afford to waste time in trying to find the street and then the number in those dimly lit alleys with their rows of interminable doors. But they carried my equipment and guided me to the house.

I mounted a wooden staircase from which a few broken bannisters projected, and entered a small room which dim candlelight showed to be filled with matchboxes. At the table sat two women dexterously pasting, folding and tying the boxes into bundles. For this, they told me, they were paid twopence farthing a gross. Without ceasing their work, they indicated with a nod that 'she was over there'. On a dilapidated iron bedstead, where slept by night father, mother and two children, lay a little girl tossing amidst a bundle of rags, feverishly gasping for breath as if eager to retain her precarious hold on a life that seemed worth so little. I gave immediate instructions for water to be boiled, constructed a makeshift tent over the child out of any pieces of wood, metal and material I could find, placed the bowl of boiling water as close to her as was safely possible, and she was soon soothed to sleep by the comforting steam. I suggested that an extra wrap should be thrown over her in the morning. 'Ain't got no hextry wrap,' was the reply, whereupon the neighbour who was helping out with the matchboxes stood up and slipped off a red flannel petticoat.

The chivalries and loyalties of the people were extraordinary. How often some battered and bruised woman, whose husband's ill-treatment had sent her to our wards, affirmed, 'Oh, Sister, 'e's such a good man when 'e ain't in drink.'

And how stoutly they would defend us if need arose. From a side ward I once overheard (to a woman who was very naturally making the most of her brief but luxurious opportunity of receiving a little attention), 'Y' oughter be ashaimed o' yerself givin' 'em so much trouble.'

'Well, they're paid for it, ain't they?'

'Not a brass farving.'

'Lumme! Wot does they dew it for?'

'Not for luv of the loikes of yew, that's for shore . . .'

'Prayer time, women – what hymn shall we sing?'

' "Let the Blessed Sun Shine In", Sister.'

And they would sing this hymn with a heartiness that was poignantly pointed up by the fact that their lives were spent in dismal hovels that were rarely lighted by the sun's beneficent rays.

The horror, the suffering, the sordidness of it all would sometimes threaten to engulf me. At such times I would escape to Wilton House in St Leonards for a few days and walk on a lonely stretch of beach, listening to the waves breaking on the pebbles. Then, lying in the sun, basking in its healing warmth, half-sleeping, half-waking, I would dream, as a seer once dreamed long ago, that I heard a gentle voice whisper, 'And there shall be no more death, neither sorrow, nor crying, neither shall there be any more pain; for the former things are passed away . . . Behold, I make all things new.'

*

But what was my lot compared to Ruth's? And yet she never complained. Not even during her 800-mile trek on foot and bicycle from Mombasa to the kingdom of Toro in British East Africa, under a ferocious sun, in melting heat, struggling over soaring mountains, riding on elephant trails, through torrential rainstorms that turned the earth into thick black mud. King Kasagama of Toro had requested female missionaries to come and help the women of his village to read and write, and Ruth and her companion were the first European women to succeed in reaching him. Her letters described her efforts at growing her own crops, baking bread, killing chickens, learning Lunyoro, the local language spoken only in the kingdom of Toro, setting up a dispensary and surgery for the many sick people who besieged her home daily. How I wished that Ruth, now living in the heart of Central Africa, at a station with no medical staff for hundreds of miles around, had taken advantage of The Mildmay's nursing training as I had tried to persuade her to do. Every letter of hers contained requests for medical information that was long past its usefulness by the time she received my reply. We couldn't help but be amused. There she was, lancing abscesses and gums, cutting tongue-tied infants, stitching up leopard-torn patients – on a daily basis. All of the requirements needed for her survival were so unlike any of her previous interests. But her spirit was indomitable.

The base at Toro was led by a more experienced Church Missionary Society clergyman, the Revd Arthur Fisher, a doughty Irishman who succumbed to malaria and blackwater fever shortly after Ruth's arrival. She had no choice but to bathe 'his poor hot body with cool water'. Not surprisingly he clung to her in his delirium, begging her to become his wife and never leave him again – to which she consented, as his temperature appeared to depend on her acquiescence, and she couldn't see how she would survive in Toro without him. Not the most romantic of proposals. But her acceptance appeared to effect an immediate improvement and the restored young clergyman refused all her protestations that they should wait at least six months.[3]

In a letter dated March 11th, 1902, her wedding day, she described the event:

> *The Prime Minister has been commanding an army of work-men since daybreak. They have transformed our mud bungalow with papyrus grass and palm leaves, and freshly cut grass has been laid all over the courtyard and on the road leading to the church.*
>
> *The native King is to act as my father. He is almost white with nerves. I am to have two little chocolate-skinned train-bearers. The capital is very full of people and our houses are crowded with English visitors. My colleague has been practising The Wedding March for weeks on my wheezy little portable organ. It is still very imperfect but fortunately it won't be heard in the big church.*
>
> *The wedding reception is to be held in our house, the guests will be seated on the floor on reed mats; we have collected all the tin cups and basins to serve tea in. I've never seen so many sandwiches, jam tarts and cakes. We have been baking for days, and the wedding cake stands high on a native stool in the centre of the table.*
>
> *The King keeps saying to me, 'Thank you, thank you for marrying my dear friend and master.'*

When the English bishop responsible for Africa gave his blessing to their forthcoming union, he also made it quite clear that from the day of their wedding Ruth would receive no further payment from the Church Missionary Society, though she was of course expected to continue in exactly the same role as before, nursing, teaching the women to read and write, and encouraging them to share the Christian faith. A married woman missionary, like any other wife, was merely her husband's chattel and must be supported by him.

In January 1903 she achieved one of her dearest personal ambitions by becoming the first woman to climb the peak of Ruwenzori, 'The Mountains of the Moon', with heights of up to 16,761 feet. She was six weeks pregnant, but had told no one, not even Arthur. My parents were horrified when they discovered the truth – fortunately not until long after the gruelling, extremely dangerous adventure was over.

*

In the spring of 1903 it became apparent that the management of Wilton House, providing rest and recreation for hundreds of worn-out missionary workers every year, from all over the world, had become too much for my aunt. Bee, as the eldest unmarried daughter, lately returned from an unhappy attempt at teaching in Bombay and not having anything better to do, was seen by my parents as her obvious successor. This was a source of wry humour to her siblings, as Bee had no knowledge whatsoever of housekeeping, and had never shown the slightest inclination in that direction. She was dreamy, disorganised and resistant to any responsibility, a fact which had not escaped my parents' notice, but they seemed to think this might be 'the making of her'. One day, though, my father arrived unexpectedly from Alexandra Road and found the guests waiting for their evening meal, nothing in the pantry or oven, and Bee in bed complaining of a headache. I was told in no uncertain terms to abandon my nursing, as there was a more pressing need within the family empire, and both Bee and Phil required my care. This I might have resented, were it not for the fact that I too could count myself a worn-out worker, and had an inkling that running Wilton House, with its steady stream of interesting guests, might be rather an adventure for two such undomesticated young ladies.

May 24th, 1903
Wilton House

My darling old Ruth

It is one of those glorious, calm St Leonards' evenings with an exquisite pink sunset and a peaceful sea, and all my thoughts go over it to my darling girl. I have been thanking God for his goodness in entrusting to your and dear Arthur's care that priceless gift – a living soul. Oh Ruth, how I love to think of you being a mother. All your grand and noble qualities and Arthur's loving characteristics will be exquisitely blended in that little life, that you really ought to be generous and enrich the world all you can.

Bee and I are always talking about it, and we get so excited. You would scream with laughter at some of our remarks. For one thing we are delighted it is happening in Toro. Fancy Sister dear if it were here at Wilton House with Pater hovering, and dear little Mater with her somewhat antiquated midwifery notions losing all patience with my 'fads', and who, of course, would have to be the fully fledged lying-in sister for the occasion. And, above all, old Dr Picard in charge, and the Vicar Stone performing the ceremonials!

There is heaps more I have to tell you, and the first must be of our experiences here last week. As you know, Bee and her friend Edith (i.e. Greenhill) are running the show under entirely new management principles, and amidst the many reforms, the entire domestic staff was swept off the premises. The new lot were not brought in until the following day. Well, my dear, for twenty-four hours we were 'domesticless' and you never in your life heard such peals of laughter as emanated from these premises during that time. There were twenty-six of us in the house and all the guests helped. My aprons were lent all round. One lady and myself started in real earnest by turning out the servants' bedroom, which they left in a proverbial state of filth and untidiness. We Monkey-Branded* and

---

* Brooke's Soap Monkey brand was a household china and metal scouring and polishing product produced by Lever Brothers

scoured every corner. I disturbed the peaceful slumbers of many a beetle.

Bee conferred her attention on the cooking, and you will hear of this anon. You should have seen the bemused looks of the tradesmen as they brought in the milk and meat. It is all over St Leonards that 'the young ladies was actually washing out saucepans'! The day started well. We laid the tables, ate the food, cleared and washed up. Every ring of the bell caused great excitement and in the middle of lunch everyone jumped up every time it rang, each of us keenly feeling our personal responsibilities. However, dinner was another matter – not quite the grand finale we had hoped for.

The vegetables planned for this famous dinner were immense, though somebody got over-ambitious and I found the greens boiling at a full-stretch gallop at 4 o'clock in the afternoon. The potatoes were peeled and put into a vast iron saucepan by a young medical student (a nice little boy I quite lost my heart to – yes, actually I!) who, never having cooked a potato in his life, followed this example and set them too to boil furiously.

Bee had manufactured one of her famous soups and was so enthusiastic that she went to ring the gong at 7.20, at which exact moment I hopelessly caught sight of the two massive joints in the oven, making not the slightest appearance of being ready for use for fully half an hour. Regardless of their half-raw state I set to to dish them up, but found nothing to manipulate them with and finally had to dig the toasting fork into the 22lbs of beef to get it safely landed on the dish. To top it all the gravy went all lumpy.

One young man in the house was fortunately on a dyspeptic diet and was not allowed meat, so volunteered to work the dumb waiter lift for me from below. Four jolly girls, quite unknown to me, dressed up in caps and aprons and did the waiting on. This gave Bee an awful shock as she at first thought they were the new maids and was indignant at their impudence

*in appearing like this unbeknown to her. I finally appeared in
the dining room when dinner was half-way through, feeling
dead-beat but not defeated. Few appeared to mind the rather
bloody meat and its mushy accompaniments.*

*Well, the climax of our dinner was reached at the dessert,
when one poor old lady took a huge mouthful of one of Bee's
special 'noirs noirs' and discovered it was sprinkled with
cayenne pepper instead of nutmeg. The poor old girl appeared
nearly burned alive. Bee declares she was innocent, having
simply found it in the spice box with the cloves etc.*

*After we had washed up all the dinner things, we had coffee,
served in the kitchen, and so closed one of the jolliest days of
our Wilton House experiences. Oh, but really we do have great
times here, and the thousands of times we wish you were with
us, darling.*

*Last week was the annual meeting of the Railway Mission,
when Phil, who has been on compulsory bed rest again,
received special permission from Dr Berry to go there and back
in a fly, and stay for quarter of an hour, just to thank all those
dear people for their prayers for him. Dear Mr Habershon[4] was
to give the address. Well, you can imagine what a warm recep-
tion they both had.*

*Phil and I left punctually after the quarter of an hour, but Mr
H asked Bee to wait and walk home with him. Well of course
he came right up to room 10 where dear old Phil was, and
although I was in number 11 and just getting into bed, he
insisted on seeing his 'little Gracie' too. Well, darling, I got into
one of Bee's swell Indian dressing gowns and got a most lovely
kiss from him, the first I have ever had, and so appreciated, as
we thought the Habershons had forgotten us since they have
become so grand and been made such a fuss of in town and do
things in such big style now. Well he stayed talking with us
three till 11.30, regardless of keeping us all up, and then at last
he went after another kiss, the likes of which, if Edith Greenhill
had had one, we should have heard the echo of, 'Oh Beatie,*

Beatie, Beatie' for a week. Bee saw him out and I came in for
her share of ecstasy at the portico door.

We were not at all surprised to get a letter two days later to
say he had to come down to represent Lord Kinnaird,[5] the
footballing baron (!), at the YMCA council meeting here and
could he invite himself to lunch. It ended, darling, in him stay-
ing the night here and Bee and I seeing him off to Brighton by
steamer the next morning. I had a most lovely talk with him on
the beach. He is a dear man. He talked to me like a father and
says he always means to watch over his little Grace, and
emphatically puts his foot down on my going abroad, for Phil's
sake – and a little bit for my own! He wants me to be a very
clever little nurse and make the most of myself and go to the
London Hospital. It did me a lot of good as he didn't say
stupid things to me like that I 'ought to be married' and all
that, and so of course, I liked him, and better still when I saw
him off from St Leonards pier and he said, 'Good-bye darling'
– which I am going to say to you too now, my old darling, for
it is very late after supper and your little baby, Grace, must go
to sleep.

Always yours.
Gracie

Belonging to one large, happy family meant that relations amongst
us evangelicals were generally affectionate, and we girls, more
than most, were not afraid to be demonstrative of our feelings.
Even so, it was perhaps not altogether wise of Mr Habershon to
encourage three such impressionable, single young ladies in their
frivolities. I rather suspect I was tease enough already, judging
from the great deal of unwanted attention I seemed to attract. But
oh, how tired I was of being constantly reminded of looming
spinsterhood, of being told that I was simply too particular. But
my suitors, however eligible, all appeared naive, ingenuous or just
plain shallow. Why should I yield my precious freedom and independence to become the property of some immature, unworthy

youth, who failed to understand why I should want to dedicate myself to caring for the sick, which, according to Florence Nightingale, was a far superior calling to marriage?

So their many attempts to thaw my frozen heart with flowers, presents or even lamentable poetry was to no avail. I received one such poetic offering on the occasion of the Boat Race in 1901, from a young lawyer friend of Phil's, who fancied himself in love with me. It is indicative of the fact that conjuring up the name of Mrs Pankhurst, or revealing any suffragist sympathy, reliably sent them running back to Mother.

I was walking one day down the Fitzjohn's Parade
That place for boys and girls
When who should I meet but a dear little maid
Whose face was encased in curls.
Now this chanced to happen on the Boat Race day,
Which was very unlucky for me.
For we mutually decided that straight away
We'd take on a bet, you see.
Now with great trepidation we longed to know
The results of the racing crews
She assuredly affirmed that the darks would go
For the chaps in the lighter hues.
When evening came I learned my fate,
So straight to a shop I went,
And bought some gloves, and it being rather late
My steps homeward I bent.
I retired a sadder yet wiser man
Than I'd ever been before,
Determined when I think of the risk I ran
To bet with the girls no more.
For now in this world, we can see at a glance
That the girls are outshining the men,
And so we must meekly watch the advance,
Of the powerful 'new women'.

And then, when I least expected it, at the spinsterly age of twenty-seven, my world was turned upside down when my father's celebrated friend Henry Grattan Guinness, house-hunting for his daughter Lucy, took a room with us for several nights.

Three years earlier, on August 14th, 1900, he had scribbled the following words on a piece of paper, which he kept folded in his wallet:

After a quiet day of prayer in the woods at Eisenach, had a very vivid dream in the night. I had prayed that God would bring me a wife suitable for me and had endeavoured to trust him to do so. Dreamed she came to me in the night, and sat on my knee and kissed me – with a bright smile, her own act. Not given to dreams! Will wait, and wait on God. Through his grace.

When I heard about this later I asked him to show me the piece of paper and, dating it June 11th, 1903, added the following postscript:

. . . and Grace came and sat on his knee and kissed him! My own act.

Part Two

The Letters 1903–10

Our Short Courtship

Sunday, June 14th, 1903
Wilton House, St Leonards

My Ruth, my darling sister

*At last! The awakening has come, and your little Grace is
transformed, and she is really in love. Oh how I have longed to
cable this to you, or at any rate the date of our wedding, July
7th, and yet I dared not for fear it would come as too much of a
shock to you just now. But the relief to sit down and tell you all
about it, knowing that you and Bee will at least understand it
all, and so what do I care for all the other criticisms? Fancy,
Ruth, that Dr Grattan Guinness (he is 68, darling!) has been the
one to break down the barriers I was building round my little
life, barriers I thought unforceable until I met him here just a
few days ago.*

*I must tell you what happened. He called on Wednesday
morning, June 10th, for a room for two or three days as he was
house-hunting for his daughter, Lucy, and her baby boys, who
are living at Cliff College. I attended to him, as dear Bee was in
bed, recovering from a nasty fall she had from a horse.*

*Well, his magnificent presence appealed to me very strongly,
his handsome, clean-shaven face and white hair brushed back
off that great forehead of his. He tells me his first impressions
of me were, 'What a sweet girl', and from that moment we felt
most strongly drawn to each other. He watched me a great
deal at lunch. Harvey Harte was sitting next to me and
noticed it. Edith Greenhill sat at the head, and of course she
noticed it!*

*Well, after lunch we had tea as usual, and everyone went out
but the doctor and me, and strange to say I did not feel in the
least afraid of him as the great Dr Guinness, as everyone else
seemed to be. He took my hand and asked me a little about
myself and what I was doing here, then invited me to sit on his
enormous lap, which I did, without a second thought. After
which he gave me a kiss – such a kiss – and I loved him and felt
I never wanted to leave him, but never for a moment thought
that he would care for me like that. Such a thought never
crossed my mind. I only knew that it was exquisite to be with
him then. The future never occurred to me.*

*The next day he was with me a great deal, coming to meet
me as I came from dressing a wound of one of Dr Berry's
patients at Rothesay House, taking my hand, walking up and
down with me and talking all about his travels, and how he
would love me to see these places and how it would develop
me.*

*Then Friday night, darling, he asked me to come and have a
talk with him in the office and he drew me to him and told me
how he had loved me right from the first moment, and how for
five years he had prayed God to bring him this love, which I had
awakened in him, love he tells me such as he has never known
before. The very morning before he came to Wilton House he
had spent three hours in his room praying about this very
matter, and yet he has been travelling in France, Italy and
Russia seeking a wife, and he had met many women in high
stations of life, but somehow, God has always prevented him.*

*Well darling, as you can guess, it was all too wonderful for
me to take in. All I knew was that I loved him, and should be
miserable without him. I felt he was part of my life already –
but I could not give him an answer that night. I just wanted to
be sure, so remained in that little office in prayer about it, long
past midnight. I had such assurance and peace, and felt as if
God was showing me how all this winter of sorrow and anxiety had just been leading up to this crowning joy of my life.*

Strange how my future had been so very indefinite, the next step a puzzling one to me. You know I had thoughts of going to the London Hospital and yet had arranged nothing definite. Now it all seems arranged by God because he had this in view.

Really, I could not have thought it possible to be so happy, yet so humbled, for Ruth, I cannot understand why he loves me. Such intellect, and such a soul. And you know what a silly little chatter-box I can be. I tried to tell him of all my faults, but he only kisses me and says he has never known such love before. Well, there it is, darling. Of course I could go on writing pages about it – but it will tire you, and anyway, you understand this all so well.

Yesterday he asked me to walk towards Bexhill with him, and about halfway we sat down on the beach. And he prayed. Such a prayer! We were right up close to the water's edge and the tide was coming in and he prayed about the incoming tide of God's blessings on our united lives. And so, by the time you get this I shall be your own little Grace Grattan Guinness.

Henry Grattan Guinness

I have no idea what possessed me to sit on his knee. And then to kiss him. A man old enough to be my grandfather! Perhaps that was why – that despite the power of my attraction, I persuaded myself that it was nothing more than my usual playfulness. After all, why would such a famous, clever man have any interest in me? Other than as the daughter of an esteemed friend, of course.

Some would have deemed it forward, even improper. But I was jesting with him and laughing, and it all seemed so natural, so right. One moment I was standing chattering, my own face at his face height as he sat. The next . . . well, there was no other chair in the room. And I fitted into him so snugly, there being such a discrepancy in our size. And he didn't find it strange at all. On the contrary, he was, he told me later, overwhelmed that it so closely mirrored the dream he had held in his heart for three long years, never once imagining that the kiss would come from one so young.

Henry's first wife, Fanny, had been dead for five years, their last years together blighted by an apoplexy that paralysed her right side and robbed her of her speech. Even so, once I had agreed to his proposal for a quick wedding (why wait a day when we might have so few together?), I became quite anxious about how family and friends might respond to such an apparent mismatch.

True, his celebrity status had faded somewhat, the generation that had lived through the Great Revival now elderly or gone, his training work reduced due to a downturn in interest, and therefore subject to the same financial constrictions that now constrained my father – hence the need to find his daughter, Lucy, a house. He is forced to sell Cliff College to the Methodists, but Lucy, who loved it, had been living there with her two little boys while her husband, Karl Kumm, was in the Sudan, setting up pioneer missionary stations – until she realised how expensive it was to run, how impractical a base for her efforts to raise funds.

Nonetheless Henry was still one of the most popular writers of the age – a Doctor of Divinity thanks to his books on the fulfilment of biblical prophecy. Even Arthur Balfour, our Prime

Minister no less, had written to him to express his appreciation, claiming that he had studied them closely.

In our large social circle, even Henry's two sons and two daughters (all a great deal older than I) were widely known in their own right, their collective achievements daunting to say the least. Dr Harry and his wife Annie were co-directors of the Regions Beyond Missionary Union, sending missionaries into deepest Africa; Geraldine, who had such an influence on Ruth's own call all those years ago, had married Dr Howard Taylor, son of the great Hudson Taylor, founder of the China Inland Mission, and was a very popular writer and speaker; Lucy and her German husband Karl were the co-founders and directors of the Sudan United Mission; and Whitfield, the only doctor in the Henan province of China, and his wife Janie, a niece of Prince Bernadotte of Sweden, were building the first hospital there. Who was I to become a part of such an illustrious dynasty? Would they think me too young, or not serious or spiritual enough for their father?

We knew people would find us a strange-looking pair, but what did we care? We would laugh at their reactions, but it was necessary to convince those nearest and dearest to us that our meteoric love was as passionate and true, indeed perhaps more so thanks to Henry's maturity, as if he were forty years younger. Even those who applauded his fortune in finding so young a bride might think I was throwing myself away on a much older man. It cheered me greatly that Mrs Pankhurst had been married to a man twenty-four years her senior and that they had produced five children while she continued her campaigning work.

It was with some trepidation that I went up to town, to Alexandra Road, to see my parents. Henry had already been to ask them for my hand. The maid had barely opened the door before my parents both appeared from their respective rooms, took me into their arms and kissed me.

As soon as tea had been served in the drawing room my father admitted that while my craft seemed to be sailing gaily over calm and sunny seas, theirs had had the wind taken out of its sails. My mother, smiling, said she had almost fainted at the news, but once the salts were brought in and she had rallied from her initial shock, she had found it 'rather romantic'. '. . . if a little strange,' added my father. Others, too, he opined, would also wonder how one so young could give her life to a man so greatly beyond her years instead of to one with prospects of long life and comfort before him. But what mattered their misgivings, what mattered age, if I were truly happy and in love with Grattan? However, he still had the presence of mind to demand reassurances from Henry that financial provision would be made for me, given my now 'uncertain future'. A new will is to be made forthwith.

The following day a letter arrived here from Henry which brought such relief to us all. His family, far from disapproving, appeared delighted with the news.

June 18th, 1903
Cliff House, Calver, Derbyshire

My own darling Grace, my very own

I have read and re-read your last letters, which I found on my arrival here last night, with such love and joy, answering to your own – my wife, my life – in anticipation, and in heart, intention, spirit, in reality, how wonderful is the relation – love's secret hidden for a season in the heart, and then, slowly or suddenly bursting into bloom!

Lucy rejoiced when I told her of my appreciation of my darling. She will leave her two babes here, and come to our wedding, so all my children will be there . . . How soon they will know that you have ceased to be Miss Hurditch! Changed your name, while remaining yourself, will you know yourself my darling? When your pure, sweet life is blended with the riper life of the one you love?

My sweet Grace, I delight now in your name, which like yourself has won its way into my heart. I would not change it, if I could, for any other in the world.

I write from my quiet study at Cliff College, with beautiful memories. I was in the garden this morning and the park, and wanted to gather the best of all the flowers and send them to you. I plucked the leaves of fragrant thyme, or rather lavender and roses and wanted you to have them all. You must come here with me after Switzerland, to see the place where we have spent, as a family, so many happy summers.

I hope you will have a happy Sunday at your father and mother's house. I will not say your home, for your home, darling, is with me.

I am your own loving husband that is to be. Henry.

After I had read the letter to my father in his study, I admitted to him (with Ruth so far away, I had no one else to tell) that I had never actually read any of Grattan's books and felt it imperative I should at least understand the fundamentals of my beloved's hypotheses – especially if the Prime Minister knew of them. I might meet him one day, and how shaming to have to profess to being completely in the dark. I had repeatedly asked Henry to explain, but he had merely laughed, kissed me, and said, 'All in its good time.' My father chuckled too at the thought of a mere woman getting her head around such great complexities, but finally admitted to the wisdom of it. These concepts are indeed rather difficult, yet wonderful too, and so I attempt here a bowdlerised version.

In the 1880s Grattan had become the foremost authority in the world on astronomy and history as a means to understanding some of the more indecipherable prophecies of the Bible. This thanks to the discoveries of a Swiss astronomer called Jean Philippe Loys de Cheseaux, who was determined to establish the exact date of the crucifixion from his studies in the book of Daniel. Medieval astronomers had always maintained there was no relation between the orbits of the earth, sun and moon, but in 1754 de Cheseaux inadvertently discovered that 1,260 years, the number of 'days' stipulated in Daniel and Revelation as having great historical significance, was the time it took for the sun and moon to complete a cycle in space to within one hour of each other, bringing the solar and lunar calendars into almost total harmony.

This, my father explained, was the key to Grattan's genius. When he began to measure biblical time in lunar rather than the Western calendar's solar years, then returned to Daniel's figure of '1,260 days', with each 'day' representing a year, Daniel's 'times, time and half a time', namely three and a half years' worth of years, came to 1,260 years. The 'seven times' referred to in Daniel and Revelation is therefore 2,520 years, twice de Cheseaux's 1,260 years.

'And it is nearly 2,000 years since the death of Christ. We must be those living in the end times,' I exclaimed. 'How marvellous.'

My father agreed. We cannot know exact dates or times, he said, but in Grattan's lectures he explained that just as the earth has its own cycles measured by a very human clock in seconds, minutes, hours, days, seasons and years, so biblical time is measured by vast astronomical clocks. Understand the astronomical code, and the apocalyptic books begin to give us a sense of how history is unfolding. 'The references in the text to days, weeks, years and times are what Grattan calls [and here my father picked one of Henry's books from his shelf, skimming through his underlining in the prologue] "natural astronomic cycles of singular accuracy and beauty, unknown to mankind until discovered by means of these very prophecies themselves." '

'No wonder that his books sell so well.'

'People are hungry to see a pre-planned purpose in the rise and fall of empires, in the historical events of the past 4,000 years, and of their own time, of course. But Gracie,' said my father earnestly, 'you must be clear that Grattan makes no attempt to foretell the Second Coming, whatever nonsense others may say of him. That remains hidden from human eyes. His task has been to convince us of the reliability of the Bible in demonstrating God's ultimate control of all human destiny.'

'It is rather overwhelming,' I said.

My father squeezed my hand. 'Ah, Gracie, you see, you have chosen a most exceptional man – a Fellow of the Royal Astronomical Society and of the Royal Geological Society, a Doctor of Divinity awarded by Brown University, one of the best in the United States. His detailed astronomical tables in *Creation Centred in Christ* are now standard reference in observatories worldwide. But,' he said, rising to take my facc in his hands, 'you will be more than match enough for him, of that I am sure. In putting mind, heart and life before any other quality or consideration under the sun, in accepting the hand of my dearly valued friend, notwithstanding his age, you will indeed possess all these in no ordinary measure, and may God preserve him to you many years, perhaps aided by your very youth, brightness and care, for increased happiness and usefulness.'

Upon my return to Wilton House a few days later, I found a letter from my father awaiting me. For one terrible moment I thought he might have changed his mind, rushed to my room and tore open the envelope. Then I wept for joy to read the further thoughts he had committed to paper.

June 21st, 1903
164 Alexandra Rd, St John's Wood, NW

My darling Grace

Regarding our conversations of the last days, that this man for whom I have had perhaps a deeper affection for than any other in the world since I knew him before his first marriage, and of whose consecrated life I have entertained the greatest admiration, and for whose family I have ever held so deep a regard, that this dear friend of many years should come to me with such news and request is still almost beyond my realisation.

In giving you to him I feel I am only paying him back a part of what I owe him for much spiritual profit in my earlier years and as a further seal of the deep friendship we have cherished ever since.

Be assured therefore, my precious Grace, that despite all criticisms that may be passed (and under the special circumstances these may be expected), you have my consent and heartiest, prayerful wishes for your ever increasing happiness in the union to which you have consented, and I hope I may have grace to forgive the Dr for robbing me – us all – of so bright a jewel in our home-crown of rejoicing. I dare not think what Phil, and especially Ruth, will feel in the loss, but 'all will be well' I doubt not, and their hearts and ours will be comforted in the joyous thought that you will be dearly loved as you deserve to be (though it is your father who says it). I cannot write more now though you are scarcely ever out of my thoughts.

When are you coming up to London again? And Phil? Is your beloved coming to the Mildmay Conference? I am not going, I think, given the circumstances, it might be wiser to stay away just now.

Ma told me of Lord Radstock's warm congratulations to both of you. He declared you would make Henry a splendid wife. Age, said he, is nothing. Just what my dear friend Campbell Morgan said. Amen.

I need not add that I am delighted it has been so well received by the student family at Harley and Cliff College. I hear that they have never had such a large gathering at their annual directional meeting, as all were expecting you to be at his side when he spoke, and though nothing was said of your engagement, it was the talk in the garden afterwards. Notwithstanding all our attempts to keep the news as quiet as possible it is astonishing how quickly it has spread, reaching Scotland almost before your Ma and I realised it was a fact.

I remain your ever devoted, affectionate Father
C. Russell Hurditch

Four days later I received the most lovely, tender letter of welcome from Geraldine Taylor herself. I was, I admit, rather in awe of her, even though I am her new step-mama.

It pleases me to see that in terms of their importance in the world of mission, Henry never distinguishes between his sons and his daughters. When I tell him I want to be useful, but have no plans to be the kind of wife who sits in the drawing room all day serving tea, he laughs. He isn't, he admits, the most practical of men, and it was Fanny who ran Harley and Cliff Colleges, ensured they were in good repair, welcomed the students, saw to their needs, put food on their plates, and when money was not forthcoming, somehow managed to pay the bills. He has, he insists, no similar expectation of me.

Fanny was also a formidable preacher. She and Catherine Booth of the Salvation Army were great friends, both insisting on a woman's right to the pulpit. Henry supported them fully, even though their preaching was not always well received and that cost them both bitter tears of frustration and pain.

His daughter Geraldine was much influenced by them, he says, and is now in such demand as a speaker herself that her husband has abandoned his medical career to devote himself to looking after her. They have currently buried themselves in Switzerland, the only place she finds the peace she needs to write a long biography of her father-in-law, Hudson Taylor.

But of me, he says, it is companionship he most craves.

June 25th, 1903
La Paisible, Vevey, Switzerland

Gracie dear

How can I write to you from so full a heart? Though we have never met, I love you dearly because of your love to him. And I long to make you feel how great is our joy in the thought that so soon you will be ours!

Only this morning father's letter reached me bringing the first news of this happy event. Of course it is a great surprise, but most welcome! And Father tells me that all is arranged and even the day decided upon, July 7th. It is very sweet and good of you

*to consent to its being so soon. I am glad on dear Father's
account.*

*For he loves you, Gracie! I wish you could see his letter to me
about it. He has so much to give. The wealth of his great soul
and tender heart. And it is yours, all yours. Oh, such a heart,
Gracie! You will explore your treasures as the days go on. And
you have much to give dear, your fresh young life and love. But
he is worth it all. How did you find out so soon?*

*You will tell me all you can when we meet next week – DV.
Meanwhile, with deep thankfulness to God and warm, welcom-
ing love,*

I am your own
Geraldine Taylor (née Guinness)

When I have the time to consider it, it surprises me how easily my
dream of nursing has been subsumed in wedding plans, but then,
we have been guided, and marriage to such a man must surely be
the higher calling?

*Now, my darling [I wrote to Ruth], how I shall need your
prayers, for I long to be worthy of my high calling, and he
wants to teach me so much, and it often occurs to me how
wonderfully you could talk to him on the great subjects that
fill his mind. He is just now completing a marvellous book on
the historical sequence of the Apocalypse (and I didn't even
know how to spell it!). He has read me many portions from it.
He is always reading some beautiful things to me and has given
me a most perfect copy of Milton. In fact I cannot enumerate
all he has given. Every time he goes to London something
comes down. It was a compressed cane travelling trunk and a
canteen of cutlery last week, and before that, he brought me
back two beautiful buckles for belts, a long string of pearls
and a purse with silver corners. I have told him I don't care a
bit about these sorts of things but he loves me to look pretty
fancy.*

Anyhow, we both agree to having a very quiet wedding. At first he wanted Father to bring me over to Switzerland and be married there, but there were some difficulties. So we arranged it should be here, where we met. He would have been married in the Church of England if I had pressed it, but in consideration of his family, we arranged that Mr New should marry us at the Congregational Church by special licence and we are having luncheon at the Queen's Hotel after, then going on to Folkestone, crossing over to Switzerland the following day and after that, darling, he is going to take me to America. He had intended making a tour there before he met me. The Guinnesses have many friends in the States and he is going to take me to some lovely places.

Oh my darling, don't think me selfish talking about myself like this, but I know you will want to know everything, and so I am just writing it as it comes to mind. But don't think that everything else is excluded. One of my first thoughts when I promised to marry him so soon was, should I see you? I remembered your talk of making a tour, and I had visions of being the very first in the family to see you, for I shall insist on my darling taking me over to meet you at some point of your homeward journey. How proud I shall be for him to meet you – my magnificent old Ruth. I have read him many of your dear letters.

You know what a great poet he is. I think I must give you a most exquisite little poem he wrote me just before he went away after our engagement. Somehow I don't like that word and I wouldn't allow him even to give me a ring, for we were so completely one, and from the very first he called me his little wife, and told me that in God's sight we were husband and wife, and there was nothing for us to wait for, and so you see that is why we arranged to be married so soon.

She has come to my arms, she has come to my heart,
And the dream of my soul is fulfilled,

> *And the love that unites us shall never depart,*
> *Nor the love that our union has willed.*
> *O thanks to the Giver, O thanks for the gift,*
> *From the gift to the Giver we turn;*
> *From the bliss he bestows to Himself we uplift*
> *The hearts which with gratitude burn.*
> *There is heaven below, there is heaven above,*
> *And they answer like ocean and sky;*
> *For heaven is found in the bosom of love,*
> *In spirit to spirit made nigh.*

Now, Ruthie, what do you think of that? Isn't it perfectly lovely? I have also had a wonderful welcome from his remarkable family, so I don't feel as daunted by them as I first did. His daughter, Geraldine Taylor, sent me the sweetest letter. As did Lucy, and Harry's wife, Annie Guinness. They, and their brother, Whitfield, currently on furlough from China, are all coming to the wedding.

Now my Ruth I must say goodnight, for I have promised to read Bee something from Milton. I am sitting with her now in number 14, writing this, while she is writing to you. We have not told you before of the dear girl's accident because we thought it might unnecessarily alarm you, whereas it is really nothing serious. We were out riding and had barely started when Bee's horse backed onto the pavement and slipped down. It was the shock more than anything, especially as she is being treated already for nerves and liver by Dr Berry. This unfortunately upset her so that really, Ruth, I found it impossible to nurse her, as her nerves were in such a condition that I could simply do nothing with her and Dr Berry saw that I should quite break down under the strain, and so arranged to have her in a small private ward in the Hastings Hospital, making the chief excuse that she must be on a water bed. It has done her all the good in the world and she came back here last Wednesday. Dr Berry tells me he doesn't think he will allow

*her to come to my wedding. The excitement would undo all the
good the rest has done her. I find it extraordinary that Bee will
not have been present at any of the weddings. Perhaps it is for
the best in one way. I think the darling girl perhaps would feel
it rather.*

*Now to close and read to her. Goodbye my darling. Always
yours and ever more yours than ever before because of this new
affinity we shall have as married ladies.*

> *July 3rd, 1903*
> *Harley House*

Grace
My own darling

*The gardens here are crowded with friends and a photogra-
pher is taking a picture of the scene through the window of the
room in which I write. We have had a crowded, excellent
annual meeting – and three of my dear children spoke – Dr
Harry, Dr Whitfield and my dear Geraldine. Dr Barnado was
there. Mr F.B. Meyer gave an admirable address. It has been
very pleasant to meet so many old friends, and quite a number
of them had heard the news of our approaching marriage.
There were congratulations on every hand.*

*I have to take the chair at the evening meeting, so I have but
a few moments to write, but I will not let the day go by without
sending you a loving message. How I wish you could have
heard Geraldine this afternoon, a solemn, thrilling address
which, coming at the close of the long meeting, held the large
assembly breathless, and drew tears from many eyes. Truly, she
is a blessed woman and she already loves you. While I write I
hear Dr Harry addressing the big crowd in the garden; his voice
sounds all over the place. He is talking about what he has seen
in the Congo – the abuses of the natives by the Belgian administration. They are savagely beaten, or have a hand cut off if
they don't bring in their quota of rubber, shot if they dare to*

protest. It is intolerable and the missionaries are holding special meetings at all the stations to see what can be done to put a stop to it.

By the way I hear that Dr Harry and Dr Whitfield are to get you a travelling bag with interior useful fittings – so don't purchase one for yourself.

And now, my darling, another day of our separation has gone by, there remaining only Saturday and Sunday and Monday until we meet again.

I must close – I embrace you tenderly in thoughts – your sweet picture is before me, you are ever with me and ever shall be. Darling, God bless you and make our united life a blessing to many.

Ever your own loving Henry

On the eve of our wedding, I found myself alone for a few moments outside my bedroom door with Lucy, Henry's younger daughter. Such a dear woman. More gentle, less forceful than Geraldine her sister, and yet there is an extraordinary brilliance about her, especially when she speaks of her passion for the work in the Sudan. She and her husband Karl Kumm, were horrified to discover the extent to which the Arab Muslim slavers had imposed their Islamic religion on the north. It is now, she says, Arabic in both culture and dress. So Karl is seeking openings in the more tribal south before the population there is similarly subsumed. But this is not a safe nor suitable occupation for a woman with two small children, so she must stay behind, raising funds for the work.

She did not complain, but I sensed that while she has thrown herself into the task, yet she baulks at being reduced to such a role after so many years of freedom to write and preach and accompany her father on his expeditions around the world. 'Ah, Gracie,' she said with a sigh, as I was about to leave her for my beauty sleep, 'aren't we blessed to marry such great men? But there is no blessing without cost.'

Grace Guinness on her wedding day

Henry and Grace on their wedding day

Hastings Observer, July 10th, 1903

A wedding of considerable interest to nonconformists took place on Tuesday at the Robertson Street Congregational Church, the contracting parties being Miss Grace Russell Hurditch, daughter of Mr Russell Hurditch, Founder and Director of the Evangelical Mission in London, and the Revd Dr Henry Grattan Guinness, DD, founder of the East London Training Institution, Harley Street, Bow.

The marriage service was conducted by the Rev. Charles New. After the ceremony luncheon was partaken of at the Queen's Hotel, at which attended only the immediate relatives of the bride and bridegroom. Afterwards the happy couple left by train for Folkestone, en route for the continent, where the honeymoon is being spent.

Mr Dick Russell supplied the carriages.

Our Long Honeymoon

And so our five-year, worldwide honeymoon began, though such expansiveness was not the intention when we set out. We thought to tour Europe and thence continue only to the United States, but a Higher Providence had other ideas. It would be five years before I saw my parents again.

Henry had gone to Folkestone some days earlier and engaged a balcony room looking towards the sunset in the Hotel Metropole on The Leas, where we stayed for two days before setting off for Brussels. It was there that I had the time to give to Ruth a full account of my wedding day.

July 11th, 1903
Hotel de Belle Vue, Rue Royale, Brussels

My own Ruth, my darling girl
  More than ever in true sympathy and love with you because another link has been added to the chain that unites us. How can I write to you old girl of all my happiness – this wonderful new life.
  Surely I can talk to you better than anyone because you have so recently experienced these strange and beautiful delights. Ruth old girl, isn't the love, protection, guardianship, sympathy and affection of a good man the greatest blessing that can come into a woman's life? My beloved husband has opened up a new world to me. His love has just touched the spring of that secret chamber which I never knew existed and my happiness is complete.
  Ruth, you don't know how humbled I feel when I think of the way God has honoured me, for my darling is so good and

*clever and wonderful, and his intellect marvellous! He reads
to me and is educating me all day, but at numerous intervals,
whether in the Grand Parc de Bruxelles, or under the palms
on the hotel verandah, impresses his ideas on me with a kiss,
such a kiss, followed by some exquisite expressions of his
love.*

*Well, darling, have I given you any idea of our happiness? If
so, let me go on to tell you of how our time has passed since
the letter I wrote telling of our love story and approaching
marriage.*

*Such a wedding, simple and quiet, just the plain marriage
service read by Mr New, with Henry's son Harry and his eldest
child Whitfield, Geraldine and Howard Taylor and Lucy on one
side, and Mother, Phil, Harry, Lil and Auntie Maud on the
other in the choir stalls at Robertson St. The whole service was
over in half an hour and finished with his giving me a lovely
embrace. There were a few outsiders there, who managed to
find out where the wedding was, in spite of our endeavours to
keep it quiet. We then drove to the Queen's Hotel, where a
lovely lunch was provided, with white flowers all down the
table.*

*In case no one tells you what I wore, here goes. The palest
dove grey gossamer voile dress made over silk, with a real lace
berthe, a black velvet bonnet, with white net strings, and long
pale grey gossamer veil down the back. Everyone said, darling,
that I looked rather sweet. My beautiful bouquet was composed
of tiger lilies and lilies of the valley. After a bright, happy
cheerful time at luncheon we drove off to Westons to be photo-
graphed, sweet Geraldine and her husband coming too, in order
to pose us (both are very artistic), then we went back to the
hotel where Mother and Edith were waiting to get me into a
Bolton-tailor-made pale grey coat and skirt. (I am sticking to a
bonnet. It becomes me as Mrs Grattan Guinness!) Then off we
went to the station and had a loving send-off from Geraldine,
Howard and Lucy.*

The two families had stayed at the Queen's the previous evening with their father and did a hundred and one little nice things for me, finishing touches to his toilet. He looked perfectly exquisite in frock coat and white tie and waistcoat and top hat, so absolutely aristocratic with his magnificent face and white hair and upright figure. Really it's not surprising that people stare at us both. We are a little out of the ordinary. And whenever we go into a shop he manages to say something about his 'petite femme' so as to see the looks of approval!

Well, darling, there is such a lot to tell you. I expect dear old Bee will have written to you it all. Her beautiful unselfish sympathy and interest in my joy was touching. Dr Berry was keeping her very quiet and would not consent to her coming, thinking the excitement would be too much for her, but anyhow, I was with her a good deal on the morning, and dashed into her room at each stage of my wearing apparel.

One thing that characterised my wedding day was the rather surprising lack of excitement and fatigue. It was all so beautifully quiet and calm, and natural. I remember, old girl, the first letter you wrote to me after your marriage, you said it was all so natural and no wonderful changes had come. Well, darling, that is just about the truth of it. It is just the most natural thing in the world to be with our kindred spirit, and I'm sure you would have thought that no change had come to me, if you had seen me this afternoon in a marionette tea gown reciting to my dear Grattan, who greatly appreciates all my little funs and frivolities. Don't be afraid of his converting me into some sedate little saint, for he loves me just as I am, at least so he says!

Our honeymoon commenced at Folkestone where we stayed two days before crossing from Dover to Ostend en route for Brussels. We have had three days here and are staying over Sunday as there is so much of interest and Grattan is a great historian and is fascinated at having discovered missing links in the chain of Spanish history. He has invested in a splendid

History of Belgium and we are reading it together. Tomorrow, Sunday, we are going in search of some Protestant church and shall try to find out what is being done in Christian work here. Then we go on to Cologne and start up the Rhine Valley for Italy and Switzerland.

I say, old girl, haven't you and I had positively ideal honeymoons and positively ideal husbands?

I am keeping a diary, just writing down the places we visit, because we hope to travel much and it is bound to be an interesting record . . . While I am writing this there are about a dozen Americans twanging away nineteen to the dozen. They are talking such a lot of nonsense and in such loud tones, evidently wealthy people by the way they are talking about their travels. How trivial even travel becomes when done in this way, whereas with my Grattan it becomes an education, creates an interest and leaves a lasting impression.

Aix-la-Chapelle, 3 days later
We are staying one week here before going to Cologne. This place has wondrous fascination for Grattan (and so of course for me!) because the great Charlemagne, who built the fallen Roman Empire made this his abode. I took the mineral waters and baths, which my beloved is indulging me in. I tell him I am sure he urges it for no physical reasons, but simply because of their historical association.

Anyhow, this place will be immortalised in his memory now, as being the scene of my declamations on Uncle Podger*– which I treated him to yesterday afternoon. He screamed with enjoyment and now waits for me to go out.

Goodbye, my own precious Ruth and Arthur, from your little Grace

---

* Uncle Podger was a character created by Jerome K. Jerome in his book *Three Men in a Boat*, first published in 1889

July 23rd, 1903
Hotel Kaiserlichen Krone, Aix-la-Chapelle

Dear Mrs Hurditch

You ask me in your letter to Grace what I think about your darling child now! Well I could write eloquently on the theme, if I could only trust myself to speak out all my appreciation, I fear I should seem extravagant! We are more happy together and more united to each other than I could have conceived we should be.

She is bright as sunshine, and sweet as a spring day, practical, energetic, clever and deft in her ways, and helps me marvellously well, writes for me, reads to me (and I to her), took down an article for me today for the press on 'The Holy Roman Empire' and its connection with Aix-la-Chapelle – looks after my things, and is the most loving companion that could possibly be.

I will not add, but only say my heart overflows with gratitude to God and I am doing all I can to care for my sweet treasure, your dear child, and make her life happy.

Give my love to your dear husband and believe me, dear Mrs Hurditch

Yours affectionately,
H. Grattan Guinness

August, 1903

I went sightseeing, alone, in Ostend, lost my way completely, almost missed the train – and my beloved. But all was well in the end, and I wrote this piece of doggerel for Henry:

> *He wed me with the golden ring,*
> *And made my happy heart to sing;*
> *And now that circlet fair of love,*

Recalls my thoughts when'er they rove,
And makes me think that I and he
Are one to all eternity.

A few weeks later, my darling Henry almost forsook me for good! Imagine my terror as I watched him suddenly disappear down the mountain. I was convinced I had been widowed almost before I had time to be a wife. Such a remarkable, divine intervention. In an interview for *The Daily News*, 'the celebrated preacher, Henry Grattan Guinness', as they called him, described for them that awful moment:

I was climbing up a steep hill to visit a cavern in which some of the Waldensians took refuge during the days of religious persecution. My foot slipped and I disappeared out of my wife's sight down the steep side of the mountain. I should have been hurled over a precipice, but providentially my downward progress was impeded by a tree stump which was on the verge of the cliff. I instinctively threw my arms around it and the action undoubtedly saved my life. That was my nearest approach to death during the whole tour.[6]

September, 1903

On the 4th of this month Ruth gave birth to a baby boy, whom she called George Pilkington, in honour of the first man to translate the Bible into Luganda, the language of the kingdoms of British East Africa. She and Arthur then set off for home, a year's furlough in the United Kingdom. It was a tortuous return trek, perhaps more so than her outward journey when she at least had a bicycle. But now little George had to be carried in a hammock across the 800 miles of mountain passes to Zanzibar.

We had so hoped to see them on their way to London, after so many long years of separation to be the first in the family to introduce our husbands to each other, but it was not to be. Our timings could not be made to connect and my disappointment was immense.

So I contented myself with travel instead, happy simply to be at Henry's side, a companion and secretary, while he was my teacher and guide – in all things. From Italy we went on to Switzerland where we spent some time with Geraldine and Howard, so that while Geraldine worked on her Hudson Taylor biography, her father could complete his book, *History Unveiling Prophecy*. I am his amanuensis. Imagine it. I! It is a history of the church from its pre-Constantine beginnings through the Middle Ages and Reformation to the present day, as described in the Apocalypse. Henry explained that a scholar called Barnes compiled an extensive list of the symbols in the book, and then, using only the Scriptures, assigned a historical religious event to each of them. Henry was astounded to see that Gibbon's *Decline and Fall of the Roman Empire* appeared to follow Barnes's notes. But how could that be since Gibbon was no believer and certainly not supportive of the Christian religion? Only if the Apocalyptic prophecies, written so long before these events, foresaw them.

My eyes have been opened. For over 1,200 years, the Roman church, and we are perhaps more conscious of it here in Europe where there are many hidden monuments, has mercilessly persecuted, even exterminated, any dissenting Christians. It is deeply shocking and may, I hope, come as a revelation to many, but perhaps the book will play its part preventing such intolerance.

The book almost complete, we set off for the United States.

November 24th, 1903

> *Germantown, before my darling arose this morning:*

> *Oh she was fair*
> *with her long dark hair*

and the lovelight in her eyes
They say men deceive
About Adam and Eve
But we know there was paradise.
H.G.G.

In December we visited New York, Philadelphia and Chicago. Forty-five years had passed since Henry had last visited Philadelphia, where in the great revival days of 1859 thousands flocked to hear him preach. There were not thousands this time, though hundreds still turned out to hear him wherever he went. He found it strange to stand in the same pulpits, to meet the children and grandchildren of those converted through his preaching so long ago.

We crossed the entire country to spend Christmas in Los Angeles at the Lakeview Hotel overlooking Westlake Park. My first Christmas away from home, and yet I am at home because I am with Henry.

By the following Christmas we were in Minneapolis. But what a year we had in between – Santa Barbara, San Francisco (Henry finished writing *History Unveiling Prophecy* there on September 12th – my 'work' is over), the Yosemite Valley, 772 miles by train (36 hours) to Portland, Oregon, then Seattle, Washington, and on up to Vancouver on the midnight boat, Banff in the Rockies, then a boat down the coast, then on to Mississippi, and back up to the Saint Louis exhibition on the way to Minneapolis.

Being thrown together in one small rented room for weeks at a time was not always easy, so Henry, who always manages to see the bright side of any situation, cheered me with another, rather lovely poem he wrote for me.

Love in a Cottage, Seattle, October 10th, 1904

I ask not for the sculptured hall,
The gilded roof, the pictured wall,
Enough for me my home to call

This room and thee.
A little space, a humble board,
A shelf with mental treasures stored,
And flowers the wayside may afford
My room and thee.
For not from multitude of things,
Or hoarded wealth contentment springs;
It visits on its lowly wings
My room and thee.
A heart at rest, a heaven in store,
Suffice me, and an open door
Which floods with radiance roof and floor,
My room and thee.

By the end of the year I was dizzy with all the travelling, and not just a little exhausted, but I tried not to complain. Henry never did, despite an exhausting preaching schedule. He welcomed every opportunity with almost boyish glee.

Everywhere we go we are fêted like royalty. His former students all bless him for the inspirational training they received. Their converts are familiar with his influence and hungry to hear him. Complete strangers tell him that all those years ago he was the gateway to their parents' faith, or their faith, or to deeper faith. Others tell him his books have changed their perspective on the fulfilment of biblical prophecy, and therefore on history, on politics, on their own destiny. Each time he preaches he is besieged by crowds clamouring to thank him for the life-changing power of his words.

It pleases me to see my darling so appreciated. What wife wouldn't indulge in a little vicarious pride and congratulate herself on having attracted such a man? He is so striking with his great height, his mane of silver hair, those penetrating blue eyes and velvet tones of voice. Though it is, of course, the powerful effect of his discourse that is of greatest weight.

I sometimes wonder, when I have achieved so little in my sheltered life compared to his worldwide ministry, what it is he sees in me. I feel so superficial and silly at times, when I tease and chide him, but he assures that 'my little frivolities' are a necessary balance for his more serious tendencies.

He has sold a great number of books. *Light for the Last Days* has had to be reprinted over and over again. And now Ruth too has written a book – about her experiences in Toro. It's to be called *On the Borders of Pygmyland*. She left it with her publisher shortly before leaving England with Arthur and baby George to go back to British East Africa, this time to Hoima in the Bunyoro kingdom. Before they left, they managed to get an interview with Sir Henry 'Livingstone, I presume' Stanley, who had inspired them and so many to missionary service in that great continent. They found him very frail, but with enough energy to express his appreciation of their work. He asked if he could be godfather to their next child, but died shortly after, before he could see the fulfilment of their promise.

*

1905 saw no let-up in our hectic schedule – Toronto, Niagara, Georgia, Florida, Miami, Cuba, Alabama, Nashville, Kansas City, these listed in no particular order as I have completely lost track. Requests for Henry's preaching continued to pour in – from as far afield as Japan, China and Australia. Once his beloved Cliff House was sold he felt little attachment to England, and since we were already half-way across the globe and there was nothing to call us home, he decided to accept these invitations, fulfilling at the same time a lifelong ambition to see the work of former Harley and Cliff students serving as missionaries all over the world.

But first we made our way back to Chicago to await news of the international peace conference in Maine, chaired by Theodore Roosevelt, a last chance to prevent a further outbreak of the dreadful war between the Russians and the Japanese that would prevent our proposed travel to Japan. Henry was not fond of Chicago, 'a monster shop or warehouse', he called it, 'twenty storeys high, throbbing with life, running its currents with electric speed at blood heat – a terrible whirling centre of commercial activity'. But the Moody Bible Institute, modelled on Henry's Harley College, was such a haven in that frenetic city. Dwight Moody, the famous American evangelist, whom Henry had encouraged to come to London in the 1870s, had told Henry to regard the Institute as his American home. And though he had died, sadly, some years before, his children ensured that we had every comfort before we moved on for several welcome days of rest and recuperation to the Old Faithful Inn in Yellowstone Park, where Henry took his favourite photograph of me looking out of the window.

To My Wife's Picture, October 5th, 1905

Methinks my thoughts have gone to heaven to be,
And that its angel sisters are all like thee;
Or is that an angel wandering wide
Sits there like thee the window beside,
Searching the infinite with longing eye?
Nay, thou art woman more than angels nigh;
If this the soul of woman 'tis the same
As gentleness, Angelica her name,
Or modesty, or purity, or Grace,
For all are shining in her heavenly face,
Thy book forgotten; linger love lit there,
I would not wake thee from thy vision fair.

An international peace treaty finally signed and sealed, we set sail for Yokohama, then on to Tokyo University, where Henry had been invited to deliver a series of lectures. And so to China, continuing on up the Grand Canal to Yang Cheo (several days on those awful boats were quite enough for me – how do the missionaries do it?).

It was in the early hours of a chilly November morning that we caught sight of the outlines of Shanghai. Streams of muddy brown water intermingling with the ocean-green indicated our entry to the great Yangtze River. Passengers and baggage were transferred to a river steamer which took us the remainder of the journey. We watched as Whitfield's dear face slowly materialised on the quay. With him was his new wife, the Swedish princess Jane af Sandeburg, who, despite having Stockholm's richest men at her feet, had opted instead to be a single missionary in China, and had then been introduced to Henry's Whitfield. I was very struck by her gentle beauty. They were both in Chinese dress, which Hudson Taylor always insisted upon, but it was odd to see Whitfield moustachioed, with a shaven head and a pigtail hanging down his back.

One of Henry's first priorities was to visit the cemetery where Hudson Taylor's remains were buried. Howard and Geraldine had brought him out to die in his beloved China a few months earlier so that his remains could lie peacefully beneath its hallowed soil. To us, I must say, his grave seemed the only peaceful place in the country. In a letter home which Henry fully expected to be quoted in the press, China being always an object of fascination for the British, he wrote:

> . . . *endless meetings, meetings, walks through the malodorous Chinese cities, walks among the graves (graves everywhere), outside the city, sedan chair rides in and out, in and out, round impossible corners, between high blank walls, opium shops, dust heaps, courtyards, with Chinese eyes scrutinising, speculating, admiring, scorning, suspecting, pursuing, all round – pigtails swinging, clothes flapping, signs swinging, cries ringing, odours pervading, poverty pleading, idolatry repelling, necessity calling – voices, voices, multitudinous, like the sound of many waters – waves which have been rolling and breaking since far distant times, anteceding all European civilisations and almost all memories of mankind . . .*

An unanticipated, unparalleled opportunity for Henry to speak to the Shanghai Zionist Association in the Royal Asiatic Hall greatly cheered his spirits. A large number of influential Chinese Jews were present, complete with nodding deference and pigtail, and for over an hour Henry held them spellbound with one of his most eloquent addresses on 'Zionism from a Christian standpoint'. The entire text, promising an end to Turkish rule in the Holy Land in preparation for the prophetic, promised return of the Jewish people, appeared verbatim in a local Jewish newspaper. If this was the only reason for our prolonged world tour, it would alone have been worth it.

At 9.15 p.m. on the day of our departure, Henry noted sadly in his diary: 'Said "Goodnight" to Whitfield and Janie.' Years later I scribbled underneath, 'It would be their last "Goodnight", for they never saw one another again.'

*

March 31st, 1906

The beginning of 1906 found us back in Japan visiting Kyoto, Osaka and Kobe. Ruth has given birth to a second son, Stanley, named after the great explorer as she promised. Lady Dorothy has agreed to be a stand-in godparent for her late husband.

And I am carrying our first child.

As I was feeling rather weak and nauseous, we thought it best that Henry respond alone to an invitation from a former student to visit Korea. It was my first separation from him since our marriage and I cannot say I found it a happy experience. It was both lonely and frustrating to sit feeling far from well in a small, second-rate hotel, in a country where language was a total barrier, and I knew no one. Waiting and waiting. But it would have been churlish to say so to Henry when he arrived back buoyant, marvelling at the work he had witnessed.

With immense relief on my part we set sail for Australia on the SS *Willehad* via Hong Kong, Manila, and German-speaking New Guinea and New Pomerania – every day bringing me one day nearer to my brother Phil, who had been in Australia for the past two years, church-planting for the Baptist Church of New South Wales.

And so we docked yesterday at Brisbane and travelled overnight by train to Sydney. And there was Phil waiting for us on the platform, having come all the way from his home in Melbourne. It is so difficult to put into words the exquisite joy I felt at seeing one of my own family – after almost three years. He is little changed, though his face is fuller, his complexion better, his constitution stronger, the climate agreeing with him more, as he hoped it might.

He had used all his savings for the trip out, with nothing in the way of contacts, no work lined up for when he arrived, he told us, as he escorted us by tram through the bustling town centre to our lodgings. So he took himself to the headquarters of the Baptist Church and offered his services as a preacher, using, he said timidly, one eye on Henry, his youngest sister's illustrious connections, as a form of introduction. Henry smiled and said that it was just as well, then, that his own gifting had more than satisfied their expectations – as he had no doubt it would. Electricity has recently come to Sydney, and it is still a time of transition, said our hostess. There has been no transition in this boarding house!

May 20th, 1906

As my 'condition' became more obvious, it became harder to accompany Henry on his many engagements. People found it difficult to hide their stares, and though I had always resisted the notion of hiding myself away at such a time, I felt I might be too much of a distraction.

I am now seven months pregnant, and we thought it best for me to stay in rented accommodation in Sydney to prepare for the birth, while Henry travels on alone to New Zealand, speaking at several conferences. But I begin to have serious concerns for his health. He wrote, 'I look forward with pleasure to more thorough rest after these eight days of meetings. Seriously, I do not feel strong enough for such an undertaking – it takes too much out of me, and does not give sufficient time for the system, at my age, to recuperate. I am glad, however, to have made the experiment afresh, and the result will be a guide to me in the future.'

If only! A day later he wrote, 'Yesterday I went down to the sea shore and had a lovely time for quiet thought and refreshment on the sandy beach, the waves rolling in and making music. Do not be anxious about me, darling, for I am feeling well and up to the work. I wonder what you are doing? Making little coats or minor garments for the expected cherub? Or perhaps little purchases in the same direction – imitating providence which does the same kind of thing for us all on a large scale! How unreasonable that we should care for the objects of such care. He careth for you. So, darling, we will trust and not be afraid.'

But I do fear – for him, and for our unborn child. It is, I imagine, quite normal for a mother-to-be, but heightened in my case by the strangeness of my surroundings and my separation from all my loved ones. Poor Henry also felt our separation deeply. In his next letter, written while waiting longingly for the 4 p.m. cup of tea (*cha*, they call it, or *tsha*, or *chsha*; how shall I write it?), he wrote to his 'pet wife', as he sometimes calls me: 'I am lonely, my darling, no one I care for near me – none to go to – none to talk to – no face to smile on me with love – no echo to my heart – because you are not with me – but more than 100 miles away, and I am among uninteresting strangers, kind in a way, but with no heart for anything that stirs the soul within me. Why should I write all this? Well, I want you to know how I feel when days away from you. If you were not with me, I should not stop long, but with you I could stay as long as I wanted. Strange, is it not? But such is the heart. There's the sound of a distant train, and I wonder whether it is going to Sydney and you, and how I should feel if I were on it!'

At least his rheumatism is improved now that the heavy rain has passed.

A letter from Ruth has been forwarded on to me. She writes that there has been an outbreak of the dreaded sleeping sickness on the shores of Lake Albert Nyanza, and that the commissioner has ordered the fringe of wood, which is supposed to harbour the tsetse fly, to be cut down all along the Nile banks. Smallpox is also claiming a number of victims. The people understand it as possession by evil spirits, and their cure is a visit to the patient by all his friends, who prick each pustule with straws, then press out the fluid in order to drive away the spirit. It frightens me. I am sick with worry for her. These later days of my pregnancy fill me with all kinds of fanciful fears and horrors. May God keep our little family safe.

*

July 24th, 1906

My baby son was born safely four days ago. Henry wrote to my father:

> *My dear Brother Hurditch*
> *We sent you a telegram on Friday announcing the birth of a beautiful boy and saying that mother and child were doing excellently. We came from Japan to Australia for this, and in faith named the child before he was born – 'John Christopher' (Christ bearer). The darling boy arrived on Friday morning July 20th at 4.15. All was mercifully ordered. The sufferings of a first childbirth which might have lasted 24 hours and been attended by complications were shortened to six hours. All went well. The doctor arrived on foot as he could not find a night*

conveyance, and immediately gave her chloroform – to her infinite relief – and she knew nothing more till the child was born. The average weight of a newborn infant is 6–7 lbs. He weighed over 9lbs! I wonder how she carried him so well and used to walk about freely to the last. The milk supply is abundant and Grace radiant. I wish you could see her with the lovely boy in her arms – all the arrangements in this hospital have been perfect and everyone so kind.

I am taking meetings all around and am well, thank God, and much enjoy the continuous sunshine here – royal weather.

We are staying here six weeks from the birth to give Grace full opportunity to regain normal conditions before we go on (DV) to Brisbane. We go probably by boat – excellent steamers; preferring that to a long railway journey. After that, back to New Zealand.

I sent Philip a telegram so he knows and shares our joy. Give dear Mrs Hurditch my love. Of course, Grace sends heaps (!) of love to everybody.

I always believed God was good – now more than ever. I must close for mail leaves this night and I have more to write.

Ever my dear brother
Yours affectionately
H. Grattan Guinness

Motherhood is truly wondrous. That life, hidden from you for so many months, except for regular little flutterings, and occasional earth-turning movements, growing in a secret place inside, suddenly makes an appearance, lives and breathes – a thinking, feeling human being, as I am. No longer attached by an umbilical cord. No longer an extension of me.

He stopped feeding today, and with unblinking eyes, calmly studies my face. In her book on motherhood that Henry's daughter, Lucy sent me two months ago, she describes this searching look that says, 'I know you, don't I?' I gaze back at this new, yet strangely familiar being, trying to discern recognisable signs of his great Guinness pedigree. Does he know me, this little man-child Henry and I have made, this fruit of our love, a son of his riper years?

The midwife was excellent, quickly smothering her astonishment that Henry was my husband not my father, or even grandfather, under a bustling professionalism, deferential and solicitous in a way she might not have been with a younger man; concerned, I imagine, and rather bemused, at the impact of new parenthood on such an aged heart and body.

But at seventy, Grattan is as excited as if he had become a father for the first time. He takes endless pleasure in our babe, noting every development with enormous pride and tenderness. He delights to carry him out into the warm Australian sunshine to pick the flowers from our garden, and believes he can already see the child's appreciation of beautiful things.

September 14th, 1906

All this, I realise now, was wonderful preparation for the heavy blow that befell barely a month later – the dreaded news of family tragedy that had fed so many of my home-sick fears.

Lucy, Henry's beloved daughter, has died of septicaemia following an ectopic pregnancy. I shall never forget his tearless grief as he read the cabled message of sorrow. The pain in his face was almost more than I could bear.

All of Grattan's children were exceptional – forceful, visionary speakers, stirring hundreds to offer themselves for sacrificial missionary service. But Lucy was truly luminous, like her name: an exceptionally gifted pianist and orator. I heard her once at Keswick, long before I knew there would be any relationship between us, and few could match her for brilliance and passion. I can only imagine how moving it must have been to hear her speak of the pressing needs of the Sudan. Fifty million Sudanese populated an area between the Niger and the Nile, equal in size to

Europe, with only half a dozen mission stations on its borders. Grattan had foreseen that the Mohammedans would rapidly absorb the pagan populations of the Sudan into Islam and engulf the whole region in anti-Christian fervour.

Lucy toured England, Scotland, Wales and Ireland, storming the British churches with their responsibility to our empire, rallying the most influential ministers to the cause. She set up councils, raised funds, recruited workers and finally succeeded in establishing the Sudan United Mission. Pregnant with her third child, she was about to speak at the Moody Convention in Chicago, a wonderful opportunity to recruit young American workers, when she became aware that all was not well. Almost breathless with pain, having refused surgery until after she had the chance to preach to a packed evening meeting, she stunned the audience with one of the most impassioned, extraordinary appeals ever made, then collapsed as she left the platform. They operated the following day, but could not save her. A meteor has flashed through the heavens and crashed to the earth, extinguished at the height of its power and beauty. How was it possible? What will become of her two dear little motherless boys?

Henry was inconsolable. Day after day he went out walking along the shore of a quiet bay in New South Wales, trying to come to terms with his loss. Then one day he arrived home radiant. Sitting listening to the mournful roar of the ocean, he had finally managed to weep, he said, his face buried in his hands. Suddenly he felt the gentle pressure of a hand upon his shoulder. He raised his head and found himself looking up into the kindly, wrinkled face of an old Aborigine woman. In a strange, halting accent she whispered, 'Let not your heart be troubled, neither let it be afraid . . . in my father's house there are many mansions.'

He turned away from her momentarily looking out to sea, trying to extract fresh consolation from those familiar words. But when he looked up again two seconds later she had vanished. He scoured the beach, but there was no sign of her.

Hardly a day passes that he doesn't ponder who she was and where she had come from, and wonder whether she was not some angelic visitation sent to bring him divine comfort and assurance at the time when he needed it most.

November, 1906

In her last letter to Karl, Lucy had entrusted her two boys to Geraldine and Howard who have been unable to have children of their own. It seemed so right, but Karl, who is rather headstrong, had other ideas and has hired a German nanny. I cannot believe this is for the best, but dear Geraldine is more accepting of his decision than I might have been. Of course, motherhood can be somewhat restricting.

Much as I adore my son, I am forced to recognise that his birth has brought me the sorrow of separation from my beloved husband. He has invitations that take him all over Australia, and it is impractical for me now to accompany him. Finding suitable and reasonable accommodation for a mother, baby and nurse, when we can find one, is an ongoing problem. While Henry travels on alone, returning as often as he can, I find myself still in Sydney in cheap boarding houses or lodgings that are not as clean as I might have wished, with an odd assembly of fellow guests unsympathetic to a baby's cries, a shared bathroom with no lock on the door, unappetising food, and landladies who demand extra for basic commodities such as hot water.

I am torn between two competing demands upon my love, two contrasting responsibilities and priorities. A man faces no such challenge. For him, the arrival of a new infant changes little, demands no more than five-minute episodes of smiling and cooing, expressions of marvel when his outstretched finger is grasped and squeezed, of pride and satisfaction when it sleeps, lies quiet or blinks in response.

But the mother's world is overturned, filled with feeding, dirty nappies, sleepless nights. Her priority, once her husband, must now be her helpless, dependent child. I am no longer the playful companion of Henry's world travels, stirring his wonder with my own, brightening the dark, disappointing days, soothing away his weariness, drawing him out of his introspection. I have had no choice but to let him go. How can a woman like me, who has achieved so little with her life, refuse to share such greatness with the world, keep it all for herself? I cannot tell him so and worry him, for what importance have my little cares; but I am reduced to lonely domestication in depressing lodgings.

Knowing our time together must inevitably be short makes separation harder to bear. But what can we do when he is so in demand? He wrote to me from Wellington, 'I seem to miss you most when there is something beautiful to see or hear or tell! I wish I could find words strong and tender enough to tell how much I love you! I long to be with you again – and to take my darling in my arms, but we must put the interests of the kingdom of God above all private interests.'

*

March 30th, 1907

1907 has been spent thus far in Sydney, while Henry is in New Zealand, and I have found it exceedingly difficult. I am completely tied to John's eating and feeding habits and cannot leave our lodgings easily – except for a short walk, which takes me nowhere, to none of the sights I'd like to see, as we can only afford accommodation in the less desirable areas. I have tried to employ a nurse, but the local girls seem to have little aptitude or understanding for it, too young for the responsibility of being left with a child for more than an hour or so. And how could I leave my baby with a complete stranger?

I must not tell Henry lest I seem demanding, a whining, immature young wife who cannot cope with what I knew marriage to such a man must entail. But in the depths of my being I find I resent it all the same. People ask me constantly what it is like to live with a saint. I smile sweetly, and say, 'Oh, an immense privilege,' when what I really feel like saying is that it is hard. They have no idea how hard. Do not ever love a saint. Oh dear – how petulant I am becoming.

And now, a letter from Henry with news that he has obtained, through friends, a grant from the government of a railway ticket for 'myself, my wife and my secretary' (Mr Ingham) first class from 'any place to any place' on the New Zealand railway. So, I shall join him there for a few weeks, and am even more ashamed of my ungrateful spirit.

'It is sweet to think of meeting so soon,' he says. 'I wonder, will baby know me? I am so glad to hear that he has been bright and well in spite of rains and storms. So, he has cut his first tooth?'

The stunning natural beauty of New Zealand with its jagged mountains, rolling pastures, steep fjords, trout-filled lakes and raging rivers took my breath away. The cities are experiencing a time of unheralded expansion with electric trams, motor cars and even cinemas multiplying rapidly. And I love the warm-hearted, friendly people, especially the Maoris. Henry and I hoped to stay on until September for the celebrations of the change from colony to independent dominion, but it was not practical. With Henry dashing up and down the country, his reputation going before him – Auckland, Dunedin, Nelson, Christchurch, Wellington – preaching to great acclaim and appreciation, little John and I could only be a burden, and so my visit was over all too soon.

May 25th, 1907
Brent's Bathwater House, Hinemoa St, Rotorua, NZ

My beloved wife
So today you start back for Sydney. I wish I was with you. It will be your first experience of travelling with our darling child by sea without me. The Lord who has dealt so kindly with us will take care of you. I trust you will find suitable lodgings in

Sydney quickly after arriving. I send this as you directed to the General Post Office, but I want your house address at the earliest opportunity, and therefore I asked you to cable it – for supposing I should follow you to Sydney before securing the address of your lodgings, what should I do? How could I find you? (Really the talk of the people in the room where I had to sit makes it hard to write without making stupid mistakes, it is so distracting!) I have nowhere to sit here but the public room with all its foolish chatter, or my bedroom which is too dark to read in!!

Well, it is only for a short visit. I don't feel inclined to prolong my stay beyond next week. I have promised to preach in this place tomorrow, at the Methodist church, and may possibly speak at Auckland the following Sunday and then take the Tuesday boat to Sydney. Do not count on this lest you should be disappointed.

I sympathise with your distress over the extravagant bill at the Lesley boarding house and that contemptible letter which Mrs Hunter Brown forwarded you. Dear old lady, she writes in the right spirit – a Christian spirit – but that wretched letter she encloses misled her judgement. The writer – if the room was as we left it – must have been in a very spiteful mood, and disposed to exaggerate every defect in a most abominable manner. I think your reply, with its quiet statement of facts, is admirable! Well done little wifey – no temper, only truth! I forward your letter.

God bless you, darling, and our precious child.

Your ever loving husband

Henry

November 5th, 1907

The £30 Henry gave me as I left Auckland was swallowed up by the bill for the (exorbitant!) lodgings there, and the steamer ticket – £17 and £13. I had to cable him for more money. He sent me a postal order for £5, barely enough to cover two weeks rent in my new lodgings in Sydney as he hoped to be with me again shortly. Really, he can be so impractical. It was October before we finally met again.

But how could I force him home sooner? To see Henry is to admire him. To know him is to wonder at the greatness of his soul. We are so different. He takes all in his stride, worries little about life's contretemps, trusts implicitly in the Great Provider, while I am anxious about how to survive another day here in Sydney again with so little money. He sees good in everyone. His heart is big enough to encompass the whole world, while I am easily irritated by the pettiness of my landladies and the ineptness of the nurses I hire, such young things, so unreliable, but all I can afford – and at extortionate cost. I am constantly left feeling inadequate, petty, unable to live up to his standards. Why did he ever marry me? I must learn to be uncomplaining, to value the moments we do have, to be thankful for our beautiful baby son.

But I do so worry about Henry. He is now seventy-two, an age, if attained, at which most men are sat in their silk slippers by their drawing room fire reading *The Times*. And though his health is generally good, he fatigues easily. In June he wrote from Rotorua to say he had been taking the thermal waters every day. 'I think the terrible treatment is doing me good. The weather is too cold and stormy for excursions in the neighbourhood to see the sights. I don't much resent this having seen the Yellowstone Park. There are hot springs in the grounds close by and two miles off a volcano crater full of boiling springs, mud springs, steam vents. I have seen them and went out to an island on the lake, four miles from the shore where some Maoris live and there is a hot spring too. But none of these have much interest for me when you are not there to share them, my darling wife.'

In July he wrote to say that he had travelled south from Nelson to Greymouth to meet his cousin, Arthur Guinness, who is Speaker of the House of Parliament, as it was too good an opportunity to miss. Though they had never met, he was warmly welcomed into his cousin's home. Arthur's father, Frank, had left Ireland for New Zealand in 1852 when Henry was only seventeen, but Henry well remembered both him and his father, Uncle Hosea, who had given up his inheritance as eldest son of the brewery to become a clergyman.

In early September Henry arrived in Melbourne, and stayed with brother Phil. The plan was for Phil to come and help me pack my bags and escort me to Melbourne. 'I would go myself for you, but I should have to sacrifice important engagements here if I went – and it is no more cost to send Philip than to go.' But in fact John had a fever and wasn't well enough to travel. To my immense disappointment I was forced to stay on in Sydney, Phil's company for a week some consolation. And at least my nursing experience has its uses.

Henry wrote to say he was glad I actually hadn't joined him in Melbourne, as though it was much finer looking than Sydney, the surroundings were poor by comparison, the beach confined, poor, flat, no waves, a mere sea inlet, while the town was dusty and smoky, the air not clear, reminding one of an English manufacturing working town like Birmingham (but not as bad as that). Meanwhile, I had access to a wide open park, Bondi Beach with its real waves and all Sydney's beautiful surroundings. 'I was touched by what you told me of our darling little man missing me! How I would fly to him and his mother if I had wings . . . but the way is open here for meetings . . .'

It was ever thus!

October 2nd, 1907
The Federal Palace Hotel, 547 Collins St, Melbourne

My own darling
  All the meetings I have had here have tended to open the way for work in Victoria, where there are many important towns within easy reach of Melbourne itself with its large population. The consequence is I incline very much to your coming here for

a good part of what remains to us of our time in Australia and am going to make enquiries as to lodgings which might suit us, for I cannot happily work here for months without you. You would find the air much more bracing than at Sydney. I have found it so and have benefited by it. I cannot accustom myself to this separation – you at Sydney and I here. The places I wish to visit are within a short run by rail, and I could just go for a day or so, and return in each case. If you don't come I am tempted to overwork and the consequences are not good.

Ever your loving husband Henry

On October 4th a telegram arrived to tell me Phil was on the way back to Sydney to pack my bags and escort me to Melbourne. A servant had been engaged to look after John. On the 7th a further telegram read, 'Would parents of your girl be willing she should come stop servant here good young person but no experience of children stop don't vaccinate. Henry.'

So, no servant, but what did it matter? Henry and I were together again at last. At the end of November we finally set sail from Melbourne on the SS *Commonwealth* bound for London. Henry 'stopped off' in South Africa for two months. I had just discovered I was pregnant again and went on to Las Palmas in Grand Canary, so that I could rest.

January 11th, 1908
43 Carrie St, Jeppertown, Johannesburg

My beloved Grace

It was a great joy and relief to get your cablegram addressed to the care of the YMCA Durban, 'Settled Las Palmas', implying that you had arrived there about 5th Jan, and were going to stay in Las Palmas till I rejoin you – which I expect will be by the February boat. Meanwhile, I send you an order for £10 – enclosed – which will be accepted at any bank in Las Palmas or by the agent for the Blue Anchor Line, Blandly Brothers and Co.

So my darling, you have actually reached Las Palmas, and are with our precious 'little man' once more on Terra Firma! Thank God. I shall look for letters from you. I sent you a cablegram (costing 27/6!) giving my address here, 'Jeppertown, Johannesburg. All well.' It crossed your cablegram to me.

I have had a wonderful time in South Africa – at Durban, Petermaritzburg, Ladysmith, Pretoria and Johannesburg – all the churches have welcomed me with open arms, and the meetings have been numerous, large and important. I have taken 60 photographs, and have had them developed – very successfully – scenes of all these places.

I cannot begin to convey to you what I have seen, and how all has impressed me – but this certainly seems the most important part of our long five-year journey – the way is opened here to do a more practically important work for various classes of the community than in any of the other countries we visited. Tomorrow I address DV a mass meeting of natives in the great square of Johannesburg.

South Africa is the key to the whole continent – here are the workers for missions in the unreached regions of Africa. They speak over 60 languages. Such fine natives and many true Christians with a missionary spirit. All the ministers here met me at a breakfast two days ago and seemed moved by my address. I sent you one or two newspapers with notices of my meetings. There is a long article in today's paper also – partly incorrect – but on the whole a fair statement.

Now I must close with kisses for our darling 'little man'.
Ever, dearest Grace
Your loving husband
H. Grattan Guinness

Not long now till we are home. I never thought when we set off that I should be so glad, but this itinerant life is no longer as attractive as it was at the start. Resting in lovely Las Palmas, I am not ungrateful for these five years of travel, but the company of one's loved one is worth so much more than all the sights in the world – and I have seen them all.

The expense of staying in Las Palmas is ruinous: £10 a week for John and me and my companion, Miss Scott. Frightful; £80 for 8 weeks. I hardly know how to tell Henry. I am entirely dependent on the postal orders he sends me – £10 weekly, which is nowhere near enough (he is such an innocent when it comes to money), then £30 weekly when I said I needed more. I fear it leaves the small pot rather empty and we still have to find the money for the passage home. I try not to panic. Goodness, how many times were my dear parents in this situation, and God always provided. My father's trust was invincible, but I am not sure I have their great faith – or will for sacrifice. But Henry does, fortunately.

From Blomfontein he wrote to say: 'I had a grand and blessed time at Johannesburg – many meetings – a wide and warm welcome. I addressed on Sunday afternoon last a mass meeting of the natives, as many as my voice could reach, standing up on the seat of an open carriage. I travelled all night to this place, and spoke last night to a full hall and have to speak there again tonight and tomorrow night, and then on 24 hours rail to Kimberley – great diamond mines place – and then on DV to Cape Town.'

And, of course, some grateful benefactor has provided the resources for our journey back to the UK. It makes me feel wretched for my worrying, and grateful for the provision – all at once.

Henry is in good health, thank God. The newspaper cuttings report good meetings everywhere, though he writes from Cape Town, 'Life is hard without you. Soon may we be restored to each other.'

And we were, at last – in February 1908.

Our Last Years Together

Seeing England after an absence of five years was little short of heaven – though, as we steamed down the Thames on a grey, smoky, chilly winter morning, I had, I admit, forgotten how ugly London could be. Steamers, schooners, barges were plying up and down the river, and then a small boat came into view. We could scarce discern its passengers, but some strange impulse bade us respond to the waves of welcome. Yes, we were right. There were Dr and Mrs Taylor, Howard and Geraldine – with Karl and Lucy's two boys now in their care as, understandably, the poor, motherless boys had never settled with a nanny, Mrs Harry Guinness and her eldest daughter Gene, and later on, at the railway station, my dear father, mother and Bee.

The press was also waiting for us. I had now become accustomed to the fact that Henry was a source of public interest, but still disliked the newspaper reporter, with his photographic apparatus, insisting on getting the travellers' impressions of the world in a ten-minute interview.

In five years London had undergone an enormous change. It was an exciting, frightening new world with its crowded streets and all the modern innovations of motor traffic. I really wasn't prepared for it, and, needing some time with family again, as I awaited our new little visitor, we settled for a time in rented accommodation in St Leonards, enjoying the refreshing sea breezes of that quiet coastal town where our adventure had first begun five years ago. Bee was still involved in the running of Wilton House, with the help of a male superintendent and resident housekeeper. Phil lived there when he was home from Australia – rare these days – and my sisters Lillie and Gertie and their husbands and children came for occasional short vacations.

May 9th, 1908
Rothesay House, Clyde Rd, St Leonards on Sea

Beloved Whitfield and Jane
    A lovely boy arrived last night. 9.15. Grace bore up bravely all day. Our hearts are overflowing with joy and gratitude. We are looking for news of similar mercies granted to you also when Jane's time comes. The newborn weighed 9lbs, like his brother – 2–3lbs above the average, the doctor says.
    Grace smiles sweetly – at rest. Little John laughed to see his baby brother. We feel quite rich with these two sons.
    I think of the name Paul Ambrose. Ambrose means immortal – a sweet name. So we shall have a John and a Paul. As I am writing to many I will not add. We love to think of you both and your babes in your new house.
    Blessed be his name for all his goodness. With love to Janie.
    From your affectionate Father
    H. Grattan Guinness

The new century was filled with so many fascinating new developments that stimulated Henry's interest and curiosity. There was so much he wanted to do and see – people to meet, exhibitions to visit, endless books to write. Harley House, with his study left untouched since our marriage, provided a base in London from which he took various nephews, nieces and grandchildren to see the latest exhibitions, including the great missionary exhibition at the Agricultural Hall: 'You may judge of its magnitude from the fact that the exhibits fill that vast hall, and there are 10,000 stewards'; and the very grand Franco-English exhibition: 'a perfect dream – seven miles of roads among palaces, almost eclipsing the St Louis Exhibition'. The young people found him a charming companion and seeing the new world through their eyes was a rejuvenating experience for him.

Rothesay House
Clyde Rd
St Leonards on Sea
9 May 1908

Beloved Gershom and Fanni

A lovely boy arrived
~~last night~~ . 9. 15.
Grace bore up bravely
all day.
Our hearts are overflowing
with joy and gratitude.
We are looking for news

of similar mercies
granted to you also.

The new comer weighed
9 lbs. like his brother
John at birth — 2-3
lbs above the average.
the doctor says.
Grace lies smiling
sweetly. at rest.
Little John laughed
to see his baby brother.

(* John weighed 10 lbs at birth)

We feel quite rich with
these two sons.
I think of the name
Paul Ambrose —
Ambrose means
immortal — a sweet
~~name~~. So we
shall have a John
and a Paul —
As I am writing to
Nancy I will not
add —

We love to think of you
both, and your babies —
in your new house —
The Lord bless you and
yours — more and more
Blessed be His name
for all His Goodness —

With love to Nancy
Ever Your affectionate Father
H. Grattan Guinness.

1908

He had taken to wearing a small moustache, and, with his still abundant white hair swept off his high forehead, he cut an impressive figure in his dark frock coat and high winged collar – and I was not the only one to remark on it.

The demands on him were almost as great as they had ever been and I worried that he might not have the stamina for it. Preachers do not retire, he said firmly, when I tried to remonstrate with him. He was forever 'held up' somewhere for an extra few days, no thanks to the draw of 'inspirational' encounters, and unexpected, unmissable engagements. Our marriage appeared to have endowed him with the secret of eternal youth. He was incorrigible. 'Don't be anxious about me,' he would say, giving me the kind of sweet kiss that instantly obliterated all my arguments. There was no holding him back, no matter how hard I tried, and I was glad, at least, to have Bee for constant company.

I tried to encourage Henry to reproduce in watercolour or pastels the landscapes of our travels, for he had taken so many photographs. Drawing and painting was a lifelong love of his, and I thought it might occupy his active mind and keep him longer at home. It had been abundantly clear the moment he picked up a brush that he had inherited his mother's considerable talent, and adorning our home we now had a significant collection of angels, harbours and hills. All his life he had loved nature. Reproducing its form and shape, its light and shade, its marvellous blend of colour, was a source of immense satisfaction to him. But neither that, nor the birth of our second son, could keep him from the business of his life's mission.

I was so taken up with caring for him and my new babe that though I had noticed how frail my father had become, I had given him little of the time that I promised myself I would. Foolish, for now, quite suddenly, a mere seven months after our return, almost as if he had only awaited our coming, he died.

Gwendoline had cleared away the evening meal, and my father and mother, as was their wont, sat in saddlebag armchairs on either side of the fireplace. 'Jane,' said my mother (her parlour-maids had always been called Jane, or Emily – such fanciful names as Gwendoline were intolerable to her), 'tell Sarah she may come up and hear the young ladies' and gentleman's letters read.'

Sarah, whose long years of service with us entitled her to the privilege of sharing in the family news, now shuffled into the dining room. 'Will the master and mistress kindly excuse me felt slippers?'

'We quite understand, Sarah, and would you care to ask Jane to come up too?'

'Oh no, ma'am, these young girls know nothin' about them foreign parts.'

Then my mother read out one or two letters in the way she always did – from Africa, America and Australia, her voice alternating between preternaturally high tones and dissonant quavers, as every now and again tears splashed onto the rice paper, blurring the ink. My father in nervous haste mopped them up with his handkerchief with manly boisterousness, until the words could barely be read at all.

And then, suddenly, a spasm, a bluish tinge on his lips. My mother took his hand. 'Whatever is the matter, darling?' she asked with alarm.

'Oh, nothing, it has passed . . . but we're getting old, Mary,' he said.

'Nonsense, dear, to talk of getting old in our sixties.'

But in the early hours of that September night the call came to my father, and I expect he was greeted with the trumpet blast that heralds the arrival of every such faithful servant as he.

Little remained of my father's work. The great days of pioneering Christian social work, in education, health and welfare, had slowly ground to a halt as benefactors became hard to find. His last great entrepreneurial venture, Wilton House, had just been sold, the new owner with aspirations to turn it into a rather fine hotel. Bee moved back to London to care for Mother.

There was nothing now to keep us in St Leonards. Even Harley College was subject to renovation at the insistence of London City Council, and Henry had a fancy to move back to Bath where he had lived for several years with Fanny in the late 1860s and early 1870s. I did not warm to his enthusiasm – until I saw it on a late summer's day in all its golden, sunbathed Georgian glory. There was more life here than in St Leonards, more vibrancy and more opportunity, Henry thought, remembering those early days there, when the aftermath of the Great Revival had opened so many doors for him.

We rented Lynton Lodge, a fine house high up over the city, with exquisite views. It was I who supervised the move and the unpacking of our belongings, many of them stored in boxes in various places for the past five years. Henry hated being left alone and found it hard to settle to the new book he was writing, *The Parallelism between the History of the Jewish People and the History of the Church.*

> *November 12th, 1908*
> *Rothesay House, St Leonards*

My darling

I am glad you are at Bath today, preparing our new home, with Bee, as it takes you away from 164 Alexander Rd and its sorrows. All goes on well and quietly here. The children are flourishing. Only I am lonely – without you – not a soul to speak to. I read and write and go out and come in and pine to have you back.

So, you find yourself encumbered with books and boxes up to the ceiling. I wonder why that can be! My fear, my dread, is that you should lift weights and severely injure yourself. You know how shocking this would be in its effects. So for the children's sakes, and mine, as well as your own, don't do that.

Remember! Ever your affectionate husband
Henry

Early in 1909 Ruth and Arthur arrived back in England for several months of furlough with their three children and new baby, Shelagh. The doctor has told Ruth she will never conceive again – to her immense relief. She doesn't know how she could cope with another baby and her work, let alone manage to feed another mouth. Ah, we women are hostages to our reproductive system. But what is she to do if she loves her husband?

Seeing her again after so many years was too wonderful to describe. We wept and laughed and embraced over and over again, and it might have seemed as if we had never been parted – but for the two men at our side and the little ones on our knees. An ocean of separation had been bridged by the shared experience of marriage and motherhood and we are closer than ever.

And what can I say of Arthur? He is a gregarious Irishman, with an endless fund of entertaining stories and the most marvellous twinkle in his eye. He grew up in great poverty due to a drunken father, left home when he was twelve for an apprenticeship at the draper's shop in Tullamore, but was dismissed at seventeen for staying out until 11 p.m. at a Church of Ireland Young Men's Association dance. His boss, a Wesleyan, considered dancing the wickedest crime in the world. This is certainly a man after my own heart. How then did he end up a clergyman, I asked him. In Rathmines, he attended a mission meeting held by two converts of Moody and Sankey and decided to devote his life to God's service. He joined the YMCA, worked with homeless men, and on his £25 per year salary somehow found the fees to improve his education and his elocution until he was deemed acceptable as a minister.

He is not at all the kind of man I imagined Ruth marrying, for I expected more in the way of sophistication, but I understand what it is she loves about him – his courage, determination and kindliness. And of course, he absolutely adores her.

And then – such a surprise – a letter from Phil in Australia , our wonderful, but largely uneducated brother (now in his thirty-sixth year), to say he is to marry Hester, the youngest daughter of Dr Llewellyn Bevan, an eminent professor of divinity in Melbourne. Our family appears to delight in making unexpected matches. It seems that for the moment he plans to settle in Australia. I shall miss the dear boy terribly.

Unfortunately, Henry's hopes of more preaching opportunities in Bath have not materialised and he spends a great deal of time in London, staying with Harry and Annie in the home they now rent in Norwood, away from Harley College. The cost of the renovation work threatens the entire future of the place.

> *May 21st, 1909*
> *Woodfield, 81 Beulah Hill, Norwood SE*

My beloved Grace

London is hot and crowded and dusty, yet strangely interesting. It has paid me well to come up to Town. I succeeded in getting Mr Davidson, my publisher, to print the title of the book in gold letters, which will make it much more striking than black letters, in fact quite handsome. He had shrunk from the expense.

Then I went today to Harley House and saw the new wing, which is in full working order, and in the afternoon, I addressed the students, and much enjoyed being with them again.

Harry is away in Belgium and will attempt to see King Leopold II once more. He will request permission for a new missionary station on the Congo, but his main purpose is to challenge the King again about their lamentable practices towards the native, whose land they appropriated in the first place. I do hope the King's heart has softened. Harry was expected back today.

The little attack of German Measles at Harley House is completely over, so I have arranged to stay there over Sunday and look forward to preaching, a privilege denied me latterly in Bath, where every post is filled.

*I trust you and the children keep well – my heart is with you.
I will write you again DV from Harley House. God bless and
keep you, darling, and our precious children.*

> *May 25th, 1909*
> *Harley House, London E.*

My dearest Grace
*I have been detained in London by important business here
connected with the training of students, and tomorrow
(Wednesday) am going up to Cliff to see the place, Mr Cook
having given me an invitation to stay at the college. I may be
detained there a day or two before returning to Bath.*
*We had excellent meetings on Sunday. I spoke in the morn-
ing at the Berger Hall, where the work is flourishing, and in
the afternoon to a large, appreciative audience in Victoria
Park.*
*Harry and I have been much cheered today by the receipt of
a cheque for £1,000* towards Harley House, which will, with
more expected help, enable him to claim Mr City's promise of
£2,000, conditional on the receipt of the other sums. And so the
college is out of danger.*
*I hope you and the darlings keep well. Need I say how much
my heart is with you?*
Ever your affectionate husband, Henry

> *May 26th, 1909*
> *Cliff College, Calder, Sheffield*

*You will see from above address that I am at Cliff, which I
reached this afternoon, and have since been round with Mr
Cook, and am astonished and delighted at the improvements
and enlargements, on which the Methodists have spent £25,000!*

* About £50,000 in today's money

*The place looks perfectly lovely, with accommodation for 85
students, with tutors and their families, servants, etc. and it is
just humming with activity and good work.*

*When I think of the past here, the students we trained, the
family house parties in the summer for children and friends, the
observatory where we could gaze at the wonder of the heavens,
the hand of Providence seems so clear and evident. I think I will
send a wire to Mr Fry not to expect me Friday for I am asked to
lecture to the students here tomorrow (Thursday), and could
not be in time for Friday in Bristol. I will wire you about my
movements.*

*I am so very sorry you were anxious and waited up till 3 in
the morning for me on Monday – I regret much I did not send
you a wire, but I wrote, I think, and you should have had my
letter Tuesday. Don't be anxious about me.*

*I enclose a cheque for £5 for household expenses, and trust
you will receive it safely.*

*It brings back old times to be here again! Ever your loving
husband*
Henry
P.S. Thank you for the collars and ties

If I did not pack for Henry, something was always forgotten, his
mind perpetually on higher things. Geraldine told me that years
ago he had once promised to come for her and walk her home
after one of her night classes for factory girls, but he never turned
up. She set off alone and found him on the way home, standing
under a lamp-post, pondering.

His dreaminess occasionally made him a hazard. A new
acquaintance in Bath informed me that during his train journey
home she had been witness to a rather worrying event. Henry had
joined her, and a young couple with a new baby girl, in their
carriage. Failing to notice that the couple had placed their precious
bundle on the carriage seat, dear Henry lifted his coat tails and
proceeded to lower himself. At which point the young father

caught his arm, but only just in time. Registering my horror, my informant said, with a twinkle in her eye, 'But don't worry, Mrs Guinness, it would have been such a heavenly end for her!'

I was even more loath to let Henry travel alone, but the needs of my boys had to come first. Days later he went back to London and preached to a full St James's Hall, and was sent to speak to the overflow as well, which nearly filled the polytechnic hall, including its gallery. He stayed with Mama, to Bee's chagrin, for she was forced to share a room with her. My mother, he said, seemed well and contented, and never lonely. 'I suppose we are differently constituted.'

To his immense satisfaction, Henry was finally invited to deliver a series of four lectures on the second coming on December 3rd, 10th, 17th and 24th at St James, Bath. I was glad too, for it meant he would spend some prolonged time with his family – though he worked extremely hard to prepare. Now that he at last had an opportunity to speak in his home town, he must give it his very best. And was indeed very well received.

Reporting the lectures in full, The *Bath Herald* said, 'Dr Guinness has a very striking personality, an almost limitless acquaintance with the countries of the world, together with an extensive knowledge of their history, and of theology.' He was, it said, unhappy with the 'Romeward movement of the Church of England', with 9,600 'ritualistic' clergymen in the country. Spiritualism was a false system, America a hotbed of weeds, such as Christian Science, and the Germans, who took the lead in the Reformation, now leant as far away as they could from their great theological tradition. The *Bath Daily Chronicle* claimed that the series 'quite deservedly caused considerable attention . . . Beyond question it is an intellectual treat to hear Dr Grattan Guinness.'

Henry was delighted with the attention and, given the physical stamina, would have rushed into the next opportunity, but he was extremely fatigued and the doctors warned him that the series had severely overstrained his heart. If he continued to tax himself in this manner, it would prove fatal. He had no regrets that his public ministry had cost him his health, yet nonetheless, for my sake and that of the boys, he cancelled all future engagements. They were delighted to have some time to romp and play and have stories and outings with their Papa.

January, 1910

On a cold, wet night Henry set out to fulfil an obligation to our postman, who had begged him to go to his house to say a few words to a gathering of friends and relatives. It was a foul night and I begged him not to go, but he insisted. A promise was a promise. He caught a severe chill, which quickly turned to pleurisy and confined him to his bed. Terrified I might lose him, I nursed him as devotedly as I knew how.

To make matters worse, it was time for Ruth to return to British East Africa. Helpless, I watched her make the heartbreaking decision to leave George, six, Stanley, four, and her little Geraldine, three, behind in England. George had almost died in the extreme heat when he was two and she was loath to take such a risk again. Mother and Bee had no room in their home. The children barely knew Lillie or Gertrude, neither of whom were particularly keen to have them. Henry and I were desperate to find a way to accommodate them, but it was becoming increasingly obvious that Henry was now too frail for me to consider such a possibility.

Ruth entrusted them instead to the care of a generous Church Missionary Society supporter, Winifred Baring-Gould, who looked after her elderly father, the famous novelist and hymn writer Sabine Baring-Gould, at Meadow Grange in Guildford. Miss Baring-Gould bought a cottage a mere quarter of a mile away and installed the children in it with a housekeeper and a maid, who would ensure they acquired a rudimentary education. It hardly seemed a satisfactory solution, but it would have to do.

Tuesday evening, March 8th, 1910
164 Alexandra Rd, St John's Wood

This is our last evening in England, and my final written
message to you, Grace. Little sister, my heart feels torn and
aching. I am leaving you at the time of your sorest anxiety. If
only I had one evening open I should have come to you. Perhaps
God allowed it thus in his tender love, because parting again
with you would have been probably more than I could bear
after the severe struggle of the past few days.

Dear Henry, I am so sorry that he is suffering. He has just the
sweetest nurse, and that is a joy to me. We shall continue without ceas-
ing to pray for him and you. Will you send me a line whenever possible
– a few words on a postcard – address Uganda, East Africa only.

Your parting message has been an inspiration to me, darling.
Joy, joy, joy when your own heart is so troubled. Yes, my Grace,
I will take home your God-given farewell message and feel all
behind and before is well. 'This God is our God forever and
ever. He will be our guide, even unto death.'

A long farewell embrace, my little Grace
Your own Ruth

Despite my careful nursing, pleurisy turned to pericarditis, an
inflammation of the heart. Henry declined slowly, but though in
intense pain and unable to lie down at times, there was no fear and
he was as mentally alert as ever. I knew in my heart, though I couldn't
bring myself to admit it, that the end was creeping close. To catch
hold of every precious moment, I noted down everything he said.

April 21st, 1910, 4 a.m., Lynton Lodge, Bath

Henry awake and reflective.

'I was thinking about those beautiful flowers, those lilies.
What a lovely little book I might have written called *Down*

Among the Flowers – up to the stars and down among the flowers.

'How I love to think of the progress of the kingdom of our Lord and of his Christ, God's love for the world, for dear humanity, the love that embraces every class, every variety of character, the rich, poor, sinful and degraded, the love that found its highest expression in Christ and the cross. God is love – it is the essence of his character. He was before, he is in and he is after all things, therefore so is love. Love is everywhere, whether life or death, Love is there. With child-like faith we must just fling ourselves into the arms of Love. Come there, my darling. Man was made for God and cannot rest until he rests in him.

'I wrote a book called *On This Rock* and I know I am on it. A dying Christian man was once told he was sinking, and he said, 'How can I sink through a rock?' Ah, whatever changes come, the truth remains.'

May, 1910

Howard and Geraldine have come to Bath to be with their father and to support me, for as long as we need them. It is comforting to have a medical man so close at hand. And Geraldine is and always has been Henry's soulmate. He opens his spirit to her.

And Ruth's first letter from Toro arrived, bringing her sustaining presence to my own spirit. 'Although so far away I seem to stand with you at your watch by his bedside and to feel your soul's tension as you watch your beloved on the threshold of life infinite and eternal.'

Oh how I wept as I pondered every precious word, and let them fill me with the strength to carry on. 'Darling, it seems that the call has come to you to lay your sacrifice at the feet of him who is LOVE. Some of us are honoured to be asked to give an offering "very precious". My own tears recently help me to feel as I never could otherwise, something of the unthinkable ache of your own heart. Your Henry is surrounded by love – his most precious ones are with him, and those little innocent pet boys are a fit parting heritage he gives to the world, symbolic of the true, pure life he has lived.'

She ended by offering to come to me if I would like her to. An offer indeed, given the 6,000-mile journey.

June 3rd, 1910, Lynton Lodge

From 10.45 to 11.30 a wonderful time with Henry. First, a personal reference as to his desire that his first family should, as far as possible, be a source of help to me. Then, again, how during this past illness there has been a deep and constant consciousness of the love of God. And then he reviewed his life – redeemed from sin, tried and tested, chastened and blessed; the desire to go as a missionary to Patagonia, that was not to be when he found himself at the centre of the great spiritual awakening, his regret of his intense preoccupation with books when he might have been preaching, yet rejoicing in what his books had meant to others.

Later on he referred to a seeming eclipse of the number of Christians. He smiled radiantly and said, 'Does the sun cease to shine when briefly clouded over? Believe in the Bible from the beginning to the new heavens and new earth, read the experiences of the patriarchs, prophets, saints and martyrs all through the ages and believe their one testimony. Oh, if only I had the strength I would sing aloud his praises. And if I have suffered at times, I've thought, "Did not Jesus suffer? And why? Because of love, infinite love. Oh the wonder of it."'

Then of Geraldine and Howard, 'What more fitting than that she, my only living daughter, should be a mother to you and the children. You cannot find better friends than you would have in them. Geraldine is like me. I was very like her as a younger man and I am glad she loves my darling boys. And Howard loves them too. I want them to be an influence in their lives.

'Now, darling, I may see you in the morning. I believe I shall. Howard and Dr Wilson think I may be spared to do further work, and oh, if I could preach for a thousand years it would be the same theme – Jesus, Jesus, Jesus. [His face shining.] But I am happy and ready to go or stay, and darling, I commend you to the word of his grace, as the Apostle Paul did when he was about to depart.'

June 20th, 1910, Lynton Lodge, Bath

We wheeled the invalid couch from the drawing room, where he was during the seventeen weeks' illness, into his study and as he spoke to me he was facing that lovely extensive view over the city of Bath which he loved to see from his study window. Geraldine came into the room, and he still smiled that beautiful smile which so often illuminated his face. We had noticed it again and again – a beautiful light on his face. He smiled at us and said, 'I am too weak to talk, but have strength enough to meditate. I think over the history of the world, the history of redemption, the progress of Christ's kingdom, the important issues of this great World Missionary Conference in Edinburgh at this very moment, under the leadership of my old friend and former Harley student, John R. Mott. Geraldine and I have long dreamed of such an event. And then I think of our own missionary work in the world and all that has grown out of it, work in America, on the continent, in China and Africa – and I think of what my dear ones have been enabled to do, and of my own life with its shortcomings.'

When Geraldine left the room later, she turned back to her father and was very struck again by his face. As he smiled back at her in the evening light, it almost seemed transfigured. And throughout the day we noticed it, the light of his soul shining through.

It was the last time I was alone with my beloved husband.

June 21st, 1910

This beautiful midsummer day my precious Henry passed peacefully and quietly to rest at 10.45. I was not with him at the end, nor was Geraldine. Strange, after we had been with him so constantly. It seemed we were not to say goodbye; I had gone out early that morning to engage another night nurse.

He had spoken to me before I left and said, 'So weak.' Howard alone was with him at the end. Three times the arms were uplifted and outstretched, as if in flight. We believe he saw a vision, for the final time he sat straight up in bed and raised his arms with a rapturous look. He kept his arms raised for some moments, then they dropped; he fell back upon the pillows; his spirit passed into the life beyond as with an expression of pure rapture on his face he raised his arms to heaven once more.

Extraordinary, when yesterday he had not the strength even to raise a hand.

Henry died, as he had been born, in the year of Halley's Comet, a happy coincidence for one who had spent so much of his life studying the signs in the heavens.

I wired the Edinburgh Missionary Conference with the news, and Dr Mott read the telegram to the vast audience assembled in the main auditorium. Almost every delegate present could claim that Henry's ministry had touched their lives in some way or another. The entire congregation rose spontaneously to its feet, and after a minute's silence, with a volume which shook the building, sang 'For All the Saints Who from their Labours Rest'.

The funeral was conducted at St James Church, where he had so recently delivered his series of Advent lectures, by the vicar, the Revd Moore, Henry's nephew, the Revd Percy Guinness, and Revd Campbell of the Presbyterian church. In a very brief oration, Revd Moore said, 'Those who valued his teaching will have a real sense of loss, but also praise and thanksgiving for a life, for which I can hardly find words, for a life now taken from our midst. And what a life. It has been a privilege to have him among us.'

July 8, 1910.   T.P.'s WEEKLY.

GRATTAN GUINNESS:
An Echo of a Great Duel.
By T.P.

Grattan Guinness! When I saw the announcement of the death of this distinguished divine the other day in the papers it immediately set going in the brain some cells of latent memories from that far-off time when, as a reporter on a stoutly Conservative journal in Dublin, I used to hear all the great preachers and apostles of the Protestant communion and the Tory faith. Grattan Guinness was a famous preacher in those days, always attracted large audiences, and was a shining light in the world of home and missionary effort. It was not, however, till I took up a copy of the "Freeman's Journal" the other evening that I realised with what memorable events in Irish history the distinguished clergyman was associated. Grattan Guinness —it is a curious combination of great Irish names; and, as a matter of fact, Grattan Guinness was related to the family of Henry Grattan, one of Ireland's greatest patriots and orators, and to the Guinness family, whose wealth and munificence are part of Irish history of the past and of to-day. Grattan Guinness's ties howe....

Parliament against emancipation. O'Connell retorted by speaking of it as "a beggarly Corporation." At that moment there was a member of the body who stood out both in character and career from the rank and file. D'Esterre was at the time a provision merchant and of bankrupt fortunes, and harassed by the cares of a wife and a large family. But before he had settled down to this prosaic and anxious existence he had been a middy, and when the mutiny broke out at the Nore had given proof of the most dauntless form of courage. Refusing to join the mutineers, he was condemned to be hanged. The rope was put around his neck, but he was offered a last chance to save his life by joining the mutiny. "Hang away, and be d——d!" was his reply. His courage saved his life.

II.

Small of stature, thin of figure, he was all alertness and fire, knew well the use of firearms, was reputed to be a deadly shot, and there were frequent

Henry Grattan Guinness' obituary

We buried my beloved Henry in the Abbey Cemetery overlooking the city of Bath, beneath an Irish cross. On one side I had Fanny's name inscribed. (She had died at Cliff College and was buried in the Baslow churchyard.) I left the other side blank – for myself. One day I shall lie next to my beloved husband again, both sheltered by the large and lovely copper beech tree that hangs over the grave.

Obituaries appeared in *The Times*, the *Daily Express*, the *Daily Mirror*, the *Daily Telegraph*, the *Westminster Gazette*, the *Yorkshire Post* and the *Sheffield Telegraph*, as well as in many other local and religious newspapers. Many included photographs. The *Bath Herald* said:

The doctor's commanding figure will no longer be seen about Bath, which he made his residence for the last two years or more, and Bath will be the poorer, for Dr Guinness was a man of intensely human and wide sympathies, a member of all churches – not one single denomination can claim him as their own. One who knew him well has described him as a great thinker, a powerful writer and forceful preacher, one who gave up his life to missionary work and found in it the greatest happiness.

They described his distinguished career as a writer, preacher and founder of missions. Some referred to his brewing connections and to the old story of how his mother's first and truculent husband had been killed in a duel by the Irish revolutionary Daniel O'Connell. 'Curious that the stepson of the old fire-eater should have been the one who devoted his life to the great work of bringing to the heathen the Gospel of the Prince of Peace.'

Most harked back fifty years to the days when he had preached to thousands from an open carriage in Northern Ireland. All paid tribute to his vision and achievement. He was held up as the first to include the study of tropical diseases in the curriculum of his colleges. Another described him as the first to call attention to the atrocities perpetrated on natives in the Congo by the evil rubber traders. Along with Spurgeon and Moody he was hailed as one of the three greatest preachers of the nineteenth century.

When they recalled his life's work, referring often to Dr and Mrs Guinness, they meant Fanny, his wife for over thirty years, who oversaw all the domestic arrangements at Harley and Cliff, founded the Regions Beyond Missionary Union and was a force in her own right. *The Record* said, 'Over the tender ministries of his home life, a veil must be drawn.' It was as if, having no public ministry of my own, I had never been his partner in the fullest sense, as Fanny was. Or perhaps the newspapers were simply uncomfortable with the disparity in our ages. Though their disregard pained me, I knew what Henry and I had been to each other, how indestructible the bonds that bound us, and resolved to fasten my feelings to that alone.

In time, I was glad there had been no formal farewell between us. For Henry, the other life was such an immediate, vivid reality. Only the tenuous thread of time divides the dead in Christ from their loved ones. Knowing how little time we would have together, he wrote me a poem to prepare me for the temporary moment of separation, to remind me that the love we shared would never, ever die.

> *Love links the living with the dead,*
> *The dead who only are departed;*
> *For lingering still when joys are fled*
> *Love binds around the broken-hearted*
> *A sense of that which never dies*
> *A tie that reaches to the skies.*
>
> *For from beyond the shadowy veil*
> *Sweet voices cry, we love you still,*
> *For heaven-born love can never fail,*
> *Or cease the holy heart to fill,*
> *And souls that love are sundered never*
> *But one on earth are one for ever.*

We love you still

Love links the living with the dead,
  The dead who only are departed ;
For lingering still when joys are fled
  Love binds around the brokenhearted
A sense of that which never dies,
A tie that reaches to the skies

For from beyond the shadowy veil
  Sweet voices cry, we love you still,
For heaven born love can never fail,
  Or cease the holy heart to fill ;
And souls that love are sundered never
But one on earth are one for ever.

A. P. P.

Part Three

The Diaries 1910–63

I Am Alone

1910–13

I must now awaken from my seven-year idyll, and provide for my two fatherless little boys. John, a gentle, reflective child, is old enough at four to understand the finality of it all, but remains dry-eyed and slightly bewildered. Paul, whom Henry referred to as 'a child of energy and purpose, with a vivacious temperament that helpfully balances the quiet, more meditative tendencies of his elder brother', keeps asking for his Pa. Geraldine and I have tried to explain that Papa has gone to heaven, and it settles him for a while, until he expects Henry to appear back from one of his travels. Which we all do.

Grace with her sons Paul and John

I am thirty-four years of age and have £4,000, and any future royalties from Henry's books. This includes Geraldine's share of her father's inheritance. Her biographies, particularly that of Hudson Taylor, her father-in-law, earn more than enough to fund the China Inland Mission and provide for her and Howard's simple needs. She says she discussed this generous benefaction with her father, and this is what she promised to do. Even so, I cannot see how it will be enough to keep us indefinitely. I shall have to find cheaper lodgings, and some way of earning my living – though with two small children, this may prove difficult. Though I am a trained nurse, The London will not have me back. There is no place for a married woman in their employment. This was why Florence Nightingale upbraided her girls as selling themselves short when they sold out on their careers for a man. Despite the promise of my progressive education, opportunities remain very limited. I have become invisible. Without even the right to vote.

My mother deplores the unladylike behaviour of Mrs P's suffragettes, marching and heckling politicians, chaining themselves to railings, spitting at the police, breaking windows, slashing paintings, setting fire to buildings, throwing bombs and going on hunger strike when they're sent to prison. But Ruth and I have always nursed a secret sympathy for them, aggrieved that we should be denied so many rights – moral, legal and social – simply because of our gender. I would love to parade through Whitehall waving banners – but my family would never recover from the shock. I told Bee I could always resort to a life on the streets. She wasn't amused. But if a woman's place is in the home, how am I expected to keep from starving in the home now that there is no man to provide for us? Perhaps, though, the working hours of a nurse are too demanding when my boys still need me so. The only other skills I possess are derived from running Wilton House, which, I must say, provided an excellent introduction to the pleasures of budgeting, administration and household management.

As my situation is a little unusual for a married woman of my background, I shall keep a diary of my quest, insofar as time will permit – so perhaps only the key events and circumstances.

*

1911

A temporary situation finally presented itself. Robert Wyndham Guinness, Henry's younger brother, invited us to Rathdrum on the eastern coast of Ireland, where he is rector, to act as his secretary and housekeeper. He is ageing, the rectory is vast, and Dora, his wife, not as well as she might have been, in need of companionship and a little basic nursing care. To live with them for a while, until the way ahead becomes clear, would appear the ideal solution for all concerned.

The vicarage at Rathdrum

Robert and Dora are in their seventies, elderly in attitude, but kindly in manner. Percy Wyndham, their son, known as 'Wyn', who preached at Henry's funeral, is a rather fine young man. He has followed in his father's footsteps and is a curate in Birmingham, while Flo, their maiden daughter, is very much the child of the village rectory, simple, sweet and loving, devoted to our two small sons. She leads them in daily drill and many other delights, rides and drives, picnics and walks in and around the beautiful bays of the Irish coast. In fact, the pleasure and freedom of it appears to have made her blossom like a flower in the sun, and has brought colour to her rather pasty cheeks. We have long talks about my past life, and it may be possible that my coming to the rectory after world travel and the seven years spent with so great and wonderful a man as her Uncle Henry is bringing her a larger outlook on life.

The boys are so happy here. We spend hours on the vast stretches of golden sands. I take off my shoes to paddle, let my hair stream down my back, so that the wind blows it every which way, and romp around like a child myself. Occasionally, I confess, I feel that happiness is near, but just outside my grasp. Life without Henry will and must go on – for my boys' sake. They will save me from self-absorption in my grief. But I will never love another as I have loved him. How could any other man compare?

A strange happening – two weeks ago, in a dense and moonless darkness, I found myself completely lost in the grounds of the rectory, after leaving 'the Den' where I worked (in quarters that once were part of the stables, where, in bygone days, the rector's hunters were stalled). As I came out, the wind blew out my hurricane lamp, and no matter how I fumbled to find my way, only encountered hedges and trees. My natural instinct was to panic, but instead I forced myself to stand absolutely still and 'coo-ied' gently.

From nowhere there appeared a little girl who took my hand and brought me to within sight of the rectory, where the lights

I Am Alone

On the beach at Rathdrum

With cousin Flora

flickered through the windows from the oil lamps within. Her cheerful assurance was a rebuke to my panic and despair. I have seen her several times since, but never questioned her about her wanderings at such an hour. Nor have I told the rectory coachman of the incident, for I fear his child might get into trouble for being in the grounds so late at night, when probably she ought to be in her bed at the lodge. I was only immensely grateful that she wasn't.

On the Rathdrum estate

Horse riding around the Rathdrum estate

1912

In my heart I knew we could not stay forever in this heavenly seclusion from the world, and slowly developed a notion to return to Switzerland where Henry and I had been so happy at the start of our long honeymoon. I took the boys with me to Vevey for a holiday, where we stayed at the Chardonne Pension. The proprietor, M. Pélot, begged me to try and reconcile a dispute between the English and German guests. 'You see, Madame, my difficulty: the English come down in the morning and open all the windows, and the Germans come first to the *salle à manger* and eat all the butter.'

The dispute, which I successfully resolved, reminded me so forcefully of the delicate negotiations forced upon me at Wilton House that I thought, surely it could not be too difficult to run a boarding house. That would enable me to pay my way and also keep my boys with me until they were ready to take up the places they had been offered at Christ's Hospital, where they had been awarded bursaries as 'orphan children of poor Londoners'.

Meanwhile, as I explore the possibility of buying a suitable property in the Swiss Riviera, I am taking up speaking engagements, a rather new departure for me, from churches anxious to hear from Grattan Guinness's widow about their foreign travels.

Tuesday, March 25th, 1912
at Bognor Regis Baptist Church, Canada Grove

A Lime-Light lantern lecture on 'Japan' (from personal observation) by Mrs Grattan Guinness. Admission by programme – sixpence

The magic lantern has made it possible for people who might never travel beyond their own homes to see real-life pictures of places they only see in their dreams. Henry transferred all our wonderful honeymoon photographs into projected images for both public and domestic use, all carefully hand-tinted by such clever women colourists.

Japan is always the most popular topic for a public lecture – so strange, so exotic, and yet such a force amongst the world powers.

Lanterns are expensive – about a week's wage, but many churches have acquired one so that they can offer their congregations not only illustrated missionary talks, but also a 'Service of Song', the words displayed so that everyone can sing along.

How the images transport me back to those precious moments with my Henry. It is all I can do to hold back the tears and proceed, which I manage, bravely, for I know he would have wished it.

Grace

With their father gone, fearing the next generation of Grattan Guinness cousins would barely know each other, Harry decided to recreate their idyllic summer holidays at Cliff, and rented a large house in Newquay for the entire month of August. All of Henry's progeny are gathered – Harry, now the patriarch, and Annie, as efficient as ever, organising the entire event, with their nine children and first grandchild, Karis, daughter of Gene; Whitfield and Janie on furlough from China with their three children; I with John and Paul; Howard and Geraldine, and Karl Kumm with his two boys and new bride, a charming, petite Australian called Gertrude.

That last addition might have made matters difficult. Karl's marriage came as a shock to Howard and Geraldine. The letter containing the details of his engagement never arrived, and the first they knew of it was a telegram: 'We are to be married at once, and are coming for the boys.'

After six years of raising the boys as her own it was devastating news. How could Geraldine simply hand them over? Yet they were not hers. Her only real choice was to relinquish them joyfully or reluctantly. Geraldine could be rather reserved and strait-laced (she never approved of the way I tucked my skirt into my waistband and revealed my ankles as I paddled on the beach with my boys), but she was not small-minded. She wanted only what was best for little Henry and Karl and with a total lack of self-interest had graciously prepared them to love their new Ma.

'Handing over the children to Karl and Gertrude was the hardest thing I have ever had to do,' she confided in me last night when the rest had gone to bed. She had been intent, I think, on checking on the welfare of my eternal soul, as she does whenever she sees me, but I managed to steer her round to her own emotional well-being. 'The boys were my very soul,' she admitted. 'When I parted from them something died within me. There is a peculiar joy in having children of your own. You live outside yourself, and when it is cut off, you are very solitary. It is different to parting from anyone else.'

Henry and Karl, however, are blissfully unaware of any tensions amongst the adults despite the almost ceaseless rain. There are games, walks, paddling and play on the beach, and endless, real-life tales of hair-raising adventures in far-away places.

My Ruth, too, has to live with the continual absence of her own children, apart from baby Shelagh, who is back with her in East Africa. Miss Baring-Gould is to marry and has written to say she can no longer be guardian to Ruth's three children. She has found a leading and well-to-do evangelical family, the Barclay Buxtons in Ware, Hertfordshire, who are willing to take Geraldine, now aged five, as a companion for their own daughter. She will have ponies to ride and a governess to share. Sadly, she could find nothing for the boys, both at Edgeborough Prep School in Farnham during term time, but needing care during the holidays.

I would offer, but struggle to provide for my own two boys. My mother has not the room nor strength enough to have them. Lillie's silence speaks for itself and is not unexpected. Gertrude, complaining that the onerous responsibilities of a vicar's wife – her Bible class, a Women's Wednesday service, a Women's Working Party, chairing the Queen's Nursing Association, and the Enfield Deanery Moral Welfare Association – must come first, nonetheless at last agreed to host them in her very generous vicarage.

1913

This diary is rather more sparse than I intended. There are too many other demands on my time. Suffice it to say, I run a small *pension* in the picturesque little village of Combloux in the Pays du Mont-Blanc. It is very quaint with its dear little chalets on stilts and has a pretty baroque church with an onion-bulb bell tower. In spring the meadows are lush and verdant, the balconies bedecked in multicoloured flowers. The spectacular views, the abundance of delicious food, the joy of having my boys with me frolicking in the snow or marching through the flowers up the verdant mountainsides, has made my lot, by comparison with Ruth, seem an almost perpetual holiday – were it not for the fact that catering for the needs of grumpy guests and moody staff is much harder work than I realised.

I am teaching John and Paul to cook, clean, wash their clothes and dishes, and make their beds, as I want them to be self-sufficient, not dependent on a wife or servant to do all the domestic chores for them. John has become quite adept at sewing on buttons.

Following Ruth and Arthur's move to Gulu in the even more primitive north of Uganda, Arthur became desperately ill once again with blackwater fever. Ruth had to supervise the urgent building of their new mud hut as the heat of the tent would have killed him. To add to her worries, she was, despite the doctor's prognosis, pregnant again.

I had never heard her so despairing. She says she would never have moved to Gulu had she known this was a possibility, and took thirty grams of quinine to induce a miscarriage. To no effect. She asks, why is it that a woman's love for her husband should be her worst enemy? Would that there were some way of limiting our fecundity.

A baby girl has now arrived – two weeks early. The government-appointed visiting doctor was six days' travel away, so Arthur, who had never as much as seen a baby bathed before, delivered it himself, carefully following all Ruth's instructions. There were no complications, thank God. But perhaps delivering her own child was no real trial for the first white woman to climb Ruwenzori, and who had taught herself five African languages.

The natives were delighted, beating the drums for three days to summon folk from miles around to have a glimpse of the first white baby born in their country and to claim her as their own. They call her 'Larema' or 'covenant friend'.

Three days later Ruth's milk ran out. Her diet is woefully inadequate to feed a new young life, she writes. There was no milk to be had at the mission station and their young houseboy had to walk all night through the jungle, every night for three weeks, to fetch smoked milk from his home until tinned milk finally arrived from an Indian store. Oh, how I worry for her. How spoilt I am here by comparison. Her troubles make my difficulties trifling.

This year no one offered to have Ruth's boys for their summer holidays. I wrote post haste about the situation to both Lillie and Gertrude and was told a family decision had been made to send them to a home for the sons of missionaries near Colchester.

It didn't seem the most caring of solutions, and I was proved right. George and Stanley were put on a train to Victoria by their headmaster's wife, but no one met them there to escort them across London to King's Cross. The station master found them a taxi, and nine-year-old George helped his seven-year-old brother onto a train to Colchester. They were met, I gather, by the rather unpleasant woman in charge of the home, which was a dreary, unwelcoming place. On George's birthday, the old biddy took him into Colchester for an outing, then deducted all expenses from his pocket money. It was the first time one of George's letters to Ruth had even hinted at possible unhappiness. 'My poor, poor boys,' she wrote. 'It breaks my heart.'

This has been the final straw. They are making plans to return to England as soon as a parish can be found for Arthur; which may prove difficult after his twenty-two-year absence. Appointments are made by bishops based on who they know, their family background, school and university tie. Some hope for Arthur – an Irishman and without a shining academic record at Eton and Oxford. Randall Davidson, the Archbishop of Canterbury, whose good offices had been sought by Lady Dorothy Stanley, replied (rather tartly, I thought) 'Vacancies do not arise to order.'

We Are At War
1914–18

Ruth and Arthur are back in England and have rented an unfurnished house in Kensington until a living becomes available.

I haven't seen Ruth since my beloved Henry's death almost four years ago and long to go to her, but the political situation is very worrying, making me anxious about travelling with my boys, finances are tight and I have responsibilities to my guests who have come to climb and ski for what may be one last Christmas if war is declared.

I have had another of those extraordinary experiences I can only describe as 'angelic'. A small party of us, including John and Paul, aged eight and six, had taken the train to Bern for a day's outing, climbing one of the high mountains around Adelboden. We started out in sunshine, then, in the late afternoon, a heavy mist completely enveloped us and, as the wind had dropped, there seemed no chance of it clearing. The adults became extremely anxious, but happily the children expressed no fear, as we yodelled and continued yodelling with all our might. From nowhere, a tiny child dropped down out of the mist, the sound of the snow having masked any sound of approaching footsteps. She guided us down the steep slopes and, after a long descent, we finally and joyously struck a mountain path. The child then gaily wished us goodnight and was soon lost to view as she climbed back up to her mountain chalet, wherever that was.

It reminded me so forcefully of the incident in the grounds of Rathdrum Rectory. Thereafter I never read the words in Isaiah 11, 'And a little child shall lead them', without recalling both of these 'other-worldly' encounters.

*

August 4th, 1914

Britain has declared war on Germany. Perhaps it's just an extension of the disputes I intervened in at the Chardonne pension? Oh how I hope so. They say it will be over by the summer.

It is unlikely there will be any more guests at the chalet for the foreseeable future, so I have been forced to sell and must now think once more about how to earn my living.

Arthur is now vicar of All Hallows in Leeds, a grimy, rather depressing town, where huge chimneys belch black smoke into the lowering sky. There are no endowments to supplement his tiny stipend, so the finances to feed so many little mouths, number five having just made her appearance, will be tightly stretched. Ruth, who is feeling very alone, and would love to have me closer after so many years apart, has sent me an advert from the *Church of England Newspaper* for the post of matron at St Aidan's Theological College in Birkenhead.

September, 1914

So here I am in Birkenhead, which, it seems, is little more than a sprawling dockyard, and not much finer than Leeds. But the job gives me the freedom of the academic holidays. During term time, John will board at school and Paul will live with Ruth and Arthur, where he can join Stanley, Geraldine and Shelagh, whom Ruth tutors herself. At least she and I are only separated by a train journey through the gloomy Pennine Hills.

Founded in 1847, St Aidan's Theological College in Birkenhead was a rather fascinating experiment that saw a small private seminary transformed into a substantial academic institution, providing many hundreds of ministers for the evangelical wing of the Church of England. Built in 1856 on Shrewsbury Road, it is a large, impressive, if draughty place, all spires, turrets, crenellations and chimneys. In the past two years, under the leadership of the Revd Frederick Sumpter Guy Warman, it had expanded substantially in facilities and numbers to cater for the academic, spiritual and physical needs of eighty students, some accommodated in its attic rooms, others in lodgings in the town. Looking back wistfully, as the staff and students do, those pre-war years now seem the halcyon days, when a large number of earnest young men, sharing the same hopes and dreams, were reunited in the boyish camaraderie, the extension of the work-hard, play-hard of their schooldays, before they were subsumed in the serious business of their calling. Long hours of lectures, study and practical ministry were balanced with den suppers, sing-songs, table tennis, football and common room 'rags'.

As long as there is no shirking of hard work and duty, the 'old Prin', as he is known, Guy Warman, closes his eyes to any high jinks. Certainly, no sympathy is shown to the slacker by a man so dedicated to his work that he never takes a day off. High standards are expected, and restless students in his classes made to stand in the corner of the room. But it is impossible not to respect a man as erudite and well read. No one is afraid of him, but no one dares to take liberties either. I find him rather sympathetic, his aloofness merely masking a certain shyness. I have, as I am wont, teased the old dear once or twice, which I'm not sure he quite apprehends.

It is wonderfully refreshing to be in such a stretching academic environment – even if the world of peace and happiness that once prevailed here is now overshadowed by the clouds of war. Already, at the start of term, one staff member and seven students have gone to the front, and there is much uncertainty as to the position of the young men in relation to national service, and not a little searching of heart and conscience as to the path of duty.

There is drill every day, and route marches. And of any spare time, most is spent digging for victory. Every Friday the college hosts a concert for the Cheshire Regiment, in the library. As long as there are enough able-bodied men to compose a team, football will continue for the time being on Saturdays. In fact, life carries on as normally as it may, given the difficult circumstances.

Henry's nephew, dear Wyn, who is now chaplain to the forces, 3rd Cavalry Brigade, is the first clergyman to receive the DSO – Distinguished Service Order – for acts of bravery and life-saving at the front:

Illustrated War News, March 17th, 1915

On 8th November, 1914, at Kruistraat, the 16th Lancers were experiencing heavy losses. Ambulances and stretcher bearers quickly became overwhelmed by the numbers of casualties. In the front line men were left to lie where they fell as it was too dangerous to try to carry them to safety. And then the word was passed from mouth to mouth, 'the Major's hit'. He lay mortally wounded in the trenches. Whilst precious time was lost in deciding what to do, their chaplain, the Revd Percy Wyndham Guinness, set off alone on his own initiative into the battle under heavy fire. Such was the bombardment that he saw at once that the Major couldn't be treated where he lay, and had to be got to a dressing station. So he lifted him gently, put him across his shoulders, and carried him away from the heavy fire to the ambulance.

Later that same day, an urgent dispatch needed to go from the 5th Hussars to the headquarters of the 3rd Cavalry Brigade. Being the only individual with a horse, Wyn offered not merely to lend his horse, but to take the message himself, galloping out into the open space between the trenches and the enemy under heavy fire, snipers' bullets whizzing past him and shells rending the air. Flora wrote to tell me that her brother sang at the top of his voice, 'Cover my defenceless head, With the shadow of thy wing,' from the well-known hymn 'Jesu, Lover of Mankind', and that as he flew the last few yards to cover, felt that his hoofs were beating out a song of profound relief and thankfulness.

We certainly join him in that.

THE ILLUSTRATED WAR NEWS, MARCH 17, 1915.—

THE FIRST CLERGYMAN TO GET THE D.S.O.;
THE REV. PERCY W. GUINNESS.

The Rev. Percy W. Guinness is stated to be the only
clergyman who has ever won the Distinguished Service
Order and to have been mentioned in despatches on
several occasions for acts of bravery and life-saving at
the front. Two other clergymen have been returned in
a recent casualty list as having been wounded.

The newspaper cutting in Grace's diary

April, 1915

The YMCA Wirral Hut on the Bebington Showground has opened
as a centre for the troops on home leave or just off to the front. We
provide them with pens, paper, even a post office, bagatelle boards,
draughts, and a dry canteen, serving endless cups of tea. At 7.30
there is an entertainment. Tonight, little Bert, aged eight, son of a
sailor, sang 'What Can a Little Chap Do, For His Country and
For You?' It was so touching. I, when persuaded (regularly as it
happens), recite comic verses, sing favourite music hall songs, or
give character impersonations of well-known commanding officers – a source of great hilarity amongst the men. A childhood
training in playing for an audience is now proving exceedingly
useful.

The students give a closing message to prepare the men for the grim realities of the front and their possible death. It is heartwarming to see them crowd forward for New Testaments; 250 have thus far signed a pledge to follow the King in abstaining from alcohol for the duration of the war.

June 24th, 1915

Harry, my beloved stepson, has died, worn out from his Congo campaign and the tropical diseases he contracted while he was there. But he died at peace, knowing he had achieved his goal. Three years ago King Leopold II sold his interests in the Belgian Congo, and the appalling abuses perpetrated by the Belgian authorities upon their slave labour on the rubber plantations finally came to an end. Harry had been so incensed by the abuses he saw that he had twice gone to Belgium and had an audience with the King. On both occasions he was assured the injustice would cease forthwith. Empty promises. So he crossed the Atlantic to meet with President Theodore Roosevelt and personally ask for his support. Finally, thanks to Harry and the Congo Reform Association, in which he played such a key role, a tragic example of colonial exploitation and oppression was brought to an end.

I am so glad Henry was spared the loss of his son. Lucy's death was painful enough.

Meanwhile, I do all I can to support our boys here who risk their lives for King and country.

National Newspaper, July, 1915

Smith, William Gerald Furness, aged 26, Lieutenant, 3rd Bn North Staffordshire Regiment, tutor at St Aidan's Theological College, Birkenhead, second son of the Rev. George Furness

Smith, of 14 Riverdale Road, East Twickenham, died of
wounds received in action close to Ypres, after recovering a
trench when in charge of a party of bomb-throwers on 5 July
1915.

William was such a dear, sensitive young man, and now, it appears,
exceptionally brave as well, willingly laying down his life for his
comrades. What greater love? How these men find their profession of faith put to the ultimate test. They say he was reading the
college magazine as he crossed the Channel just a few months
ago. His example is so touching.

General Allenby to General Sir John Keir:

Will you please convey to the officers commanding the North
Staffordshire Regiment our appreciation of, and gratitude for,
the gallant behaviour of Lieutenant Smith of that regiment,
with his grenadier party who came to the support of the 41st
Brigade yesterday morning, and in a counter attack on the
Germans who had demolished a barricade, rushed a trench in
the left of our line. I would also express our deep sorrow on
hearing that this brave officer has died of wounds, and would
offer our sympathy to his regiment.

And now another of our most brilliant tutors, the Revd Robert
Wilmot Howard, a veritable whirlwind of a man and one of my
favourites for his irrepressible good humour, has left to serve as
chaplain with the British Expeditionary Forces. Anxiety and fear
besieges us, threatens to overwhelm us on every side.

When I can, I escape to Bidston Hill. The view across the
miles of golden gorse and soft greenery to open country and
beyond to the white-flecked cobalt sea restores my calm amidst
so much quiet grief. On a clear day I can see the hills of Wales.
When our tutors and students are at the front, fighting for their
country and their lives, do they ever think of the hopes and

dreams they left behind? Or imagine their lives would come to this?

We women increasingly fill the gaps the men leave behind, in the schools, businesses and factories, as well as on the home front. And we prove ourselves well capable of it – though we still have no voting rights and are referred to in many a journal and magazine as 'the weaker sex'.

Here in an all-male theological institution, with no access to the studies the men regard as their right alone, I am fearful our students might take this erroneous and ridiculously outdated notion into their sphere of influence in the church. What do they think we do all day? In whose hands do they leave their families, and indeed the country, when they set off for the front? I myself am forced to work for my living, and raise my two fatherless boys alone. It is no easy task, but we women show ourselves quite up to it.

I was so cross at this refusal to recognise our contribution to society that I resorted to verse, and dear Prin Warman allowed me to publish it in the college magazine.

Trinity Term, 1915,
The St Aidan's Theological College Magazine
The Weaker Sex – By One of Them

We thought the above-quoted term had become obsolete in these enlightened days, and were it not still being used in an up-to-date journal of far-reaching influence, we should have let it pass without comment. But for the sake of the younger generation, who might be misled by the misnomer and deluded by the fallacy that strength is to be measured by the dimensions of the biceps muscle, we would endeavour to show in the following lines of doggerel how the law of compensation has brought about the most perfect equality of the sexes, manifested in varying degrees and in ever-widening spheres, but proving indisputably that there is neither stronger nor weaker, but absolute equality.

We will leave the opposite sex to write up the case from their standpoint, while we confine our observations to Woman.

When man a helpless infant lay,
A fact which he can ne'er gainsay,
Who nursed, bathed, dressed him every day?
'The weaker sex.'

When intellect began to dawn
Upon his little soul new-born,
Who nurtured it from early morn?
'The weaker sex.'

And when his muscles stronger grew,
He ventured out a step or two,
Who praised him, gave him courage new?
'The weaker sex.'

When kicks and tumbles did their best
His heart's strong action to arrest,
Who healed those wounds, so ably dressed?
'The weaker sex.'

When dawned the joy of Love's young dream,
And earth like Paradise did seem,
Who brought this joy – this love supreme?
'The weaker sex.'

Through all the 'ups' and 'downs' of life
That come to every man and wife,
Who nerved him, braced him for the strife?
'The weaker sex.'

And when old age came creeping on,
And he 'fell out' from 'mong the throng,
Who tended, cheered him right along?
'The weaker sex.'

If you the page of history scan
For deeds heroic done by man,
Eliminate them – IF YOU CAN!
'The weaker sex.'

From Deborah to Joan of Arc
(You brand them 'weaker'? – Save the mark!)
Who ruled the Empire – millions dark?
'The weaker sex.'

So though 'tis said by a DD,
We really can't with him agree;
E'en Samson proved them not to be –
'The weaker sex.'

G.G.G.[7]

The poem generated a lively, if not altogether sympathetic, debate on the subject. Perhaps the war will achieve what my poor musings, and all dear Mrs Pankhurst's campaigning can't.

I have taken on the role of College Bursar in addition to my other duties, since it is hardly worth the college advertising the post. The few students who remain regularly go down to the docks to visit the ships, talk to the crews and bring them spiritual comfort. Conditions are appalling – so cramped and cold, that they need, primarily, comfort for their bodies – warm clothes and small treats. So I have agreed to accept the role of National Organising Secretary for the Ladies' Guild, the 'active daughter' of the British Sailors' Society. One of my duties is to address crowds up and down the country to enlist workers and raise funding. My aim is to raise its membership to over 21,000 by the year 1917.

Wednesday, April 26th, 1916, at 8 o'clock,
Brassey Street School, Birkenhead

Mrs Grattan Guinness will speak on 'Our Eastern Allies' (illustrated with lime-light views). Chaired by the Principal of Birkenhead College – Dr Guy Warman. Collection for Blinded Soldiers Fund.

This is the text of an article I sent to the newspapers, and was gratified to see reproduced in quite a few.

'What is the Guild?' you may ask. Look in imagination at the throngs of people streaming from the Picture Palaces and Theatres of a big northern city. Among them you will see ladies with sailors' hats in their hands, filled to the brim with money . . . (More than £200 – a Trafalgar Day record!)

Or again, it is summer time. Music fills the air, songs and recitations delight the guests gathered in an old world garden. Competitions are keenly contested for; the bluejackets who are the principal guests, carry off most of the prizes. Now they listen to stirring words from a padre in khaki, then from an old 'Sea salt'. Tea follows – a war-time tea, but how those tars enjoyed the strawberries and the cigarettes! And what ringing cheers went up for the Ladies' Guild. Then if you ever read those tragic little stories of torpedoed crews, you will have another clue to the answer. Somewhere in those pitiful true stories, you will be sure to see such phrases as, 'The men had been for 36 hours in open boats, many of them half naked: 517

articles of clothing were distributed from the Society's store.'
All thanks to Ladies' Guild.

In a basement bale upon bale of woollies, piled high against
the walls, some of them labelled with the name of the ships –
His Majesty's Trawler, His Majesty's Submarine. I confess that
I can never think of all these multitudinous pairs of socks and
gloves and jerseys and chest-protectors, merely as 'articles of
clothing' any more than I can think of the poor boys lying in
the cots of one of our Red Cross wards merely as 'cases'. For
me, there is always a certain individuality about each one – the
imprint of the Maker's hand is always there.

17,000 torpedoed sailors are being looked after by the
Society at Homes of Rest, and the supply of knitted garments
has never failed. Strong, thick, good – you couldn't buy socks
like ours in the shops! Hundreds of socks, miles of stitches
– days of monotonous toil. Yes, but look closer. Look at the
touches here and there, little differences; sometimes it is
only that supplies have run out and the foot has to be finished
off in wool of another shade. Wool is not so easy to come by
nowadays. And it always costs money. Sometimes money of
those who have not overmuch to spare. There's more than a
hint of self-denial – I had almost written the big word sacrifice
– in these bales of woollies. The sailors know the painstaking
toil, the labour of love that has gone into the making of these
socks and comforts. 'It is not only the comfort your gifts bring
to us, but the fact that we are thought of by our women at
home that makes us most grateful.'

I've seen some pairs of socks with little presents tucked
away in the toes – a packet of cigarettes, a tiny book, a card
with extra wool for darning the holes that will come.

And just as I pride myself in hearing that the Ladies' Guild now
has 21,750 members, some sorrowful news from Madras:

February 4th, 1917, The New York Times
Cricket Loses Hurditch

Word was received in metropolitan cricket circles yesterday of the death of C. Percy Hurditch of Typhoid Fever in Madras, East Indies on Jan 30th.

Hurditch, although absent from this country for some time, had been one of the leading figures on the creases of New York and Philadelphia, and had played cricket in many countries, including England, Canada, West Indies, East Indies and the USA. Hurditch was regarded as one of the best wicket keepers New York ever had.

Hurditch was a good punishing bat, and won the batting championship of the Metropolitan District Cricket League, with the highest average for the seasons of 1896 and 1904. He attained his highest mark in 1904, when he compiled an aggregate of 1,026 runs.

Dear Percy. Almost forty-eight. I had not seen him since he left to make his way in the USA so many, many years ago, where he had finally become a successful businessman. I gather that it was Cricket Week in the Madras Presidency shortly after his arrival there on business with his American wife, Daisy, daughter of Colonel and Mrs Kopper of New York, and their young son. It soon became known that he was a former captain of the New Jersey Sports Club and that he headed their batting averages, holding a record of 555 runs for one season, so he was invited to play against a visiting team. He agreed with alacrity, but on the day itself felt unwell. He told his wife he couldn't let the team down by withdrawing, and he died of typhoid two days later. There is little more to say than that he gave his life for a game. A fitting end for so keen a sportsman, dying with the financial and sporting success he had set out to find lying at his feet.

Thursday, 22nd February, 1917

Mrs Grattan Guinness is to speak at the Presbyterian Church of England Women's Missionary Association at the Lundie Hall, Beech Street, Fairfield, Liverpool. Secretaries are asked to do all in their power to secure a good attendance of their members and to have the conference announced from the pulpit on Sunday.

28th February, 1917

Wyn Guinness has been awarded the Military Cross for his bravery and is now a national hero. Robert and Dora must be so proud of their son, and Flo of her brother, and even happier that he has survived intact – so far.

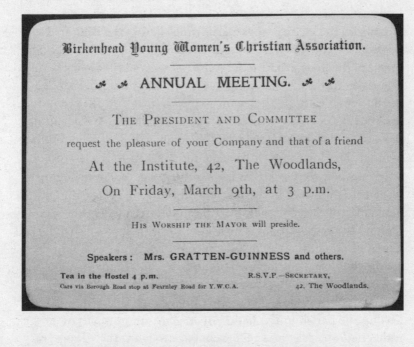

Birkenhead Young Women's Christian Association.

❧ ❧ ANNUAL MEETING. ❧ ❧

THE PRESIDENT AND COMMITTEE

request the pleasure of your Company and that of a friend

At the Institute, 42, The Woodlands,

On Friday, March 9th, at 3 p.m.

HIS WORSHIP THE MAYOR will preside.

Speakers : **Mrs. GRATTEN-GUINNESS and others.**

Tea in the Hostel 4 p.m.   R.S.V.P.—SECRETARY,
Cars via Borough Road stop at Fearnley Road for Y.W.C.A.   42, The Woodlands.

March 9th, 1917

Mrs Grattan Guinness will speak at the annual meeting of the Birkenhead Young Women's Christian Association, presided by the mayor. Collection for the Ladies' Guild of the British Sailors Society.

April, 1917

Only the new principal, the Revd Frederick Cheetham (Guy Warman having gone to be vicar of Bradford), and one tutor remain on the resident staff. There are so few students that chapel is closed and we attend the local church, Christchurch, Claughton, for Sunday services. The dining room is also closed and, due to increasing austerity, very simple meals are served in the Principal's Lodge.

College and charity work permitting, I cross the Pennine Hills to visit Ruth in Yorkshire whenever I can. I worry about her. She seems perpetually exhausted, trying to feed and clothe her family, especially in these straitening times. In May last year she gave birth to their sixth child, Bryan. Arthur left shortly after to spend seven weeks in France with the French Expeditionary Force under the auspices of the YMCA, travelling from camp to camp holding services, offering comfort, serving out thousands of cups of tea.

Meanwhile, the Leeds Battalion of the West Yorkshire Regiment was heavily involved in the battle of the Somme. Hardly a family here is untouched by grief. Will the toll of the dying never end? Despite her responsibilities at home, Ruth tirelessly visits all the bereaved families in the parish. In one family alone, a widowed mother has lost all of her six sons, one by one. I can't imagine the pain of losing one, let alone both my boys.

Arthur has reported to the War Office once again this month, leaving the parish in the hands of his consumptive curate and a rather neurotic deaconess. He went back to France as a Temporary

Officer in the Army Chaplain's Department. He was barely gone when Ruth fell down stairs and was told at the infirmary that she had suffered a miscarriage. 'Suffered' was not exactly the right word. It came as such a relief to her that she found it difficult to maintain sufficient earnestness to respond to the condolences and sympathies of her many well-wishers.

Arthur's reports from the front are printed in the parish magazine.

May 12th, 1917, the 7th General Hospital

Here are men of every order, of many nationalities, and of all branches of service – resting, billeting, going to and coming back from the fight, going to and coming back from leave; continual streams of transport, gangs of German prisoners; bands playing, bugles announcing fresh convoys of wounded; and above all the continual drone of the aeroplanes overhead, the roar of the guns, and the distant glare of shells bursting. We have over 3,000 men in hospital, half of them on the 'danger' list, while all fields and ground around are used as overflows. Mumps and measles patients alone occupy a plot as large as Woodhouse Moor. The wards are arranged according to the nature of the wounds – one all arms, another all legs, another all head wounds, two others for those suffering from shell shock, another cerebra-spinal fever patients. One tries by going through all the wards twice a day to get in direct touch with every man.

Meanwhile, his little family struggles on without him, desperately trying to live on their tiny means. Food is becoming increasingly scarce and very expensive, and their diet appears to consist of little other than potatoes.

But so many are suffering, so many returning maimed, missing a limb, blind, or with appalling facial injuries. So many young men gone for ever. So many women grieving their lost husbands, sons, brothers, fiancés. Had I hoped to marry again, which I do not, fortunately, for no one could compare with my Henry, there would be little opportunity for it now.

November 2nd, 1917

A most extraordinary and wonderful event. 1917. In *Light for the Last Days*, the most popular of all his books, that was the year that Henry, from his reading of the prophet Daniel, pointed to as the year of the collapse of the Ottoman Empire. Nothing would then stand in the way of the return of the Jewish people to their homeland.

And now, fourteen years after he had first written to Henry to say that he had read his books, Lord Balfour, Foreign Secretary in David Lloyd George's wartime administration, has publicly stated today that, 'His Majesty's government view with favour the establishment in Palestine of a national home for the Jewish people, and will use their best endeavours to facilitate the achievement of this object.'

November 29th, 1917

Henry's great work, *Light for the Last Days*, first published in 1887, is republished today due to public demand.

The new preface says:

It is in bad times that the church of Christ has ever turned back to the great Apocalyptic portions of Scripture and sought to kindle her dying hope at their flame. Once more the cataclysm of world drama, unparalleled in modern history for sheer horror, is compelling men of faith and goodwill to inquire for the seer whose eye can pierce through the mists of time, and for the interpreter of his vision. They alone can meet the hunger of the human heart for a large and deathless hope. Man cannot live by history alone and a morality founded on a merely moralistic view of life. The human soul needs the poetry of outlook; it needs the bow in the cloud, the throne above the firmament, the vision of a great war in heaven giving meaning to the struggles of earth, the New Jerusalem descending to justify man's effort for righteousness. It needs apocalyptic literature.

December 12th, 1917

Such news. I can hardly believe it. The British forces have indeed finally taken Jerusalem. (Would that my beloved Henry could have known of it – which, I have no doubt, in his heavenly home he does!)

The Middle East campaign has been so long and bitter that we barely thought it possible, the Allies under General Sir Archibald Murray suffering such a humiliating defeat at Gaza, as the Turks, aided by the Germans, held on with an iron grip.

A note from 1939

I insert here a cutting from 1939, pasted into my diary because it is so remarkable, and to ensure its correct chronological order. General Sir Beauvoir de Lisle, KCB, KCMG, DSO, on leave for ten days from his command in the trenches, read in *The Times* that his old friend, Field Marshall Sir Edmund Allenby, had been appointed to take over from Murray as Commander-in-Chief of His Majesty's forces there. Few would envy Allenby his appointment, so Beauvoir de Lisle took a cab to the Grosvenor Hotel where Allenby was staying. And this is how he described their conversation:

'No cause for congratulation,' Allenby said in his gruff way. 'Had to give up a jolly fine army to take over a rotten show. Archie Murray is a good man and if he could not succeed, I don't see how I can.'

'My dear Allenby,' I replied, 'you are on velvet. You may make all the mistakes in tactics or strategy, but nothing can prevent you from being in Jerusalem by the 31st December.'

'How do you make that out?' he asked.

I told him of the book 'Light For the Last Days' by Dr Grattan Guinness in 1886, in which he had stated that the interpretation of the three prophecies in Daniel, Ezekiel and Revelation all pointed to the same year, 1917, as the end of the Gentile times, a period of 1260 years – time, times and a half a time. 'At the same time,' I added, 'don't forget your big guns.'[8]

It is interesting to note that Beauvoir de Lisle had said his farewells and was at the door, when a thought occurred to him and he turned back and said, 'When you get to Jerusalem, Allenby, I hope you will not ride in state, for that is reserved in the future for One higher than you.' For today, we read that when he reached the gates of Jerusalem, the triumphant Allenby got off his horse and walked into the city.

February 6th, 1918

We have the vote, finally, and also the right to become Members of Parliament. The Representation of the People Act gives to women 'over 30 who occupy premises of a yearly value of not less than £5' the same political rights as men. I presume St Aidan's College is worth more than £5 a year!

What an opportunity we women now have to make a real difference to the workings of our country. No longer to be passed over as the men make the decisions on our behalf.

No amount of marching or protest broke through the bulwarks

of male prejudice. It is the war that has enabled us to prove ourselves, to demonstrate that 'the weaker sex' can do work that we were thought incapable of performing. Why has it taken so long? How can anyone think that a mother who knows what is best for her child would not also know what is best for the country?

Mrs Pankhurst claims that campaigning will not cease, however, until we eradicate the pernicious nonsense that bars younger and poorer women from having their rightful say in the running of the country. Quite right too. Such a senseless distinction.

June, 1918

Only thirteen students are enrolled for next year. Forty-five St Aidan's students have been in the combatant forces. Others have served in various spheres, twenty-eight as serving chaplains. Seven have been killed, apart from those almost mortally wounded.

In addition there are the already serving clergy who trained at St Aidan's who went out to the front as chaplains, too many of them to be named, who are now dead, or have returned maimed or were gassed.

And then all those might-have-been students, who planned to train but will never do so now. A local magazine reporting the death of the poet Wilfred Owen, who grew up in Birkenhead, claims that in a letter dated 1910, contemplating what he might do when he left his secondary school, he wrote, 'I see nothing I should rather do than enter, if possible, St Aidan's.'

Just as I thought there was little left for me to do here and I should start to seek other employment, the newspapers report a worldwide outbreak of a virulent new strain of influenza. It is accompanied by the most violent symptoms – rib-cracking coughing spells, intense pain, a haemorrhaging from the skin, eyes and ears, a cyanosis of the skin such a deep blue that the like has never been seen by the medical profession before. It is horribly like the Black Death.

The principal has asked me to stay on a while in case we have an outbreak here, for unlike most varieties of the flu, this one spares the very young and the elderly, but extinguishes twenty- to forty-year-olds. This is a new enemy – one over which we have no control. If it were visited upon a small, enclosed community like our college the results would be catastrophic. If ever our small band of warriors here gave themselves to prayer they do so now, at the same time religiously following the somewhat fatuous advice in the newspapers:

The News of the World, November 3rd, 1918

Wash inside the nose with soap and water each night and morning; force yourself to sneeze night and morning, then breathe deeply. Do not wear a muffler; take sharp walks regularly and walk home from work; eat plenty of porridge.

Monday, November 11th, 1918, Armistice Day

Hostilities ceased at 11 a.m. this morning. Every church bell rang out the news and business came to a standstill.

After he had read out the terms of the armistice in Parliament, the Prime Minister, Mr Lloyd George, concluded by moving that the House adjourn until this time tomorrow and proceed to St Margaret's to give humble and reverent thanks for the deliverance of the world from its great peril.

After our own short service of thanksgiving in the chapel, the students, tutors and I took ourselves down to the docks, where all the ships were beflagged and the sailors danced for sheer joy.

December 2nd, 1918

Just when we thought it had taken itself off, we find ourselves in the throes of a second, deadlier strain of this pernicious flu epidemic. Our Armistice Day celebrations – shoulder to shoulder, hugging and kissing – have exacerbated the situation. We have all taken to wearing masks across our mouths and noses, though what good it will do . . . Some advocate Vick's VapoRub to keep open nasal passages and loosen any mucous, though, as a nurse, I'm not confident of its efficacy. How advertising exploits naivety and fear. Oxo is supposed to fortify the immune system. Prayer seems the better protection.

Schools, churches, moving picture houses, theatres, places of amusement and public gatherings of all kinds have been closed in an attempt to bring the epidemic under control. It could be months before life returns to any degree of normality – though whether anything will ever be 'normal' again after such prolonged disaster remains to be seen. Ruth says the war has severely shaken the faith of many in their parish.

I Am My Own Woman

1919–37

May 8th, 1919

Several months have passed and nothing in my diary. Little to say except that life goes on, as it must, slowly closing over the wounds of grief and loss. My annuity has been whittled away by the war to almost nothing. A lifetime of genteel poverty confronts me, but for the work of my hands. I am now completely dependent on a salary.

Here at St Aidan's we quietly get on with our task of preparing men to restore lost hope, rebuild shaken faith and bind up the broken, and are much encouraged by the many applications for the new intake in September.

I am delighted to say that Arthur and Ruth's exceptional qualities are finally being recognised. Last month Arthur was approached by the Admiralty for his help with a confidential report on British East Africa. They are paying him for it, which makes me wonder whether the Secret Service Bureau hasn't some hand in it. Perhaps I shouldn't say so.

And Ruth goes today to 12 Downing Street at the request of the Government Chief Whip, as a 'friend', or rather representative of Liberal supporters of the Prime Minister, to contribute to discussions on 'certain questions of policy'. Lunch is provided, so at least the dear girl will get a decent meal.

June, 1919

Following the lunch at Downing Street, Ruth wrote a long letter to the Prime Minister, describing the desperate plight of the people in the north from her personal experience in Leeds. The men returning from the front have been unable to find employment, causing familial hardship and humiliation, which has added to the psychological damage caused by the war, while the women responsible for running the country in their absence have once again been relegated to the home, their gifts disregarded and wasted. She suggests a new political movement is needed to represent a newly emerging society.

Lloyd George wrote back immediately inviting her to stand for Parliament in one of the Leeds constituencies. He is very keen that women take up the new opportunity we were given last year. The first woman elected to Westminster, Countess Markievicz, has not taken her seat for she is an Irish Republican and fancies her absence a form of protest. Such an ironic waste. So typical of the contrary Irish.

Ruth declined on the grounds that £400 a year would be swallowed up by lodgings in London, extra help in the house and her train fares, contributing not a penny to the feeding and clothing of her six children. Upon which, she received a very persuasive letter from Lady Nancy Astor, who is a candidate for her husband's seat upon his succession to his father's peerage and seat in the House of Lords. Since financial constraints are hardly an issue for the Viscountess, she had failed to see Ruth's point.

November 13th, 1919

Our dear mother has died and was buried today. How we shall miss her gentle, steadying presence. Brother Phil delivered this tribute:

With her exquisite refinement – for she was a perfect lady, with her culture, geniality and handsome presence, she might have aspired to social eminence; instead she accepted a humbler position and elevated it by her contented and gracious spirit . . . Entirely free from vulgar ambition, pride and selfishness . . . she was never known to lose her temper, as her children have testified. Was there ever more perfect self-mastery? To be in her company was to me to breathe the atmosphere of rest.

And then tonight, Bee announced that she is indeed a secret Roman Catholic. It would have been Mother's worst nightmare, but now there is nothing to stop her following her feelings, and she hopes we, her siblings, will accept her decision. Ruth went to her, put her arms around her and said, 'Monsigneur need not be afraid that I am going to try and cool your ardour. My own conviction is that *any* church is only a symbol; the real thing is the Person – Christ.'

I have mixed feelings, however, remembering Henry's abhorrence of the history of the Roman Church and its persecution of so many true believers.

1st December, 1919

Lady Astor has taken her seat in Parliament, the first woman to do so. Winston Churchill MP, such a silly man, said he blushed at the sight. 'It was as embarrassing as if she burst into my bathroom when I had nothing on with which to defend myself.'

And to think, it might have been Ruth.

January, 1920

Both of my boys are now boarders at Christ's Hospital, and so it suits me to move back south where I can more easily dedicate myself to their care during the holidays.

Home for the holidays

I miss the small, intimate community of St Aidan's terribly, but
have taken a post as bursar at Whitelands College. Founded by
the Church of England National Society, Whitelands College in
the King's Road in Chelsea is one of the oldest higher education
institutions in England, pre-dating every university except Oxford,
Cambridge, London and Durham, and is regarded as one of the
foremost women's teacher training colleges in the country. Its
avowed aim at inception eighty years ago was 'to produce a superior class of parochial schoolmistresses'.

At no time has this been more necessary. Over a million of our
young men are dead, and another million maimed or disfigured or
suffer from more hidden wounds that seem to afflict their minds
and deny them any form of useful work. Educating a new generation is a vital necessity as we confront the reality of the cost of
war. And that is a job women do best. Teaching, nursing and clerical work are the only means of gainful employment eligible to

women of a more genteel background with no expectation of marriage, enabling them to make their own way in the world. And there is no doubt that of the three, teaching may be the most 'useful'. In addition, the sociable hours and longer holidays allow those who have taken on financial responsibility for elderly parents, now that the son and breadwinner has been taken from them, to contribute to their care.

The chapel at Whitelands is of particular interest. In 1874, the then principal, the Revd John Pincher Faunthorpe, enlisted the interest of the great Victorian art critic John Ruskin, who not only gave numerous gifts of pictures to the college, but also approached William Morris and the eminent Pre-Raphaelite artist Sir Edward Burne-Jones to design artefacts for the newly erected college chapel. Burne-Jones created several beautiful stained-glass windows and William Morris the splendid reredos.

I have joined a rather interesting, stimulating mix of staff – presided over by dear Winifred Mercier, the vigorous and imaginative head – all single ladies, of course, except for myself, though some, sadly, have lost fiancés, not to mention brothers, cousins and friends. One cannot but admire the way they throw themselves into their work, with little complaint or self-pity.

22nd November, 1920

I have so little time to write in my diary these days, but must just simply note the tragic, deteriorating situation in Ireland. The newspapers report that yesterday morning fourteen British intelligence operatives were assassinated in Dublin. In the afternoon the Royal Irish Constabulary opened fire on a crowd at a football match, killing fourteen civilians and wounding sixty-five.

God grant that we are not at war again – and with our own. Henry was so proud of his Irish ancestry. The events of yesterday would have broken his heart. I wonder how his cousins in Dublin fare?

1921, Whitelands Guild Annual, College Notes

Mrs Grattan Guinness, the present Bursar of the college, has for many years been interested in educational and missionary work. She has already given an interesting lecture on Japan, in aid of the Whitelands Thank-offering for Peace, and her social and administrative gifts are much appreciated in the college.

I must make mention of the new English teacher – rather a departure for us all. Amy Ida Louisa King is a mulatto and much adored by the girls already for her inspirational lectures. She arrived in England from Trinidad some twenty years ago, studied at Girton College, Cambridge, and, as with every woman student, was awarded only a diploma, 'conferring the title of Bachelor of Arts', rather than the full degree itself. Such sacrilege, but especially for a woman of Miss King's brilliance. She must be blessed with exceptional inner strength to have conquered the prejudices of such an institution. She has the most beautifully modulated speaking voice, one I must try to emulate as I do so sound like a chattering parrot. Her brilliant brain is, I'm afraid, probably beyond my powers to attain – though she has touched me, as well as our girls, indeed everyone in her orbit, with a determination to widen our knowledge of literature and philosophy.

October, 1921

Ruth writes to say that dear Stanley, a frail child at his best, has diphtheria. There has been an epidemic in the parish and a number of children have died, so she is beside herself with worry and never leaves his bedside day or night. The doctor has administered large doses of the new antitoxin injections, unavailable to my brother, Phil, when he contracted the disease, and we must hope for the best. Have we all survived the war and the flu epidemic only to be robbed of our loved ones by yet another, deadly pestilence? I do wish they could find another parish, for how can anyone thrive in Leeds? Such a dreadful, depressing, grimy town.

1923

How the years pass – almost before I have a chance to record what they bring us. No, I am not the best of diary keepers, but there has been little of real excitement in my life to record in these past two years.

Arthur and Ruth have moved to St Philips, Norbury, in South London, a somewhat pleasanter environment with cleaner air, and less germ-ridden, than the industrialised north, I truly hope.

She and I have committed ourselves to the campaign for birth control, as we both feel rather strongly about it – even if it does offend the finer feelings of her new parishioners. The first birth control clinic was opened two years ago by Marie Stopes, and has been the centre of a great deal of controversy. Ruth and I had both read Mrs Stopes's book, *Married Love*, which we had acquired with some difficulty, it not being a 'seemly' topic for women of our refinements, and therefore only privately circulated. And we were far from the only ones to do so, though no one, certainly not our own sisters, ever admitted to reading it, of course. Bee is single and a Catholic, and Lillie and Gertrude decided long ago that Ruth and I are beyond the pale.

I have always sympathised with the notion that for the sake of her mind, body and independence, a woman must try to keep herself from perpetual child-bearing, but became more convinced of its indispensability when my dear sister told me something I should perhaps not commit to a diary, except that it contains a salutary lesson on the need for contraception.

She told me that within two months of Arthur's return from France at the end of September 1917, to her absolute despair, she discovered she was pregnant again, having already had a miscarriage the previous May. She was weary beyond belief with coping with six children, one still a baby, wondering how they were all going to survive the increasing deprivations of war with its shortage of food and money. Besides, at forty-two, she was not a young woman any more.

She had some lecture to deliver in the centre of Leeds, and being a little early, and feeling very miserable, went into a tea shop – such a rare luxury. Sitting opposite her was a complete stranger, who must have sensed her unhappiness and drew her into conversation, and before long she found herself pouring out her troubles. The sympathetic stranger gave her the name and telephone number of a doctor in London who would help her.

The moment she arrived home, she made an appointment, arranged for the cook and maid to take charge of the children for a night, told Arthur she was staying with Bee who was unwell, and went to London by train. After the procedure, the doctor told her to get the first train back to Leeds, go immediately to bed, and send him a telegram to let him know that all was well. Thankfully, it was.

Ruth knew that the doctor was breaking the law, but in her heart could only admire a man who had risked his all to help a poor parson's wife in wartime. I asked if she had any regrets, especially in these later years, but she said not. It was the only solution and best for her children, and she has always held to that. Though it has been hard to keep such a secret from Arthur all these years.

I could not bring myself to condemn my poor, dear sister, though she knows many would. I could only guess what such a decision must have cost her. And then understood why she was so insistent we support the introduction of birth control clinics – a far better option than the one she was forced to take.

How perverse of God, it seems, that a husband and wife should find their love blighted by the very bodily expression of their affection. Most are forced to rely on withdrawal or periodic abstinence, which are both very prone to failure, and disastrous for the families of the poorer classes, as Ruth saw only too often in their Leeds parish. But what is a woman to do?

The new clinics will introduce female barrier methods which have a much greater chance of success, and can therefore only enhance the marital relationship. Though why some, particularly those of religious persuasion and largely men, of course, remain oo oppooed to the idea, I cannot imagine.

'*No woman can call herself free who does not own and control her body.*' So says Margaret Sanger, American doctor and campaigner for birth control.

1924

Little time for my diary this year, so let me simply record the over-arching event that cost me my writing time, and almost my sanity. On April 30th, Christ's Hospital informed me that my son was in the school sanatorium, having developed blood poisoning from a cut from a rusty nail while working on the school farm. I rushed to the school almost out of my mind with worry, and found him receiving the best of care. But his situation was grave. Nothing to do but wait and hope and pray that God would not take my lovely Paul from me. My boys are my reason for living, my very life itself. What would I do if I lost one of them?

There was some discussion about removing the infected finger altogether, but in the end the doctor decided to wait and see how the situation would develop. What use to put him through such trauma when he might not survive?

And so I sat by his bed day and night for over a week, each minute seeming a year, until, without warning, he appeared to turn a corner. It was months before he was fully well and strong enough to leave the sanatorium, though, missing all the end of year exams – a small price to pay for his life.

So for me, this has been a year of fulfilling my bursarial duties while to-ing and fro-ing between my tiny room and Paul's bedside.

'My big lads'

How strange God's ways – how unfathomable, for meanwhile, on July 7th, Calvin Coolidge Junior, son of President Calvin Coolidge, just sixteen years old, the same age as Paul, died of blood poisoning following a blister from wearing tennis shoes without socks. What a dreadful condition this is. It strikes without warning and even the President of the United States is helpless in the face of it. What must his dear wife be feeling? She loses her boy while mine is restored to me – something I cannot account for and that humbles me beyond measure.

1925

I am in my forty-ninth year, and now that my boys are grown, John at university in Oxford and Paul too soon to fly the nest, I rather felt that after ten years of working in educational establishments, I should spread my wings and re-establish my independence. Why not offer my administrative and housekeeping skills to the service of greater personal freedom?

The remainder of the legacy Henry left me, much of it evaporated by the economic recession that was the aftermath of war, has been just enough, with my savings, to acquire 8 Courtfield Gardens in Kensington at a cost of £400. My plan is to run a rather exclusive private hotel along the lines of Wilton House. But it is rather a gamble.

Courtfield Gardens, completed in 1881, is regarded as one of the most beautiful garden squares in London, the houses originally intended for the use of the wealthy during the London Season. I feel myself very fortunate to be the proud owner of such a prestigious property and only pray I might find enough 'guests' to pay the wages of my staff and what will no doubt be other, extortionate bills.

£400 is around £20,000 in today's money. A one-bedroom
flat in the house would now cost around £1,250,000

May, 1926

I never imagined life could be so busy. I have four paying guests in my little family here – a kindly but lonely Major, who has never married, daily relives his wartime experiences, and somehow manages to block every exit of mine in his need for conversation; a nervous former governess, a shy, spinsterly lady, who smiles at us sweetly before she buries herself in the book she always brings to the meal table; a young woman from a Brethren family in Ripon who has taken up nursing at the London, manifestly finds us very dull company and is enjoying, if I am not mistaken, some rather un-Brethren-like outings on her free evenings; and a forceful retired headmistress, who addresses us all as if we were a school assembly. All my guests expect me to cater for their every need, if not whim, and the headmistress and the Major both seem to think they know better than I do how to run the place. I am sure they could indeed improve on my efforts, since I have been forced to take on a rather deadly administrative job in the Registry Office to supplement my income and cannot supervise the staff as closely as I would like.

August, 1926

I am heavy hearted. Unlike his older brother, my beloved Paul, now eighteen, having had a disrupted education because of the blood poisoning, has decided that the academic life is not for him. He has joined the government colonies scheme for the migration of public schoolboy settlers to New Zealand, as approved by the National Headmasters' Conference. He always loved working on the farm at school, and now he will make his living out of it. He leaves in a few days' time and I have no idea when, if ever, I shall see him again. I do so hope it wasn't his experience of our rather varied and strange extended family life that has given him the desire to leave home so soon and travel so far.

I comfort myself that Henry would have understood. He recognised in this younger son of ours, even when he was a toddler, an outgoing nature and yearning for adventure that matched his own. I cannot curb Paul's intrepid spirit any more than I could ever hold his father back.

October 4th, 1926

Paul's first letter from on board the SS *Ruahine*, en route for Panama, says, 'Darling little Mother, Just a short letter to tell you that everything is perfectly ripping. The other public schoolboys seem jolly nice. There are twenty of us altogether.' What an experience for such young men. They appear to be having a grand time of it, as young people do, unlike those they leave behind to mourn their departure.

Ruth, as ever, is my sister in sorrow. George, her eldest, upon leaving Oxford University, joined the civil service and has just arrived in India. What a pair of desolate mothers we are, grieving for our beloved sons.

December 27th, 1926

In August Ruth gave a talk on the BBC on the Pygmy people, whom she encountered and befriended when she was in Uganda.

Not to be outdone, I have today, from 4.00 to 4.15, read out on radio some 'Letters of a Public Schoolboy Emigrant', which I had compiled primarily for my own interest, but, following Ruth's success, submitted for broadcast. Here is an excerpt:

> I have come to one of the nicest little places imaginable. It is only a small farm and will give me time to get acclimatised and used to the conditions before launching out on to a big place where I should be more on my own.

Our daily programme is somewhat as follows. Out of bed at six with bread and butter and tea. Milk the cows, separate the milk and wash the separator. Breakfast at eight. Feed the cows then do lots of odd jobs until dinner at 1.30, such as tree felling, carting gravel and timber, planting trees and hedges to form quick shelter, attending to the orchard, building small sheds, cutting rushes and carpentering – incidentally, I am becoming quite an expert hand with an axe. You should see my rippling muscles. I ride everywhere.

In the afternoon milking again, then saw and chop wood – by moonlight usually – until high tea at seven. Then write letters, talk or read until ten. I am not lonely as there are always plenty of people calling.

John, meanwhile, informs me that he has exchanged his theology course for medieval French. He maintains that the 'higher criticism', casting doubts on the authenticity of the biblical texts, and very much in vogue in the theological corridors of Oxford, has provoked a crisis of faith. He no longer feels called to be ordained. This is exactly why Henry deplored the liberal approach to theological scholarship. Those foolish, stuffy dons in their rarified world have thoughtlessly demolished my son's evangelical beliefs. I am angry and disappointed, as I think Henry would have liked this more gentle, reflective son of ours to take holy orders. I also fear that a degree in French might take another son from me too, but I must learn to let my boys pursue their own destiny.

Ruth's Stanley has been accepted for ordination training at Cuddesdon Theological College near Oxford, a course lasting only a few weeks because he already has an Oxford degree. Why that should prepare him for church ministry, I cannot imagine. Nor can Ruth or I understand why he should want to attend a High Anglican college, but suspect it was the influence of that Auden friend of his, one of the arty, poetic set he got in with on his floor at Christ Church.[9]

National Newspaper, January, 1927

Mrs A.B. Fisher, formerly of Bunyoro, will talk on Uganda
Yesterday and Today, accompanied by her lantern pictures.

And this to a packed Royal Albert Hall at a meeting to commemorate
the Church Missionary Society's Uganda Jubilee, from 1877 to 1927.

The chair was taken by the Archbishop of Canterbury, and the
speakers included Sir Frederick Lugard, the Administrator of
Uganda from 1889 to 1892. Dear Ruth. What a wonderful honour.
Especially for a woman. She was a little overwhelmed, but spoke
marvellously, holding an audience of over seven thousand spellbound. And as I watched her so proudly, an image of our father
flashed before me so strongly that the words came to mind: 'He,
being dead, yet speaketh.'

April 26th, 1927

Today the sad news that Whitfield, Henry's youngest, died on
April 12th at the age of fifty-eight, a death that reflected his lifelong selflessness and dedication.

Janie writes that one night a man arrived at the door obviously
suffering from typhoid fever. It was a freezing night and Whitfield
would never turn anyone away. Nor could he risk an epidemic at his
hospital where there were so many wounded because of the near
civil war in China. Whitfield took him in, stipulating that he alone
would take care of the patient, and by the time the order to evacuate
reached Kaifeng, was seriously ill with typhoid himself. 'My heart is
breaking with sorrow,' Janie says, 'but full of peace. I praise God for
all the love of these twenty-two years. Such perfect happiness.'

He was buried on April 17th, Easter Day, in the English cemetery
in Peking. Will China ever know what it has lost in such a man?

June, 1927

Stanley, newly ordained, has set off for India like his elder brother –
to teach at St Paul's, Darjeeling – laden with presents for George and
his new wife, Marjorie, whom George met on the boat on his way
out and married last November. So Ruth has now said goodbye to
two of her boys. That is how it must be. We teach our children to
spread their wings, only to find that one day they fly the nest and
leave us. Our only consolation is that God maps out their flight path.

July 25th, 1927

It is too awful to be true. I cannot take it in. George is dead – so
soon after his arrival in India, not of any tropical disease, but of
playing polo. He had a terrible accident and died shortly after, a
mere five days ago, with Stanley still at sea and only two days
from Bombay. He was to travel on to Saharanpur to visit George,
who was assistant magistrate there.

Handsome, vibrant George, whose luminous career was anticipated by all who knew him – dead at twenty-three. It doesn't seem
possible. I cannot bear the pain in my beloved sister's face and
cannot find the words to say. What consolation is there for such a
loss? All that wasted potential. Why, oh why? Where was God's
protecting hand in which she had so put her trust?

July 28th, 1927

How strange. A letter from George arrived today. Ruth hardly
dared open it, her grief is so raw. She held it out to me, unable to
read the words through her tears, and I took it and was struck
from the first by the extraordinary reassurance and comfort it
contained, as if he were speaking to her from beyond the grave.
He says he is lonely, but: 'There is a loneliness which brings with

it a sense of dignity and a wonderful peace because it springs from a deep communion with all life ... Sacrifice, sacrifice – where is love and happiness without it? It alone gives them meaning ... unhappiness and worry don't enter into my philosophy. What must be, must be, and all will ultimately be for the best.'

December, 1927

Ruth has received the most lovely poem from Stanley, who is so creative and clever. He had received the terrible news of George's death by cable from Marjorie when he arrived at Bombay, and was too late for the funeral, so continued on to his school at Darjeeling. But somehow he could not settle without seeing George's grave in Roorkee Cemetery in Saharanpur.

As he sat there quietly he found himself writing this poem for Ruth, and it has brought her such comfort – at last.

> *And then*
> *A blue jay flashed across the sun and left*
> *The unearthly colour standing in my eyes*
> *Long after it had passed, until I felt*
> *Like Saul of Tarsus on the Damascus road,*
> *Blind to the busying destinies of dust.*
> *There was a mother once who laid her son*
> *First in a manger and afterwards, a tomb;*
> *She came on such an eastern dawn as this,*
> *Bringing sweet spices and a bitter grief,*
> *And took away a joy no years have dimmed:*
> *She found the grave a sanctuary of God.*
> *'Here lies one of India's lovers' – No!*
> *Though death police the lips and puts a stone*
> *On the twin sepulchres that were his eyes,*
> *We shall arise and go this way to find*
> *Thus early, in the morning of our sorrow,*

An unimagined vision in the empty tomb,
Empty of our too soon imagined loss.

1931

And so the years have passed since I last put pen to diary – difficult years as Ruth comes to terms with her loss, and I hanker after
my Paul, whom I have not seen for four long years.

In September last year he left New Zealand for good, having
decided farming was not for him after all. He travelled by ship to
Vancouver and journeyed 2,500 miles overland through San
Francisco and Los Angeles, a route that his father and I had once
taken so long ago, and is now in Texas, training for ministry in
the church at Dallas Theological Seminary. Not at all what I
expected of this adventurous, outward-going son of mine. So one
of our boys will follow in his father's footsteps after all. Oh, how
I long to see him after all these years, to tell him face to face how
proud his father would be.

Meanwhile, upon leaving university John took up acting and
joined the Liverpool Repertory Company. John, my quiet, thought-
ful introvert! But then Henry's mother was on the stage in Dublin
for a while – at a time when it wasn't exactly a suitable profession
for a well-brought-up young woman. He currently understudies
the actor John Gielgud, who apparently said to him, 'With your
looks and my voice we could go far!' Not that far, I suspect, as in
his last letter he seemed very uncertain about whether the lifestyle
really suited him – which doesn't surprise me at all.

I work by day in town, and by night at Courtfield Gardens,
seeing to the needs of my various guests, who come and go (except
for the Major!) and are as eccentric as a host of Dickens charac-
ters. The young nurse is long gone, ordered back home I shouldn't
wonder, replaced by a dapper, elfin man of indiscriminate age
who works in fashion in the city, and regularly brings back a
motley crowd of rumbustious young male friends, who, because

of his unfortunately prominent ears, refer to him as Mickey Mouse. My head teacher passed away suddenly, vacating a place for 'Uncle George', an elderly widower, who is rather too fond of the opposite gender and regularly gives me chase around the kitchen table.

In June Ruth required surgery for suspected cancer of the breast, though I was the only one who knew the real reason for her stay at the St Luke's Nursing Home for the Clergy. She told Arthur it was simply 'one of the little things women have to face from time to time'. Only afterwards, when the large lump had been removed and proved not to be cancer, did she tell her family the truth.

> *26th June, 1931*
> *St Luke's Nursing Home for the Clergy,*
> *Fitzroy Square, London*

My precious sister

While you are all sleeping I am up, feeling very fresh in this bright morning sunshine, singing in my heart Te Deum Laudamus.

You, darling, have been a revelation to me of what love is. You have poured out the riches of your love upon me and mine, denying yourself so many things that you must want to have, giving me so much of your time when you have your own large household to see to, and John leaving so soon too. I can't tell you what all this has been to me during the past fortnight.

I have been going back over the almost-miracle of you treating me to that expensive day at the Hurlingham Club in Fulham, the headquarters of world polo, so that I could at last enter into my beautiful boy's ecstatic joy in it and understand. When we had been hoping for a holiday in Italy! How wonderful that we had a change of plan. That day was well worth two weeks in Italy.

The necklace and the clasp are simply beautiful – they tone with my complexion and blend with the frock. And in

*themselves they are lovely. I shall keep them as a sacred
memento of this time.*

*I did love having your John here yesterday. Others were
coming and going but he stayed on and was a darling. My
darling Grace, I feel more than I can say about this last giving
up of yours – with Paul gone and now John off to Africa so
soon. Your two splendid boys, with all the wealth of their
different natures and their full experiences are out in the wide
places to make their contribution to the perfecting of the
Divine Plan – so little comprehended, yet apprehended by both
of them and us.*

*Our home is always yours. You are the one loved by us all,
and a warm heart welcome will always be there for you and
John when he returns.*

Your ever devoted Ruth

September 4th, 1931

It has indeed been dreadfully hard to part with John, who, through
the offices of some highly connected Oxford friends, has been
appointed deputy district commissioner for the Ivory Coast. Oh,
how I miss him, such pleasant, undemanding company when he
was home, a supportive, calming presence at Courtfield Gardens.
I asked the maid to clean out his room, to make it ready for a new
guest, but cannot bear the idea of someone else in it. Chin up.
Needs must – though the tears flow at the very thought of it.

And then news from Paul that cheered me enormously. He has
met a very special young woman at Canadian Keswick. He was a
speaker there to the young people, thanks to an introduction from
Geraldine who now spends a great deal of time in the United
States and keeps a maternal eye on him for me. There were a few
titters, he says, when the quaint elderly lady in almost Edwardian
garb introduced a twenty-three-year-old in her plummy English
accent as 'my brother'.

Jean, his new interest, is from a good, English-speaking, Baptist family in Montreal. And of special interest to me – she will commence a degree course at Wheaton College, Illinois, this autumn. A bright girl, by the sound of it, taking up the new opportunities for women to further her education.

No chance of seeing Paul in the near future, I fear. It will be a sad Christmas this year without my boys. But no doubt my little Courtfield family will keep me busy. Some consolation that is!

January 2nd, 1932

Such news. Paul travelled all the way from Texas to Montreal to ask Jean's parents for her hand in marriage. And has been accepted. On condition that they do not marry until she finishes her degree.

Wheaton College, where the men and women are strictly segregated, appears to be a rather strait-laced environment, by the sound of it, bound by the same narrow restrictions I knew in my childhood. But have no fear, Paul writes, for Jean is a rebel – raising the length of her uniform skirt, wearing her beret at a jaunty angle, and even sporting lipstick. She endures because her parents insist she must, and she does want a degree at the end of it. But she is subjected to regular 'talkings to'.

It is hard for them to be so far apart.

April 14th, 1932

I am beside myself. A cable received today tells me John has contracted blackwater fever and is not expected to survive. He is being shipped home – accompanied by his coffin.

Too devastated to write more. I can but pray and wait. With God's help.

April 20th, 1932

No news. Is that good news then? This waiting is unbearable. This is the second time that, like Abraham, I must be prepared to offer up a son. Unlike Abraham, I am unwilling. Yet I have no choice in the matter.

The guests are behaving. They try not to bother me. It is hard for them too. Most knew and loved John. They creep around, uncertain whether to ask after my welfare or keep silent. The tension in the house is unbearable.

May 2nd, 1932

Still no news. I cannot eat or sleep. My poor boy is on the high seas somewhere, desperately sick, alone, without his mother. God watch over him for me, since I cannot.

June 3rd, 1932

I must record my thankfulness, my gratitude, for John is home. The fever had passed by the time he docked, the coffin dispensed with! But he is still weak and needs nursing care. Fortunately, I had not let the room.

I am indeed blessed to have my son restored to me – in every sense. The second time I have almost lost one of them. I cannot help but think, why me and why not Ruth? Why did God hear my prayers and not hers? These questions are too hard for me. I cannot find any answers, except that Henry used to say that it's the what-for, rather than the why-for that matters. What must I learn from this? That everything I have is a gift to be held on an open palm and never taken for granted?

September 7th, 1932

Harry's eldest daughter, Gene, very kindly suggested that John recuperate with her at Brickwall, the progressive school she runs at Northiam in Sussex for the education of girls aged seven to nineteen who struggle with speech and reading – the first such school in the country. It was the holidays, so John would have the rather lovely landscaped park and gardens virtually to himself.

As it happens, he was forced to share them with Karis, her daughter, and the upshot is he has decided to stay on at Brickwall as a teacher. I'm not sure whether the attraction is the post, the place, or Karis – but suspect it is the latter.[10]

February, 1934

The reason I have had so little time for my diary is that I have been recording the events of my rather unusual childhood amongst the 'Peculiar People'. John is urging me to seek out a publisher, but why would any publisher want my poor scribblings? I merely intended to commit my memories to paper for the next generations. But then, I was incensed some years ago by the publication of a most unhappy memoir of a child raised in the Plymouth Brethren called *Father and Son* by Edmund Gosse. My parents knew the Gosse father well, and were mortified that he should be portrayed as such a repressive tyrant when he was a gracious, gentle man who adored his boy. The home, not unlike ours, was full of love and fun, despite its restrictions. Perhaps I should set the record straight? To spare the memory of my dear parents, I am using the pseudonym 'Septima' – the seventh child.

Paul has completed his ministerial training and will transfer to North Western University in Illinois in November so that he can take a degree close to his beloved Jean.

October 22nd, 1934

My doodles have been sent to several publishers. I hold my breath. For myself, I am an avid reader, and if I had my way would spend the entire day with my head in a book, and nothing would get done. Novels, art books, politics, spirituality, my taste is very eclectic. Havelock Ellis, Dean Inge, H.G. Wells, J.B. Priestley, Irving Stone, Vera Brittain, Winifred Holtby, Matthew Arnold, Jung, John Donne, Charles Morgan, and Evelyn Underhill, whose brave letter to Archbishop of Canterbury Lang, requesting he call his clergy to a deeper spiritual life, was published in our newspapers. There is no competition between the choice to read or write. Which is why there is so little in my current diary.

Time, in later life, for Arthur and Ruth to take on something a little less demanding. They move today to the more rural parish of High Hurstwood in Sussex, on the edge of the Ashdown Forest – a quieter, 'waiting room for heaven' church, as he is now sixty-six and Ruth nearly sixty.

May 6th, 1935

I am determined to keep my new diary more up to date, starting with the Silver Jubilee of King George V and Queen Mary.

In my seventeenth year, forty-two years ago, I saw them on their wedding day, from the shop window of a chemist on The Strand. Today, with my niece and only godchild, Larema, I watched from the Westminster Bank, opposite the Law Courts. It was a warm summer day. The sun shone continuously on a most wonderful procession and crowd. Not a hitch in the magnificent organisation. Good temper, eager enjoyment and enthusiastic outbursts of cheering and waving for all and sundry, including all the king's prime ministers, headed by Ramsay MacDonald with his daughter Ishbel.

The cheers rose to a crescendo when the royal carriages passed with the Duke and Duchess of York (in jubilee blue), and the two little princesses (in Margaret Rose pink), both waving their hands; followed by the Duke and Duchess of Kent (Princess Marina looking lovely in beige with a large picture hat, which, alas, she was obliged to hold on to), then the Prince of Wales, the Duke of Gloucester and the Princess Royal. Finally, our King and Queen – the King in naval uniform and the Queen looking positively lovely in regal white satin and silver.

Through the broadcasting apparatus we were able to follow the procession and the service at St Paul's. The crowds had now filled the streets and were passing in a continuously moving stream, but as the first strains of the national anthem came through the various wireless sets, everyone instantly came to a standstill, men bared their heads and all on the stands rose and stood to attention.

A truly wonderful day. To those of us who had seen the Diamond Jubilee of Queen Victoria with all its majestic pageantry and worldwide representation, this seemed quite an intimate little family affair. Most of the great European potentates of 1897 have passed away, some murdered, others in exile. Dictators have arisen, but our King remains on the throne, holding the loyalty of his people.

May 19th, 1935

A constantly recurring theme in all types of books, magazines and newspapers is the need for a spiritual renaissance. Modern science has, to a large extent, cut a swathe through the foundations of religion, the church has lost its sway over the people. There are no great seers or prophets and the masses are like sheep without a shepherd. What is the result? That every nation is seeking to satisfy its soul with political ideals, and the two countries that have made a fetish of politics are the two most bitter in their persecution and intolerance of the old accepted religious beliefs – Russia and Germany – substituting the worship of Communism and Nazism.

Can the soul of man be satisfied with this? Does not the failure of the League of Nations and all the future efforts made for Peace and Disarmament point to the need for a fundamental change of heart in man?

My intention in this diary was mainly to comment on newsworthy events, but to record only what one thinks and not what happens is to omit an important part of one's life. There are certain days when one seems to strike the rock bottom of doleful experiences – and these should be recorded if only to prove how one can live through such sad experiences, philosophically accept them, and subsequently see how very insignificant they were in relation to life as a whole.

May 20th, 1935

Within three weeks, four maids have given notice to leave. Two left after two days, despite the fact that they were on monthly wages, finding the work all 'too much'. Did no one tell them that being 'in service' involves a great deal more than delivering tea in the parlour? So slapdash and empty-headed, these girls. Each was more incompetent than the last, and I had to watch the house getting dirtier and dirtier. But an inferior maid is better than none at all, and the climax came when my only standby, Annie the cook, failed to turn up one morning as well.

I have no strength to cope with it after a day in the loathsome Registry Office. But we all need feeding, so no choice but to roll up my sleeves and set to work in the kitchen. I have never really had a chance to master the art of cookery. My achievements are plain and simple, and will have to do.

To make matters worse, when I arrived home today, I was confronted by the postman who handed me a packet containing the manuscript of childhood memoirs. Rejected for a second time!

May 22nd, 1935
To the Editor of The New Yorker

Dear Sir

The statement in your issue of April 20th that 'the man in the street isn't thinking about the Jubilee at all, it means nothing to him, not a thing, and the newspaper ballyhoo about it actually bores him', is so obviously untrue as proved by the actual happenings of Jubilee Week, not only in London, but throughout the British Isles and indeed the whole Empire. An estimated 250,000 gathered outside Buckingham Palace, shouting themselves hoarse with repeated calls for the King. Such enthusiasm makes the reading of your London Letter both ridiculous and false.

Yours faithfully
Grace Grattan Guinness

June 15th, 1935

Paul and Jean graduate from North Western University today. I am so proud to have a future daughter-in-law, albeit a Canadian, who is a graduate.

It seemed fitting that I should be at Whitelands (new) college reunion, among past and present students. Among my old colleagues, it was a pleasure to meet again Miss King, the brilliant mulatto teacher of English and Drama. But oh, how I missed dear Winifred Mercier, the one-time brilliant principal – now dead. It was she who masterminded the move of the college away from the grime and noise of the King's Road to West Hill in Putney, a more conducive place to study. Convinced that nothing but the best would do for future teachers, she persuaded the college council to employ Sir Giles Gilbert Scott, architect of the magnificent Liverpool Anglican cathedral, to design the new college, opened by Queen Mary in June 1931. It is one of the finest specimens of his grand, spacious style, quiet and dignified, standing in around thirty acres in Putney, with a vast panoramic view over London to beyond the Crystal Palace and the Surrey hills.

I went to evensong in the beautiful new chapel (the Burne-Jones windows and the William Morris reredos had been transferred with the move) and prayed for Paul and Jean. I didn't hear a word of the Bishop's address. He was old, with a weak, thin voice – and spoke at considerable length (such a mistake with all those young teachers present).

June 22nd, 1935

A sudden heatwave in London today that made me long for open spaces, trees, flowers, the smell of earth and flowering shrubs. There was Kew, of course, within easy reach. So off I went, forgetting that the luncheon hour would let me in for strap-hanging crowds on the underground. But they thinned out at Hammersmith, and Kew never seems crowded.

I found a bench under the shade of a tree, an elderly lady sat at the other end. I felt there was a tacit understanding that neither of us wanted to converse. I had my book (Robert Graves – *Claudius the God*) and she her paper. I removed my shoes and put up my feet. She did the same, without removing her shoes. The air was heavy with the scent of flowering shrubs, and the heat drew from the earth that lovely mossy smell that makes one long to lie down and let the cool grass touch one's skin. Then I thought of rheumatism and lumbago and all the risks of lying on the grass in my sixty-first year, but a coincidence made me risk it all. My primitive instinct only needed the goad of a couple coming and sitting on the same seat, polluting the air with the odour of their perspiring bodies . . . so I moved on and lay on the grass.

I slept for an hour – and was filled with a deep sense of peace as I gazed up through the laden boughs of the trees and became strangely conscious of our dear, precious father, who, every

Saturday (as I remember him doing all my childhood), went to Kew or Richmond and walked for miles along the towpath, meditating and thinking out his 'addresses' as the Brethren called their sermons, in the open air. It seemed to me he walked in the gardens today.

Almost an omen, for when I arrived home a letter from publishers Heath Cranton awaited me. I steeled myself as I opened it, convinced it was yet another rejection, but no. My stomach turned over with excitement. They feel there is real potential in my little book, and plan to have it ready for publication in two months.

June 23rd, 1935

Two of my sisters, Lillie and Gertrude, on holiday, have written to me this week on the same subject – their difficult husbands! These are my remarks by way of reply.

> *It only confirms one of my strongest convictions that married couples should be parted from time to time. I cannot understand in these days of advanced psychology that you do not realise the need of this. Everyone needs not only change of work and surroundings, but of people.*
>
> *There are times when I feel I shall scream if I have to listen to one more fatuous remark of the Major's – after five years of my guest – so I pack up and come down to you for a day or two, then return and think what an asset he is to the house!*
>
> *Men are much more conservative than women and dislike being uprooted. The change upsets them and their irritability reacts on their wives (nice handy, passive resisters). Really it is all a 'set-off' against their repressions – primitive creatures that they are. And you foolish women do exactly the wrong thing, because you think it is your duty to stick to them, instead of taking the only wise course of leaving them from time to time. (As a matter of fact, they can be happier with their daughters*

*for a time, after they reach a certain age. The wife reminds him
too persistently of his lost youth, while a daughter restores it
– he is parasitically rejuvenated.)*

*My dear husband was clever enough to know this advantage
of occasional separation without expressing himself in words.
More than once he and I were parted, especially after John was
born (a natural reaction on the part of the man against the
other's absorption in her child – seeking consolation elsewhere). But usually, wives are too afraid to run the risk and so
stick to their husbands like leeches, with the disastrous irrita-
bility you get as a recompense. (Most of them are much too
afraid to be adventurous, and the clergy more so than others in
this respect.) Then, when you get together again you rediscover
the freshness and joy of it, and it makes life pleasantly possible
and you both come to realise how indispensable you are, one
to another.*

July 3rd, 1935

Paul arrived home from New York today for a short stay prior to
his marriage in Montreal. He motored up from Plymouth to
London and arrived at exactly 8 p.m. as indicated in his morning
telegram. I have not seen him for almost eight years – this handsome son of mine, tall and broad-shouldered and looking so like
his father. I stood for some time, unable to decide whether to look
at him or hold him.

He tells me that Jean has done magnificently in her BA finals
and that he came third in his BSc out of ninety-seven. Following
his wedding, he and Jean will come to England as he has accepted
a curacy in Sussex with his older half-nephew, Gordon Guinness,
one of Harry's sons. I shall have both my boys within my reach at
last, thank God. And two new, lovely daughters by marriage.

Paul and Jean's wedding

John and Karis' wedding

August 24th, 1935

Paul has sailed on the *Empress of Britain* for Canada, and his marriage on September 7th. I am so sad neither to have the fare, nor indeed the staff available here, that would enable me to accompany him.

How curiously reticent one is to put into writing the things that most deeply touch us in life. This is doubtless due to the fact that a diary may be read by others, and one shrinks from sharing one's own thoughts with an unknown person. Yet surely, all the world should know the joy of a mother's heart in seeing her sons in love and being loved by the sweetest and best of daughters-in-law.

John's wedding to Karis on July 26th this year was quite the most lovely wedding I have ever been present at – and I have been to many. Its setting – the old parish church in beautiful Rye – its simplicity – and the presence of all those dear pupils from Brickwall School.

Now this is the rather extraordinary thing, and it causes no end of hilarity in the family. In marrying his eldest half-brother's granddaughter, John has made Karis her own mother's aunt, one of the anomalies created by Henry's siring two separate families so far apart. Imagine their surprise when they discovered they were related and had met, many years before, at a family reunion in Newquay.

August 26th, 1935

On the eve of Paul's departure six advance copies of my first book, *Peculiar People*, arrived. Curious, my reactions. I could hardly bear to see anyone handle it. I wanted to snatch it out of Major Festing's hands and hide it. I did not so much mind his cousins having a copy – which I gave him for all his kindly interest and in getting the woodcut done for the jacket. But I felt that even he wouldn't read it. I don't want anyone to read it. And yet, here

I am furiously addressing hundreds of envelopes and sending notices to everyone about it. I positively have a pain when I read my publishers' letters that some copies have already been sent out for review and more will go next week and more the week before its date of publication (September 20th). And I'm miserable, for despite the publishers' optimism and the family's praise (but those who have given praise would praise anything I did, so this doesn't count), I am conscious of its terrible shortcomings, its feeble literary merit and its limitations and utter lack of accepted literary standards. I know the critics – those who deign to read it – will pounce on all its glaring faults and shortcomings and my misery will be complete.

Whatever does one write for?

September 19th, 1935

It is amusing to note the different reactions of those in this house – and the family – to my book. 'Uncle George', before it was even in print, ordered six copies. 'Mickey Mouse', after reading a review, said, 'I should like to read it; have you a copy you could lend me?' I thought of my publisher's remark, 'People will beg, borrow or steal a book, but not buy,' so suggested that he should buy one. 'Maybe, after I have read it,' he said cautiously.

Lillie wrote from Leigh on Sea. 'I shall not send off any order forms for your book until I have read it, but anyway it is doomed so far as this town is concerned as there is a sect here called "The Peculiar People" – most dreadful freaks.'

Gertrude made no remarks at all, until I chanced to ring her up one day and she said, 'Of course, my dear, we shan't be able to give your book to any of our friends as they would at once recognise it was our family.'

Bee is proud of it – but forgets to tell me any of her reactions, saves up all the reviews and circularises all my friends and relations. It will be a wonder if anyone ever speaks to me again.

September 26th, 1935

G.K.'s Weekly (G.K. Chesterton)

Not a novel but an indefinite kind of biography hard to pigeon-hole . . . As a sidelight on the men and methods of the religious revival 1858–62 it is immensely attractive. Its attitude is gently broad. It sees both the strength and defects of this rebellion against tradition, that, supplying no control or authority in church government, failed in understanding human needs . . . It is an interesting slant across a Victorian sub-section, and a sidelight on a Protestantism more dogmatic and infallible than the Pope at whom it publicly and painstakingly shuddered. Odd though, to note that, for all this loathing of the Pope and the City of Babylon, the preacher father could not keep away from it for one of his rare holidays. Perhaps he wanted to collect relics of abandonment, for quite a haul was made, including a plenary indulgence. I wonder if he brought that home in a cage?

October 1st, 1935

My book has also been reviewed in the *Daily Independent*, the *Daily Telegraph* ('a lively and demurely amusing chronicle'), the *Daily Dispatch* ('charmingly described by Septima, who has a fine sense of humour'), the *Daily Sketch*, the *Glasgow Daily Record and Mail* ('the regulations imposed upon the children read curiously today. How could her eldest sister have been sent away for going to a performance of Gilbert and Sullivan?'), the *TLS** ('the whole book is marked by understanding and by charity . . . It would be unreasonable of course to compare it with *Father and*

---

* *Times Literary Supplement*

G. K. CHESTERTON

G.K.'s Weekly

September 26, 1935

" Peculiar People " by Septima is not a novel, but an indefinite kind of biography hard to pigeon-hole. Under a slight veil it describes the life of a preacher who did much to popularise those Saints " saved by grace sealed in the heavenlies—holy and unblameable," that is, the Plymouth Brethren. As a sidelight on the men and the methods of the religious revival of 1858-62, it is immensely attractive. Its attitude is gently broad. It sees both the strength and defects of this rebellion against tradition, that, supplying no control or authority in church government, failed ' in understanding human needs.' It is full of strenuous preaching, mission rallys, baptism by immersion—when feminine converts were embarrassed by the way their bridal garments would float upward as they entered the water—of musical evenings of " The Better Land " school enjoyed by a big and jolly family. It is an interesting slant across a Victorian sub-section, and a sidelight on a Protestantism more dogmatic and infallible than the Pope at whom it painstakingly and publicly shuddered. Odd though to note that, for all this loathing of the Pope and his City of Babylon, the preacher could not keep away from it for one of his rare holidays. Perhaps he wanted to collect relics of abandonment, for quite a haul was made, including ' a plenary indulgence '—I wonder if he brought that home in a cage?

The review in G.K.'s Weekly

Son. In spite of its literary distinction it lacks the richness that marked Gosse's work; but nevertheless, with its sincerity and faithful reconstruction of a strange world it makes an impression of comeliness that remains in the reader's mind'), the *Bath and Wilts Chronicle* ('the casual reader will enjoy its frank and easy style, and will reel in the passages which illustrate how long and how difficult was the path to feminine emancipation'), the *Guardian* ('it is written with great charm and is a delightful picture of one side of nineteenth century religious life and its inevitable reactions'), the *Nursing Mirror*, and *Woman* ('the story is delightfully told and one could have wished for far more of such fascinating reminiscences').

The Whitelands Manual made it their 'book of the year', while the St Mary Magdalene parish magazine in our old haunt of St Leonards sounded one of the few snooty notes ('we are not given to advertise the change-over of converts from other forms of faith to our own, but it ought to be known and remembered that there is a constant migration and procession into the Church of England from all sides which never stops'). Other rather negative comments, largely from evangelicals, accused me of derision and wondered why I wrote such a travesty – unless I was inspired by *Father and Son* to another distasteful attempt at undermining my parents' faith.

But I have had scores of excellent reviews in both the secular and religious papers, and was the subject of two articles in the *Daily Graphic* in the USA.

October 15th, 1935

Today I received a letter from Sylvia Pankhurst, with whom I have been in correspondence for some time, (together with a list of her books), saying that we women should all unite to oppose the growing Fascism in Europe. I don't agree with Sylvia on this, as I feel dictatorships may sometimes be an appropriate expedient to meet a national emergency.[11]

Repressions of the "Peculiar People"

PECULIAR PEOPLE. By Septima. (Heath Cranston, 5/8).

" Not for many years has there been so much grave and deep apprehension; never has the future seemed so incalculable as at this time. In America there is universal prostration and panic. In France the political cauldron seethes and bubbles: Russia hangs like a cloud, dark and silent, upon the horizon of Europe ; while all the energies, resources and influences of the British Empire are sorely tried."

You might think that this refers to the uneasy state of the world to-day. It doesn't. It was written in 1857. And the result of this general unrest was a great outbreak of religious Revivalism in 1858-62. This phenomenon is picturesquely described by Septima in " Peculiar People ".

Daily Independent, 23rd September

October 16th, 1935

I read in yesterday's *Daily Sketch* that the head of a big lending library declared that the sex novel is as dead as mutton. What people ask for now is romance with a definite uplift. This is no doubt thanks to the enormously popular Oxford Group Movement, founded by Frank Buchman, stressing a life-changing personal and social regeneration. Thank heaven for it. Paul and Jean are great fans.

Unexpectedly and for reasons the man in the street finds hard to understand – a general election is upon us. The present government so surely has the nation behind it, that one has the uncomfortable feeling that political machinations are at work in this precipitate decision. True that the immediate outlook is extremely critical with Italy's cruel invasion of Abyssinia upon us, but why plunge our country into the electioneering vortex at such a time?

My ignorance of politics prevents me from reasoning out the implications, but my instinct resents the facts – a party returned to power at a time of crisis is not a representative one. It can only be an ominous reflection of the gravity of the present and uncertainty of the future.

The outlook is dismal indeed, with all the nations arraying themselves in groups against the others over sanctions against Italy. We are right back at 1914 once more – then it was Serbia and then Belgium – and there was world war.

Friday, October 18th, 1935

This afternoon I was asked to propose a vote of thanks to Doreen Wallace, author of *Barnham Rectory*, who lectured on 'Country Novels' at this month's literary talks series organised by W.H. Smith and Son.

Kensington News and West London Times

Mrs Grattan Guinness, who has recently written a book called *Peculiar People* under the nom de plume of Septima, moved a vote of thanks to the speaker, saying Miss Wallace was 'the glorious justification for the none too seemly efforts of my generation for the emancipation of women. She is indeed the perfect product of a new woman – an MA from Oxford, writing books at the rate of two a year, and reviewing on average six a week, with politics and gardening as recreations and still in her early thirties, the mother of three young children under ten, the youngest a girl who promises to be brilliant, she proudly told me over the tea table.'

of 37) was one with an intimate knowledge of the Country, as one would expect from a Yorkshire farmer's daughter. She touched on others, whose names were quite unknown to me, so limited, of necessity, is one's knowledge of those thousands of authors whose books are ~~flow~~ swelling the great literary flood-tide –

In conversation ~~with~~ Of course, Miss Wallace touched on Politics, *her over the* her pet subject, and the Tithe, in her ~~after~~ *Tea table,* conversation with one.

In proposing a vote of thanks I referred to her as "the glorious justification for the none too seemly efforts of my generation for the emancipation of women. She was indeed the perfect product *of the New Woman* – An M.A. of Oxford, ~~passing out her fascinating~~ *writing* books at the rate of ~~about~~ two a year, and reviewing on an average ~~of six books a~~ *three*

Excerpt from Grace's diary, October 18th, 1935

October 31st, 1935

What strange whims may possess an electorate when one considers that Oxford has rejected Sir Gilbert Murray six times – though he is their greatest Greek scholar and most ardent supporter of the League of Nations – but returned A.P. Herbert, *Punch*'s humorist, at his first parliamentary candidature. In his maiden speech he spoke of the Matrimonial Causes Bill that aims to reform the 'indecent, cruel, hypocritical, and unjust marriage laws of this country', making it easier for women to seek divorce, broadening the grounds from adultery alone to include permanent desertion of one's partner, and incurable and severe mental illness.

He swore that it should be passed before this Parliament was over. My addenda May 29th, 1937 – 'It was – and about time.'

January 1936

Congregational Quarterly

Peculiar People is a much happier story than that of Edmund Gosse. The reader gets an excellent idea of the earnestness and narrowness of the Brethren and the clash between two generations . . . We scarcely see the purpose of pseudonymity; it would be easily possible to identify all the people mentioned.

(I hope they don't try.)

January 13th, 1936

Tonight, my two daughters-in-law met for the first time and I realised how blessed I am as a mother-in-law. I was so proud of them, on either side of me at dinner, both in evening dress looking so attractive. Each so different from the other, but so absolutely and entirely fitted to be the wife of such opposites as my boys. As I sit writing alone in my room, I am conscious of a most perfect contentment and gratitude, that there should be two such sweet girls for my sons. I feel as if the whole load of their future has been lifted from me and that all the past struggles and single-handed efforts have been worthwhile, to have arrived at such contentment of spirit as is mine tonight.

January 14th, 1936

Have been chuckling all day at one of Jean's little anecdotes that she recounted to us last night. Paul took her to meet Geraldine Taylor, who apparently grilled her as to her suitability as a wife for her protégé. (A bit late now!) She fixed her eyes on Jean, as she does, filleting flesh from bone, and asked, 'Jean, dear, can you sew? Jean, dear, can you cook? Jean, dear, can you type?' Jean's answers in the affirmative seemed to satisfy her, fortunately. I patted my daughter-in-law's hand and said, 'Jean, dear, she is very naughty, as she has never done any of those things in her life. Howard always does them for her. What's more, she asked me exactly the same questions before I married her father!'

January 19th, 1936

Our King, in his seventieth year and with signs of cardiac weakness, cannot possibly be long with us. Our concern is something so intimate, so personal, that it is as if a member of our own family were ill. I can recall this same sense of personal loss at the death of our dear Queen Victoria in 1901. It is wonderful how deeply the feelings of the nation are interwoven with those of our royal family. It is their intimate personal relationship and interest in the lives of their peoples that has brought about this bond of sympathy, and which has done more than anything else to give unity to our empire.

January 22nd, 1936

And so he has died – a peaceful ending at midnight on January 20th. Was ever a king so widely mourned and so deeply loved?

The Prime Minister's broadcast the evening of the 21st was the most wonderful tribute that could be paid to any man, for he showed most supremely that the King's greatness lay in his simple devotion to duty. He said, in a tone of deep reverence, 'I think I can tell you without any impropriety that at the end, during brief intervals of consciousness, the King sent for his secretary and asked, "How is the Empire?" The secretary said, "All is well with the Empire," and the King gave him a smile and relapsed once more into unconsciousness.'

This sentence will surely pass into history.

It reminds me of a personal coincidence at the time of my beloved Henry's passing, when he uttered two words during a moment of returning consciousness – 'Dear humanity.' Is it possible that as earth-consciousness recedes and associations fade out, the dominating passion and devotion of life fills the conscious mind?

I went to the lying-in-state in Westminster Hall. The majestic beauty of it can never be described in words. Sunlight shining on the massive carving of the oak-beamed roof, and in the midst of the great, misty emptiness below, the tall catafalque with the coffin, over which was draped the Royal Standard, on which lay the sceptre, the orb and the crown, glittering with diamonds. Thrown over the foot was the King's velvet and ermine cloak, and at its head the Queen's wreath.

Three quarters of a million persons went by in ceaseless procession for four days, all day and most of the night, paying their last homage.

February 3rd, 1936

Peculiar People featured on the BBC's *Books of the Week* programme. Ruth wrote to Bee, 'What a crown to Grace's labours to have had that broadcast. And the way Ellis Roberts spoke about Father's character only confirmed what I felt all along – how all uncon- sciously she has drawn a most beautiful character sketch of him.'

Unconsciously!

February 27th, 1936

I have been reading *Saints, Sinners and Beechers* – the lives of the Beecher family. Brother of the famous abolitionist, Harriet Beecher Stowe, who wrote *Uncle Tom's Cabin*, Henry Ward Beecher filled his Plymouth Brethren church of Brooklyn with over 2,000 people for thirty-seven years by touching their emotions. 'We all have hearts and emotions, while comparatively few of us have minds and thoughts,' he said.

I ask myself, does this apply today? I doubt it. People are better educated and have developed their reasoning powers. There is far less emotionalism in preaching. Religious revivals were the order of the day in the 1860s. All the world went to church because there was nowhere else for the masses to go. Only a few churches are crowded today and though one must not forget that millions may listen in, broadcasting cuts out emotionalism and the man who broadcasts successfully must look to the quality of his address for its appeal.

May 4th, 1936

I was reading my old diaries yesterday. How curious to read one's thoughts of many years ago. It is hard to recognise oneself. Indeed, I could hardly believe what I did think then, which makes me real- ise that there always remains an inner self different to the self that tries to express itself in words.

During those seven wonderful years with Henry I seemed to be someone else. Was that my true self or an extension of his?

One of an imitative nature like mine may perhaps unconsciously use the expressions and even assimilate the thoughts of another person, especially when one loves and admires that other person, so that in time, we may grow to be like them, or our personality may be absorbed by their stronger personality. The process may be gradual and complete, or temporary and partial, but need not be feared, so long as the personality that influences us is of the essence of goodness.

But who have I become without Henry's influence? More myself, I think, but perhaps not so good.

May 13th, 1936

I wonder what is wrong with me that no matter how much I invite it, none of my friends, except the most intimate, call me by my Christian name. The eternal Mrs Guinness sounds so horribly formal. Why not Grace? Madge, a retired milliner to some of society's best families, has been here at 8 Courtfield Gardens for over three years and it is still Mrs Guinness. Is it my fault or my name's fault? Grace is rather formidable, perhaps; or maybe I have imbibed so much of my beloved husband's personality and there is so much Guinness in me, that the name sounds more familiar to friends than my own Christian name. I am sure psychologists could explain why some persons are always addressed by their Christian name, and others never. Possibly it's just a Victorian throwback, my age, and that I am married.

May 15th, 1936

Mussolini addressed a wildly cheering throng of 400,000 men, women and children and 20,000 troops in Rome, proclaiming, 'Italy has at last her empire – a Fascist empire.'

A Te Deum was sung in nearly all the principal churches in Italy for the triumph of Italian arms in Abyssinia. 'We Praise Thee, O God' – the irony of it – for success over a wretchedly equipped, nominally Christian people, fighting for their existence and freedom against modern aeroplanes, poison gas and all the latest military equipment of a highly civilised, so-called Christian nation. The Bishop of St Albans has surely voiced the feelings of the whole civilised world when he says, 'I dare to say that Signor Mussolini and those associated with him in the government of Italy have made the name of the so-called civilised white man stink in the nostrils of native peoples, not only in Abyssinia, but in every part of Africa.' Now I do agree with Sylvia Pankhurst's outspoken support for the Emperor, Haile Selassie, though her interference hasn't won her much support in the higher echelons of government.

June 28th, 1936

From the peaceful beauty of the gardens of High Hurstwood Vicarage, where I am now installed with my beloved Ruth and Arthur, I look back on those last days at Courtfield Gardens without a regret for the necessity that was increasingly forced upon me of giving up the work that took eleven years to build up. It is done – and the strength to continue it; so, having served its purpose and met the needs of that period of my life and the boys', providing us with independence, security and a lovely home, it was ripe for dissolution. My major consolation is that it will continue as a private hotel – though the new owners have employed three people to do the administrative and managerial work I did single-handed alongside my work at the Registry Office.

But what a sordid experience the divesting of it was! The view day, the sale and the final stripping when all the worst elements in human nature seem to be made manifest. Like vultures, swooping down on a dead carcass, the dealers gathered round and even when they had claimed their pound of flesh, those others, whose personal relationships would entitle one to expect some sympathetic understanding of what the loss means (for one always suffers loss at dissolution), disappointed one by their avarice and greed. My reaction was to give them a surfeit of it. Take every fitting, unscrew every rod of brass and chromium; take this picture and that mirror, tear up all the leftover pieces of linoleum, take the electric fondants.

My move here is temporary – until I find suitable alternative accommodation. Ruth seems to welcome the companionship, however, for she has often said that Irishmen are convivial, but not companionable.

I am already turning my thoughts to the re-creation of some other work, and have had an interview with Sir Robert Evans, Director of Education, and set before him a big scheme of a country house for retired schoolteachers. I was so tired on the appointed day that I only got through it with the help of taxis, and the psychological revival of spirits by means of rouge and lipstick. The interview, however, was most satisfactory.

August 15th, 1936

I have just returned to High Hurstwood from a brief visit to Bath to visit Henry's grave. I found the beautiful tombstone shining white after the cleaning which Mr Spear had kindly done for me. I was greatly impressed with the dignity of the monument that seems so befitting to the one to whose dear memory it was erected and I wonder how its beauty can remain unimpaired after those of us have gone who loved him?[12] What a problem it is, the whole question of memorials and tombstones. More and more the desire for cremation grows with its inevitable forgetfulness. Yet, as the memory of our loved ones ever remains with us, so it seems to me there should be some fitting monument erected to them. I cannot but feel the world would be poorer without the monuments to great men. There is too a quiet sense of peace and continuity in a village churchyard, a realisation of spiritual comradeship, deeper and more real even than one feels with the living within the church. So I think it is befitting that we should care for our family monuments, even as the government cares for our national ones.

September 1st, 1936, Champéry, Valais

Oh the joy of being in Switzerland once again, amidst the peace and beauty of its everlasting hills and the grandeur of its mountains. I was last here in the late spring of 1927 with Ruth, just before she had to face the dreadful tragedy of George's fatal polo accident, the news of which came from India a few weeks after our return.

Nothing has changed – even the same poster on the wall of the little railway chalet. Here is the village street with its double line of chalet-pensions and hotels, now gay with flowers on all the balconies, the green pasturelands with peasants mowing the grass on almost perpendicular slopes, and the familiar peaks of the Dents-Blanches and the Dents du Midi, with large patches of snow in the hollows and the sound of clanging of bells as the cattle graze on the mountainside.

How insignificant one feels in the presence of these glorious mountains and yet how strong. As I stood on my balcony this morning looking up at them, conscious of their overwhelming might and majesty, I thought of the wonder of man's aspiration and achievement. Man needs must scale the world's highest peaks and circumnavigate even the unscalable ones by mounting on his self-invented wings to survey them triumphantly from above. The instinct cannot be any other than the expression of an unquenchable desire for the realisation of the Divine.

Most though, most of the time, are deplorably content with staying at the bottom. The village street with its picture postcards, the daily papers, toy-chalet souvenirs and patisseries, all too easily satisfy us. But when, as tonight, the setting sun illuminates the snowy peaks with a pink glow of scintillating brilliance against a sky of aquamarine blue, the soft fleecy clouds, catching the red rays of the sun, rest in billowy softness around and above the peaks, the fir trees of the lower slopes contrast blackness with the mossy green of the valley, then all the ugliness of the world is obliterated by an all-pervading beauty.

To some is given this privilege of ascending the Mount of Transfiguration, but even there we may be so confounded by its glory as to imagine the experience must have some material expression. 'Let us build a tabernacle here,' said Peter on the Mount of Transfiguration. And we smile at his stupidity, but that is exactly the normal reaction of man to spiritual experience. He wants to organise it!

Sunday, September 13th, 1936

The English church is closed down for the season – a fact that amazes the local Catholics who cannot conceive of the possibility of any religious life outside of the church. So that when the cook saw me sallying forth, prayer book in hand, this morning, she said, '*Vous allez prier a l'église, Madame?*' I replied, '*Sur les montagnes,*' and she looked at me with a shake of the head, as much as to say, 'Poor deluded pagan.'

I climbed up the path to La Calvaire, the glorious Rhone valley with the Tête D'Or and the Diablerets and the Tours D'Aie in full view, and before me the peaks of the Dents du Midi, and I joined, with all the company of heaven, in the psalm for the day, the 68th – 'Oh sing unto the Lord and sing praises unto his name. Magnify him that rideth upon the heavens, as it were upon a horse.' Then comes that wonderful little personal touch, 'He is the Father of the fatherless and defendeth the cause of the widows.' (I remember this verse coming to me one Sunday morning many, many years ago in a time when I most needed it.)

And I was glad the parish church was closed.

September 27th, 1936
Champéry

Dear John

It was good to get your letter from Brickwall, for despite a certain fascination in being shut up in these mountain fast-nesses, one does miss the heart contact of loved ones and the stimulation from living in an active workaday world.

Yes, you are right. I do love being abroad. I sometimes wonder what it is in me that revels in the sound of foreign tongues, even when they are unknown tongues, for I experienced just the same delights when walking in the streets of Japan among the clip clop of the sandal-footed, smiling, chatting crowds, or mingling with the enigmatical more silent Chinese, and so on, throughout the world, always feeling a certain detachment and even a terrifying loneliness despite the sense of oneness with them all.

It is the same in this little village. I love to go into the chalets up the mountainsides and talk to the people and get down below the surface to the things we have in common. I forget that I am English or that I belong to any country, I feel so intimate a part of the whole human family.

Summer visitors have all departed, the village street is empty and the shops closed down. Even our 'police dog' and her pups have departed. She recently brought nine puppies into the world, but this in no wise improved her uncertain temper. Her previous maternal effort resulted in the production of one pup only and she was so disgusted that she buried it – no one knows where, but she was very proud of her second achievement. Five had to be dispensed with as she was unable to mother more than four. There were many requests for them among the villagers and much grumbling and bitterness against the various recipients. We were told that in one household the puppy had been the piece de resistance for Sunday dinner!!

Well my darling boy, there is much in your letter I would like to discuss, but how can one in the limits of a letter? Suffice it to say you have not yet converted me to Russian Communism. I am in sympathy with the type of Socialism that is evolving by natural means out of existing conditions, as the people are becoming better educated, a socialism with a definite programme and laws to bring about better conditions, but I have no faith in forcing, by revolutionary methods, a plan on a people, who may not be mentally or socially ready for it, as is the case in Russia today. But every government must work out its own salvation and create a form of government suitable to the character of its own people.

It is difficult to see how a world war is to be averted if this present armament race continues. 'And the flood came and took them all away.' It still seems to be the inevitable catastrophic method of wiping out the present order to make way for a new and better one. But I sincerely hope the new order will not be after the H.G. Wells pattern.

October 16th, 1936

I am reading the love letters of the German biologist and geologist Ernst Haeckel, who introduced Darwin's ideas to Germany, and am profoundly impressed with the strong resemblance of character which these letters reveal to my own beloved Henry. Even the description of his person and his strange absent-mindedness amidst admiring crowds is exactly descriptive of Henry. And yet how strange to think that Henry hated Haeckel's philosophy. *Au fond*, I believe these two souls would have been in perfect accord and sympathy if only they had known each other. Both were earnest and fearless seekers after truth, and yet a great gulf of divergent thought separated and antagonised them. Such superficial discords seem to demand a life to come (till we all come in the unity of the faith), where they would really know each other. But Haeckel denied survival after death.

I heard today from Jean that I am to become a grandmother towards the end of May, no longer merely a step-grandmama, which I have been since my marriage to Henry.

October 20th, 1936

Madame the cook is something of a wit. We often have chats and she imagines I am a compendium of knowledge and consults me on her ailments. 'What can be done for the asthma?' I make a few suggestions but add that it is difficult to cure.

'Not at all,' she replied. 'Death will cure it.'

'That's true,' I said. 'Death cures everything.'

'As your Mr Rudyard Kipling says,' she replied.

October 22nd, 1936

Dear John

Your graphic and realistic description of Brickwall School life has set me thinking, and I wonder how ever you can stand, or will continue to stand, the racket of it. When I thought of a dozen or more children tearing about the place and saw the proximity of your quarters and with winter coming on and little hope of outdoor releases and the sheer improbability of getting away from it all, my heart sank at the prospect.

As I ponder on these things, I can see how the whole of the British public school system, run on the lines of absolute discipline, has grown out of this very necessity for the staff to escape and opt for the quieter, idle life.

But now, you young moderns, with H.G. Wells to champion you, have condemned all that and intend to scrap it.

As I read Wells's autobiography, how first the Fabian Society failed him, and then Russian Communism disillusioned him, I think that his ego-centred Utopia will prove illusive, if 'The Shape of Things to Come' is all he has to offer. I still believe,

more firmly than ever after reading Wells, that God-controlled
lives, with the logical sequence of a God-controlled world, is
the only solution to its problems. When the church ceases to
teach the absurd duality implied in a present and future world,
then will dawn on most men's minds the fact that Eternity
begins now, and the Christian Socialist state may be realised,
the 'New Jerusalem' which John of Patmos saw descending
from heaven, 1,900 years before Wells was born.

October 23rd, 1936

It was not until I was middle-aged that I happened to notice, as I
was brushing my hair one day in front of my mirror, that I was the
possessor of a forehead that was the exact replica of my father's,
even to the way that the hair grew around it. (I can see him now,
carefully parting his hair in the middle, right down to the nape of
his neck, then brushing it back into two long chignons from a
forehead that seemed to form almost two thirds of his face.) And
he has passed this peculiarity on to me. I had not observed it
before, for it had always been concealed by a straight silky fringe
in my childhood, curls at adolescence, and now with silver-grey
marcelled waves.

So this is where my gifts of organisation reside, I soliloquised,
and any executive powers I may possess, and the desire to scribble,
scribble, scribble (Father wrote millions of tracts). Alas! Too late
I have discovered the potentialities residing within this forehead
of mine. My mind has never been trained to any consecutive
thinking, nor have my reasoning powers been developed. Such is
the lot of many women. But I console myself with the thought
that these potentialities may come to fruition in my sons and their
offspring.

Men are naturally endowed with reasoning faculties and this
generation will profit from better methods of constructive education. Hitherto, we women have been guided almost entirely by

our primitive inheritance of instinct. I will not allow myself to enlarge on some of the advantages of instinct over reason, for I should be side-tracked from my intention which is simply to say, 'Thank you, dear Papa, for the endowment of your forehead.'

November 5th, 1936

Dear Paul

Guy Fawkes Day. 'Wasn't he your founder of Sunday Schools?' an American lady once asked of me, confusing him with Robert Raikes!

Your packet came this morning. Ninepence to pay on it, alas. You would hardly credit the large amount I have paid out on surcharges during these two months in Switzerland. It's time I returned to England.

I've had a great disappointment over the post of Directrice of the Ada Leigh Homes and Hostels in Paris. The secretary wrote me yesterday to say that much to the regret of the directors, my application was received the day after the appointment was made. I have every qualification they required, and I should have loved the work. However, the psalm that came in my reading today was: 'O tarry thou the Lord's leisure: be strong and he shall comfort thine heart; and put thy trust in the Lord.'

This applies to you, darling, and all your future work as curate at Bishop Hannington Church, with Harry and Annie's dear son, Gordon, as your training vicar. 'Tarry thou the Lord's leisure.' I think if you do the work in hand with all your heart, the future will take care of itself. I often think about what you said about being disappointed with the few conversions you managed to achieve in your preaching, and I am immensely impressed with the seemingly feeble results of Christ's own efforts to win men. It's amazing when one reads the Gospels to note the difference between the crowds and the few who really became changed and followed him to the end.

*Numbers and immediate visible results mean nothing. We
must get a right sense of values. Any life spent even in the
narrowest circle of influence, amongst the humblest of people,
is capable of all the success and results that followed the life of
Christ and the Apostles . . . only after many days, perhaps.*

November 11th, 1936, Montreux

I left Champéry yesterday having been there two and a half
months, entering into and enjoying the simple life of the village,
with which one is much more *en rapport* when the season's visitors have departed.

There were the bankers and owners of the Grand Bazaar de
Champéry whose family go back to the eleventh century, Monsieur
le Père, who cashed a cheque for us one day, then died suddenly in
the night. (Not a good death, said the villagers. Without
Communion, he won't go to paradise.) Then the large family of
the Berras, owners of half the hotels and chalets in Champéry;
Denis, the church organist, who was the devoted son of a bad-
tempered old woman whose husband couldn't live with her when
he was alive, but headed the procession of women at his funeral
when he died, mourning his sad loss. Old Madame Gonnett, with
the red handkerchief over her old grey head, minding her three
cows as they grazed on her own pastureland, knitting the while
and talking as incessantly as she knitted, and her pretty daughter,
Olga, the fashionable village dressmaker, and old Pauline, our
one-time cook who I hoped would take a bath while she was with
us, but hoped in vain. I doubt if her voluminous layers of black
garments were ever entirely stripped off. Her conversation, no
matter what topic was under discussion, always veered round to
her one obsession. Poor old dear, all her life savings gone in one
of the many failures of the Swiss banks. Then old Madame
Pateroni, half Italian, half witch, they said, who went around in
fear of Monsieur the Curé, who imposed heavy penances on her

for her fortune-telling. She told us our fortunes from an old pack of greasy cards, having cleverly extracted all the information she could out of one and another of us, and then mysteriously read it in the cards we turned up. I am sorry to say I am never to have any money. Now there's a surprise.

And now all this is left behind and I am down at Montreux on Armistice Day and have gone all British. At the English church, poppy-bedecked Britishers, Boy Scouts, Girl Guides, all with Union Jacks, lustily sang 'Lest We Forget' and 'O God Our Help in Ages Past', and at the hotel, the broadcast service from the Cenotaph so clear that even the crack in the dear old Bishop's voice came over. We six grey-haired Englishwomen staying there stood to attention while Frenchwomen flitted to and fro in the lounge and raised their eyebrows, '*Tiens, tiens, ces drôles anglaises.*'

November 17th, 1936

These grand hotels, these Eden Palaces, now closed, how they conjure up the once fashionable, turn-of-the-century *haute saison*, the empty buildings and streets haunted still by the distant voices of a lavish bygone era. Shutters are drawn across the balcony windows from which dowager duchesses and American million-aires once looked out with possessiveness onto all they saw. In those heady days the world was owned by the rich. Money could buy everything – all the luxuries that the hotels could offer or the expensive trinkets the shops displayed, while the most renowned artistes came to entertain their wealthy patrons.

It was their affluence that built the funiculars to transport them to still greater heights and grander hotels. The entire lakeside was given over to the indulgent wealthy, who did little to deserve it but bear the burden of ancient titles and unearned increments, or the jumped-up new moneyed who paid for those privileges at the expense of those who never had a chance to realise the meaning of the word beauty, much less enjoy it.

Those days are gone for ever. And now the bourgeoisie have moved in. Days of youth hostels and polytechnic parties filling the sultry summer air with shrill laughter and phrase-book French. And the sportsmen who belong to all times, skiing, skating. Such are the pastimes of the world's cosmopolitans. And then there are the unclassable ones, of refined, Home Counties origin, transplanted to foreign lands, remnants of a world overpopulated with women since the war, indefinitely middle-aged and single, who seem never to have been young or to grow old, grey-haired, mostly kind and gentle women, and always staunch supporters of the church.

And the mountains and the dark, impenetrable forests remain aloof, mute and indifferent to all the changing scenes, as the generations come and go.

November 18th, 1936

There is no doubt about it, I am a misfit. I find it impossible to fit neatly and completely into any one of the variety of circumstances in which I find myself. If I stay in a hotel of my choice it must be because the proprietor has quoted specially low terms in consideration of the hope of introductions to which he imagines the name of Guinness will lead. Then the doubtful advantage of looking smart in the oldest clothes (worn by me after many transformations, or else the gifts of generous friends) gives the impression that I am in a position to pay full terms. And as I descend to dinner in the evening and meet the questioning gaze of the proprietor, I resolve on leaving the rest of my wardrobe in my trunk.

Then as regards amusements – I asked some ladies if they will come with me to the Kursaal to hear the Lener Quartette. They raise their eyebrows in surprise and say they would never go to the village hall. I assure them that Schumann, Beethoven and Mozart would suffer no desecration by being rendered in a Kursaal, and that the 'concert' hall was far removed from the Salle de Jeu de la

Boule – the infamous casino. So they came, but got even with me by asking me to join them in hymn-singing on Sunday evening. Now, to sing hymns immediately after a table d'hote dinner is to say the least a difficult performance, but when it is in a continental hotel on a Sunday evening, when the lounge is filled with many guests and day visitors, mostly talking at *haute voix* and with a Terrazini record on the wireless coming over at her loudest, then I find hymn-singing particularly difficult and embarrassing.

Then there is the matter of church-going. I have never been able to find the type of churchmanship that appeals. The Low Church is dreadfully dull. Then, if I go to the High Church, I find myself surrounded by ardent spinsters who inform me of the hours of matins and evensong and regard me with suspicion when I am not to be seen at every celebration. Nothing daunted, they tell me of tomorrow's requiem and I dare not say I haven't the least desire to attend requiems; in fact, that I am not really at my ease among genuflexing priests and acolytes, and I finally fall from grace when they see me at a street corner sympathetically listening to the Salvation Army.

December 3rd, 1936

Passing through Paris on November 20th after ten days in Montreux, on my way back to High Hurstwood, who should I bump into at the Gare St Lazare but Phyllis MacDonell and her mother? They begged me to let them know what was being said in France about the King and Mrs Simpson. It was the first I had heard of it. The Paris papers are, apparently, all saying that the King is going to marry Mrs Simpson. I thought it a piece of absurd gossip – the kind of thing the American newspaper reporters would say. For never a word appeared in the English press and no one seemed to be talking about it.

Then today it bursts on us like a thunderbolt. We bought up the daily papers of every shade of opinion and are profoundly impressed not only by their tone, but by the unanimity of disapproval for the standard of morality implied in all we know. Mrs Simpson – whose two former husbands are still living, and whose second divorce is not even made absolute until six months hence!

What will become of the country?

December 11th, 1936

Today the King announced his momentous choice between a woman and a kingdom. His abdication was read by the Speaker in the House of Commons and by Viscount Halifax in the House of Lords and the rest of the world listened in on the wireless. This past week has been a time of such great tension, such strain of uncertainty as to the ultimate outcome. And he goes, this king whose accession was only proclaimed on January 21st this year – he on whom we had placed such high hopes as the ideal constitutional monarch because of his truly democratic principles and for the place he held in the hearts of all his peoples. He has made his choice between personal love and service to his country and renounces his throne. He told us he could no longer discharge this heavy task with efficiency and personal satisfaction without the support of the woman he loves.

I have just found a letter from Ruth dated February 2nd, where she writes, 'The King's death has been a benediction after his strainful years and the loneliness of our beloved Queen Mary will be brightened by the joy of having lived to see their son reigning. But what a burden for him to shoulder.'

And now I feel let down, as we all do, having deluded ourselves into thinking him such a perfect successor. Maybe when the psychologists come to study his life they will find that marriage to this woman has been a mode of escape from the responsibilities of kingship. Looking back, I now see clearly that escape has been the ruling desire of his life – escape from the inevitability of having been born to be king, contrary to all his temperamental instincts.

He is master of his own destiny and must be allowed to make his own choices. But one regrets that in so doing he has fallen well below the dignity of kingship, first by taking another man's wife; second by involving her in a divorce from her husband where there has been blatant collusion, and third, avowing his intention of marrying her as soon as her decree nisi has been made absolute.

December 12th, 1936

I did not listen in on the wireless to the proclamation of the accession of King George VI today. The happenings of these last nine days have so exhausted one by the unexpected shock of its results, that I had no heart to listen at the close of the year to what we had all heard with such joy and high hopes at its beginning.

How apt was Prime Minister Baldwin's quotation of lines spoken of Shakespeare's Hamlet: 'His will is not his own; For he himself is subject to his birth: He may not as unvalued persons do, Carve for himself; for on his choice depends the safety and health of the whole state.'

We expect better of royalty than to shirk their duty. I am wondering now, if he could not put the state before his own needs, whether we have not been spared.

May 12th, 1937

So, the great coronation day of King George VI and Queen Elizabeth is passed. I spent the day with Ruth and Arthur in the study of High Hurstwood Vicarage, mostly listening in to the broadcasting of the wonderful ceremony from the Abbey.

When so much has been said about it by the ablest writers in the land, and through the medium of the wireless, what more can one say? It is as if all one's enthusiasm had gone out into the universal spirit of rejoicing, leaving one in a state of contented exhaustion, in the certain knowledge that after all we have been through, all is well with the Empire.

The newspapers still give us echoes of the shouting and the tumult from London. Over and above all the noise, glamour and pageantry and the din of worldwide broadcasts, there has come through and remains a deep sense of the unity of this Commonwealth of Free Peoples, and the fact that it is a unity based on moral values.

Ever and again one's thoughts turned to the king who has abdicated – tucked away in a French chateau in Tours with the woman who cost him the loss of his kingship and kingdom. What must he be feeling today? I hope he thinks she is worth it all.

May 20th, 1937

An amusing incident occurred during the broadcast of the coronation naval review and the spectacle of the fleet illuminations at Spithead. It is being treated with undue solemnity by the BBC authorities, who refuse to make a statement, though they duly apologised late that night. Meanwhile, we have all had our private laughter over the fact that Lieutenant Commander Thomas Woodroofe, who had been broadcasting with immense success and vigour all day, had obviously 'spliced the mainbrace' in the Officers' Mess of HMS *Nelson* – indulging in more than a little liquid refreshment some hours in advance of the given farewell signal from the King.

Who can blame him for dining not too wisely, but certainly well, on such a night? 'It's all lit up,' he kept repeating, 'by fairy lights . . . What? I'm sorry – I was telling people to shut up talking. What I mean is this. The whole thing is . . . fairyland.' Then a long pause, and, 'It isn't true, it's gone. The fleet's gone. Damn! It's disappeared. We had two hundred warships all around us a second ago – all gone, disappeared. There's nothing between us and heaven.'

Then the BBC chipped in and announced, 'That is the end of the Spithead broadcast. It is eleven minutes to eleven and we shall now take you over to the Savoy band.'

The entire country is up in arms, solemnly writing to *The Times* to complain, when they could simply be enjoying the joke.

June 2nd, 1937

I have now made two attempts to read Virginia Woolf. I felt I must, otherwise it seemed that my education had been fearfully inadequate. I never could find a reason for people's look of shocked surprise if anyone ever confessed to not having read her. I would try to glean some information, but never seemed able to extract more than 'Oh! Virginia Woolf . . .' which might mean anything or nothing. Then I stayed in a house when my eye fell on a single Virginia Woolf volume. With pleasurable anticipation I took it down from the shelf, only to find it was a story about a dog. It was exactly what one would expect in that house where a small pet dog was the centre of interest. Now I like dogs, good sensible terrier types, but fluffy, yelping pets I find extremely objectionable. So I was in no mood to read a book about a dog and failed to see any point to it.

Virginia Woolf has just written another book – *The Years* – and the shop windows are full of it. So I got a copy from the library. Now, I thought, settling down to my after-dinner coffee, here is something more than, 'Oh! Virginia Woolf!'

Yes, decidedly clever, was my first impression. Very neat, these vignettes. A Chekhov touch. But after about fifty pages the style becomes a little wearisome, and after a hundred, boring, and by the time I reached page 168 I was positively exasperated.

And now, I too shall say, when the subject comes up for discussion, 'Oh! Virginia Woolf.'

June 7th, 1937

I have just met my first grandchild – Margaret Geraldine – peacefully sleeping in her crib. Yes, I agree that there is just a faint suggestion of likeness to Paul, but at four days old, much is left to the imagination. And I had to accept the adoring mother's word for it that she has lovely blue eyes as she was contentedly sleeping all the time I was there. She has long tapering fingers, which suggests capability for all sorts of things with her hands.

All these thoughts of babyhood have sent me right back in thought to the days when my two boys were very young. I recall early tendencies that were extraordinarily characteristic of later development.

Our house in Bath used to come down to family prayers each morning. John, who was then about two, would rush into the room demanding, 'Book, book,' and his father would hand him any book, and John would contentedly sit on a stool, the book on his knees, silent for the entire prayer time. Paul, then about four months old, would be so active, every now and again giving such terrific leaps as to nearly jump out of the nurse's arms, that she frequently had to go out of the room as she could not sit still through his activities.

June 17th, 1937

Am reading Vera Brittain's *Honourable Estate*. She seems to me a reformer and propagandist rather than a writer. She is the twentieth-century feminist *par excellence*. I think her attitude on moral questions is representative of the views of her generation. In this book the question of a woman's chastity is expressed in one sentence by Denis. 'Chastity is only a virtue in the sense of being a voluntary self-discipline, and that not a matter of technical virginity. It's an attitude of mind.'

Chastity, merely a state of mind? What an extraordinary idea!

July 21st, 1937

I have been appointed matron and housekeeper at Ardvreck Boys' Prep School in Crieff, to start this September. My heart sinks at the thought of moving so far away from my loved ones, but what else can I do? I cannot impose myself on Arthur and Ruth at High Hurstwood Vicarage for ever. The annuity is not enough to put a roof over my head, and Ardvreck is one of Scotland's finest preparatory public schools for boys. I am sixty-one – fortunate to have been appointed.

Ardvreck is, however, in the middle of nowhere, and one of the conditions of my appointment is that I learn to drive to take the boys to and from the station if and when required. So I had my first lesson today in Tunbridge Wells – in a Morris Cowley. I drove for over an hour on country roads, then came into main thoroughfares where double-decker buses and a stream of motors rather terrified me; but I got through and was surprised to find myself on the London Road. I came to rest, as told to do, at the Pantiles, safe and sound – but almost on a Belisha crossing.

July 22nd, 1937

Went to Brighton for the day to see Paul, Jean and Margaret Geraldine (aged seven weeks). What a lovely tile house is theirs. Tiny, but everything in such perfect order.

It is curious to reach the age of seeing the complete revolution of life's circle in one's own family – birth, marriage, death and birth again: another generation coming into being, and each upheld and impelled by faith, hope and love.

July 23rd, 1937

I have had an unaccountable fit of depression all day. And nothing to do with my bank balance either, as my little annuity was paid yesterday. One cannot account for that feeling of gloom that settles on one's spirit so heavily and refuses to be shaken off. I have tried to combat it tonight (successfully) by reading Shakespeare's *Hamlet*. 'To thine own self be true . . . thou cannot then be false to any man.' The tragedy of *Hamlet* is the eternal one of character and circumstances.

I expect the weather has something to do with my melancholia. It is cold and wet with an east wind blowing and fine drizzling rain falling on the window panes. I think of Ruth's daughter, Shelagh, with her new husband, Douglas, starting out on their motor tour of Scotland in the morning. It rained for all the five days I was there earlier this month for my interview at Ardvreck. And now the school writes to say I will have the additional responsibility of overseeing the catering too – all at my age. No wonder I feel so low.

August 28th, 1937

I arrived at Gleneagles at 7.10 p.m. on August 17th, after a day in London (at Pratt's Hotel on Gordon Street – conveniently situated for Euston, from which I started at 10.15 a.m.). I was met by the headmaster in the new Morris 8 which I am to drive, and taken to Ardvreck. The padre called on me Thursday evening and I was invited to tea with two of the staff, Mrs Frost and Miss Fountain, on Friday. Found it very tiring, after the strenuous work I had commenced right away in the school, to have to go out to tea, and was unfortunately given the wrong directions as to how to get there. It must have been over a mile. People are very kind, but I would rather be left alone to get on with the job.

I am responsible for repairs and decoration of the empty boarding house in readiness to welcome back the boys for the new term, the fourth house I shall have prepared in this way, and each one declared to be the last. The usual thing – gasmen, electricians, carpenters, painters and furniture men – all seeming dawdlers. I, in despair, feeling they will never be through and that it will never be ready.

Last Saturday the doctor and his wife kindly invited me to the Highland Gathering – quite a novel experience for me. It was a glorious day and a record crowd of 10,000 were present. The great thrill to me, as to all visitors from afar, was to see most of the men in kilts, and to watch the astonishing muscular feats of the competitors.

There were pipers, among which one woman competitor, an enormous creature in a black-and-white tartan and black velvet coat and patent shoes. I cannot imagine what her chest dimensions must have been, but the doctor remarked that she would require every inch of it for the amount of wind needed for playing the bagpipes.

We did not stay for the massed pipers' band, which, Miss Fountain said later, was a pity, as it was the most impressive item on the programme. But I found one band somewhat overwhelming in volume of sound, so had no regrets that we left.

Sunday, September 5th, 1937

The strangeness of my environment comes over me at times. Living alone here in the school sanatorium, looking out on the lovely surrounding country, hills and distant mountains – the grey skies and steely grey light breaking through alternate gleams of sunlight and misty clouds, the rain, sometimes soft, sometimes strong and torrential, the eerily deep calm or strong swift storms. And I, suddenly plunged into new circles, a new way of life and new people. It is a lonely yet intimate existence, feeling as if I had always known them. Longing to be with my own dear, familiar, loved family, and yet conscious of the inevitable distance from them that the years bring – as each one becomes more involved and absorbed in their own life and circumstances. This 'aloneness' is best forgotten in absorption in the lives of others, and so, for this work I am grateful. The secret of happiness must be in self-forgetfulness.

September 7th, 1937

This climate gets me down. Gleams of sunshine slant from masses of grey-black clouds, and give a fierce grimness to the ranges of hills and distant mountains. Then the rain envelops all the scenery in a dense mist, and the trees are drenched and dripping, and the ground sodden, until I can't bear to look out on the dismal scene, and draw the curtains to shut it out, but the damp penetrates. Even the fire gives no heat. And I read in the paper of twenty hours of sunshine in the south, and tennis being played in Eastbourne in intense heat; and of a heatwave in New York!

Now I understand (and I dreamed of the horror of it) why I saw two youngish women drunk in the streets of Perth last week, and one poor dishevelled creature being taken to prison, I suppose, by two stalwart constables . . . It is this depressing climate, and the grim grandeur of the mountains that are too oppressive for the human spirit. I long for the bright, cheerful colouring and sunshine of the south of France and Italy. These northern countries are unkindly – yet what strength of character they produce. I greatly admire the types I have met. And even now, as I write these futile murmurings, the scent of roses from a vase on my table comes with a defying fragrance, as if to challenge me – for no sun-baked rose would give such a perfume as do these roses in my ugly room with its dull green walls.

I must go to bed, and try to forget, in sleep. And tomorrow I shall be busy again with all the work there is to do – electricians, plumbers, gasmen, carpenters, painters, visitors – and between-whiles I am machining and sewing. Thus I am occupied all day. Only the evenings are lonely. I read Ruth's letter three times. Contact with the old life is very precious.

October 5th, 1937

Now all that urgent preparation belongs to the past. The last big effort to be ready for the boys' return was made, and though electricians were working in the house up to the very day of their arrival (September 23rd), we actually were in readiness. *Mon Dieu*! What a rush it all was, and what unspeakable exhaustion I experienced after the strain of it all. Sleep was almost unknown for nights on end. And yet I have been strangely conscious of those prayers which I know have been going up for me. Then there is such a happy atmosphere in the school. The boys are the most enchanting little people and the staff delightful. And happiness is rejuvenating.

I love being involved in the catering, and everyone is very pleased and thrilled with the variety of it. I hope I have strength enough to continue . . .

My Trip To Egypt
February – April 1939

I have had no time to write in my diary while at Ardvreck, but must take it up again as something rather exciting has material-ised, enabling me to make up for my lack of sun these past eight-een months. I have been granted two months leave to make the journey of a lifetime – to Egypt, at the invitation of my dear cousin-in-law, Percy Wyndham Guinness, DSO, OBE, known as Wyn. He married late and his wife, sadly, died in 1930 after a mere six years of marriage, so he took himself out to Egypt as chaplain of Ma'adi, Heliopolis and Helwan. His sister, Flo, keeps house for him. Although unmarried, she has spread her wings, as I said she would one day.

Travel is no longer a rare luxury for women, the Empire provid-ing the possibility of respectable accommodation and rail and steamer transport for any woman seeking an adventure, even if she journeys alone and is rather more aged than she once was. I am already widely travelled, but it will not, of course, be the same as having Henry at my side. As part of their missionary enter-prise, his daughters, Geraldine and Lucy, covered thousands of miles as single women, to the very edges of civilisation, so I need have no fear. Besides, I am longing to see the setting for Agatha Christie's *Death on the Nile*, which I so much enjoyed. Percy has promised me visits to archaeological digs and museums, tombs, mosques, pyramids and churches, trips though the desert, and meetings with the various dignitaries, both Egyptian and European, that he and Flora have to entertain. They have a repu-tation, he says, for the liberality of their hospitality. If I postpone such an opportunity any longer, the worsening political situation may prevent it altogether.

February 3rd, 1939

I left Gleneagles by the night train for London and breakfasted with Paul at Victoria. I am always conscious of a thrill of excitement as I board the continental train, and on this particular occasion there were six Frenchmen in my compartment to supply the right atmosphere.

It amused me to watch the reactions of the stolid English porters to the amatory leave-takings of the Frenchmen. They are so much more . . . demonstrative than Englishmen. At Folkestone one of them appropriated my *Times* without asking my permission.

On boarding the boat, I followed my usual plan of retiring to the salon and going sound asleep, which renders the nature of the Channel crossing a matter of indifference to me. From Paris to Genoa I travelled by train with a young Austrian woman and a young man whom I should imagine to be a commercial traveller. His reserved place was on my side of the carriage. Thanks to the advantage of age, he chose to share the opposite side of the compartment with the younger woman, so I was fortunately able to lie the full length of the seat, and so enjoy a good measure of sleep.

The Austrian told me she was in Vienna at the time of the Anschluss, the German invasion, had escaped and was now emigrating with her husband, whom she was meeting in Genoa, to Australia. She had been in London for six months learning English. 'Ah, you English,' she said to me repeatedly, 'you do not know how lucky you are to have such freedom. I am a Jewess.'

When the question of money for incidental payments occurred, she said, 'Madam, give them your English money, they are only too glad to have it.' I, on the other hand, was none too pleased to have theirs, since thanks to inflation, most of what I had from previous visits proved worthless. '*Non buona*', or '*Pas bonne*', to every piece I proffered.

February 4th, 1939

Arrived in Genoa at 10 a.m. Brilliant sunshine, but a cold wind blowing. As we came through Turin in the early morning there was a white frost and snow falling.

Cook's agent efficiently undertook all the details of transport to the boat; but I was horrified to find myself in an impossible 'touristica' class, among the derricks and motor cars and with no salon accommodation. I arranged with the purser to change over to second class and wrote a cheque to Cook's for a return fare difference. Bang go the sixpences!

February 5th, 1939

How the Italians love NOISE! We arrived at Naples with gramophone records of dance music blaring forth from innumerable amplifiers. I had hoped for quiet after the passengers had gone ashore for the Pompey expedition, but now there was a torrent of Italian news, which, as on the voyage, was broadcast at two-hour intervals throughout the day. Only the mountains – that wonderful Appennian range – suggest peace and quietude, and the slow-descending smoke of Vesuvius rose like incense across a cobalt-blue sky. There was no terror in its mood today; not until nightfall, when we left the bay and tongues of fire leapt from its crater.

To leave Naples at sunset is to carry away a lasting impression of beauty. The town was bathed in a pink haze of light. The vast pile of buildings on the surrounding hills with medieval fortresses rising above the bay were now seen in misty outline, while the modern maritime station and destroyers and submarines formed a confused black mass in the foreground. Vesuvius took on a lurid aspect; shafts of light from the setting sun were reflected in the windows of the houses that so incautiously crept up its slopes. The island of Capri now came into view silhouetted against a flaming sky. A ball of fire sank into the sea and fantastic black outlines remained. Passengers drew their wraps around them and slipped away. A shrill laugh and the rhythmic churning of water were the only sounds that broke the silence.

How I love Italian cooking and all the varieties of vegetarian food they offer. Macaroni with a delicious range of sauces, omelette with spinach, chicory, salads and the most delectable *bomba* and ice creams, *petits fours*, followed by Bel Paese, all rounded off with Chianti Ruffino. Makes our English cuisine – particularly that of our boarding schools – so dreary and unappetizing.

If I consulted my gastronomical instincts I should choose Italy as the place in which to live.

February 7th, 1939

I am not surprised that St Paul and his 275 fellow passengers were shipwrecked here. Wind, rain and mountainous seas have been our portion throughout the night and day. I know now how much that shipwrecked crew must have rejoiced in the beauty and calm of the Bay of Syracuse. No wonder they stayed there three days before setting sail for Rome.

There were only one English and two German women among the passengers in the dining salon today. I conclude that the Teutonic races have hardier stomachs than the Latins, for I perceived that even the Italian and French priests were missing. Certainly it required a big effort to ignore the discomforts of a boisterous sea, doing its worst against its victims, who moaned and groaned as the ship pounded its way through waves that threatened to overwhelm it. 7 a.m. and we shall reach our destination – Alexandria.

February 8th, 1939

And now we have arrived. Natives swarm the ship as we moor. We try to secure one for hand baggage, which evokes a torrent of words but no service. We decide to go ashore and leave it to Cook's, happy to think there are two hours before the train departs. Cook's man smiles at our optimism, stands by and informs us that we shan't catch that train. 'If only they would let our men go aboard we would have your luggage in a jiffy,' he says. 'But they don't.' And so we stand on the quay watching the shouting, gesticulating crowds of coloured men, with 'Egyptian government' embroidered on their blue jerseys, who are now joined by crowds of shoremen offering Turkish coffee or a liberal exchange of their somewhat questionable money, which residence in the country later teaches you to check before accepting.

The noise increases as the luggage is piled up pell-mell on the quay (will yours ever turn up, you think, and how will it ever be extricated from this gigantic pile even if it does?). On every hand one hears a babel of foreign tongues with the usual accompaniment of wild gesticulations, and amidst the crowd, calm and unperturbed, one sees a fellow countryman with that 'Thank God I am an Englishman' expression on his face. 'Ever been here before?' he asks. 'You may be in time for the one o'clock train, and you can get tea, of a kind, at the station.' We thank him and take courage.

'Do look at that man with the Bank of England in his hand,' says an American woman, as a dignified-looking man in long flowing robes, which we come to know as *galabia*, strolls by with both palms extended, offering an exchange of currency.

Cook's man, however, supplies you with the necessary money for immediate expenses, and you try to distinguish *milliemes* from *piastres* and to reckon how many *piastres* there are to a pound, and you inconsequently distribute five-*piastre* pieces to all and sundry and are alarmed to find then how many porters it seems to require to carry your suitcases, rugs and hat boxes, until an angry *'imshi'* from Cook's man reduces the number to the official Cooksmen, and at long last you are in the customs office.

Neither on arrival nor on departure did I have to open my baggage; but I did have to fill in sundry forms giving my ancestral history and the purpose of my sojourn in Egypt. I tried to recall what reasons I had stated in a similar form I had filled in at Cook's in London. Evidently there was some discrepancy, for I ultimately received a form on which I was inscribed as a schoolmistress! I had met a very interesting teacher from a training college on the boat. I only hope she did not go on her Egyptian tour described as 'widow'.

I travelled on the train to Cairo with three Americans. The man of the party told us that he traded in gloves, had no opinion of English business methods, and that he made so much money he could afford to go on world tours every three years, 'according to plan', he added, in evident scorn of our haphazard English habits of wandering the face of the earth.

Wyn and Flora were on the platform to meet me. So wonderful to see them again after all these years.

February 11th, 1939

It is three days since I landed in Alexandria. It seems more like three weeks. Yet, today for the first time, I feel I am in the Egypt of my imagination. These hybrid cosmopolitan towns are not Egypt, but the result of European conquest. Latin races and the Latin tongue are everywhere. Shops, hotels, streets and even tram cars bear French and Italian names. French is the business language of Cairo and one converses in French with the educated Egyptians, rather than in English. Persian, Grecian, Roman and, later, French and British conquests have left indelible marks on the country, while the Arabian conquest has been merged into the life of the people and the Mohammedan religion has become the accepted religion of the land, and the state religion of modern Egypt.

But today we left the car and driver on the Cairo road and struck across the desert. A long string of camels was coming towards us and we followed a track in their direction.

Across vast wastes of sand there rose the long stretch of sandstone hills, the Mokattam Hills which border the eastern banks of the Nile. Westward the three great pyramids of Gizeh, dimmed by the haze of the noonday heat, were seen against a deep blue sky, and immediately across the wide and cultivated valley of the Nile was the Step Pyramid of Sakkarah, said to be the oldest existing building in the world, and south of this the pyramids of Dashur. We were at once back in the dawn of history; here were the monuments that Abraham had visited when he came to Egypt in search of pasture and corn.

February 14th, 1939

We motored into Cairo this morning. Apropos of motoring, I am told there is no driving test in Egypt. I can understand that any one test would be useless, considering that every moment of one's driving is a continuous test of one's ability to drive on roads, or rather embankments, where cars, from Rolls to Fords, many of the latter holding anywhere from six to sixteen people, zig-zag across the roads between camels, donkeys, buffaloes, herds of goats and sheep, and swarms of children, some of whom may even be asleep on the highways. One night when our car returned from Cairo, there was a country cart with a wheel off, the donkey standing guard over the seemingly dead driver, but on inspection, he was found to be peacefully sleeping. 'Allah is good. Allah keeps watch.' Such philosophy produces supreme indifference to the happenings of life.

I consulted a famous Egyptian throat specialist about my persistent throat trouble. I noticed that his walls were hung with diplomas from many parts of the world and his surgery equipped with all the latest apparatus. His diagnosis was . . . gout! And his advice: 'Gargle with salt, soda bicarb and water. Thank you. One hundred *piastres*. And now consult the English doctor.' I felt I was getting into a vicious circle, and candidly told the doctor that I had little faith in his ability to cure me. At least he had the good sense to accept this statement without offence.

We lunched at the Cairo Women's Club, shopped at Cicurello's and Ades, then, as Wyn had to use the car, Flora and I took an *arabiyeh* and drove to the Lady Cromer Clinic, which is situated in the poorest part of the Arab quarter. It was with great difficulty that we found it, and at one point we were foolish enough to ask for directions. This was to be instantly surrounded with hordes of people, who spring from nowhere when they see an opportunity of receiving *baksheesh* from some helpless European. Would that Egypt could be delivered from the pest of begging. I wrote to the *Egyptian Mail* about it.

March 28th,
To the Editor of the Egyptian Mail: A Tourist's Complaint

Sir – I was interested in reading Al Mokattam's article in today's Egyptian Mail on 'Attracting tourists to Egypt'.

As a worldwide traveller, now on my first visit to Egypt and enamoured with its beauty and historical interest, might I suggest that the greater boon that could be granted to tourists would be the prohibition of begging. The persistent demand for baksheesh – spoken or implied – mars every excursion from the port of arrival to the southernmost limits.

Let it be remembered that Mussolini earned the gratitude of all tourists to Italy when he eliminated every species of begging from that country.

An English Tourist

I do not imagine that anything will be done about it.

To the Editor of"The Egyptian Mail"

" Sir,

I was interested in reading 'Al Mokattam's article in to-day's 'Egyptian Mail' on
'Attracting Tourists to Egypt'.

As a world-wide traveller, now on my

first visit to Egypt, and emamoured with its
beauty and historical interest, might I
suggest that the greatest boon that could be
granted to tourists would be the prohibition
of begging.   The persistent demand for
'baksheesh', spoken or implied, mars every
excursion from the port of arrival to the
southernmost limits.

Let it be remembered that Mussolini
earned the gratitude of all tourists to
Italy when he forbade every species of
begging in that country.

I enclose my card, but ask leave to
sign myself-
                    'English Tourist'

I do not imagine that anything will be done about it.

20th February

I was reading the "Gazette" this morning, and in
what we should call the Court Circular, appeared the
following notice:-

      " H.M.King Faruq will say his prayers at the
      Mohammed Ali mosque in the Citadel on Friday.
      On this occasion, Sheikh Mohammed Mustapha
      El- Maraghy, Rector of Al-Azhar, will deliver
      the sermon and lead the prayers. The sermon
      will be broadcast. "

February 22nd, 1939

An Egyptian Inspector of Education (Ahmed Helmy Bey) and an English lady (Miss Gray-Thoroughgood) were our hosts for a sight-seeing tour today. Our progress through the crowded streets was very slow. At many of the shops, workmen, mostly father and small sons, were squatting on the floor, or seated on stools manufacturing their goods with tools similar to those of Egyptian history, precisely like those seen in the museum and found in the tombs of the pharaohs.

There were hand-spinning wheels on which silk thread was being spun, brass work on which young boys were hammering out intricate designs with finely pointed tools, or placing with small forceps minute pieces of ivory and coloured metals and stones in patterns of mosaic on cedarwood tables and boxes. Others were sitting cross-legged on the floor working wooden spindles with their feet, that cut and polished amber. There was a tailor pressing clothes with a huge triangular flat iron that he moved with his foot, while he balanced on the other leg and guided the iron by means of a long scythe-shaped handle.

A crowd of women in long black draperies, and with veiled faces, followed us down one of the streets, among them one dressed in European clothes. She was enormously fat and all the buttons of her coat were strained to bursting point. She proudly pointed to her clothes and then touched ours and implied that she was very pleased to be similarly dressed.

In the midst of these crowds are to be found mosques of great antiquity. Women are not allowed in except by special permit, which we have asked an Egyptian friend to obtain for us, but today, to our frustration, we may only peep through the porches of the great Madini Mosque and see the rows of superb granite pillars that once belonged to the heathen temples of the Ptolemaic period.

All round are streams of people and noisy vendors shouting their wares, some balancing large round trays on their heads, roofed over with glass, under which are a variety of comestibles; others are carrying great brass coffee jugs slung over their shoulder, or glass water jugs – for water is a valuable commodity. There are donkeys laden with market produce and even furniture, and country carts drawn by donkeys with no restrictions as to the number of passengers they carry; two-horse *arabiyehs*, the driver freely using his whip on the crowds rather than on the horse, drive American tourists through the Mouski; every now and then a daring motorist will attempt to steer through the crowds, klaxoning his way, and above a thousand noises, one hears the loud and monotonous droning of verses from the Koran by some beggar squatting at the entrance of a mosque.

From the City of the Dead and vast tombs of the caliphs we motored out of Cairo on the modern Heliopolis road and arrived at the grandiose villa of Helmy Bey. It was built in that bad period of Italian architecture, when the Italians pandered to the tastes of the commercially rich of the early nineteenth century and adopted the massive style of the Castello, with none of its simplicity or beauty. The interior of this pseudo-castle was furnished by our wealthy young bachelor host in the most ornate taste of modern Europe. We took tea in a large salon; there was an abundance of genuine Queen Anne silver on the table and 'Famille Verte' plates were laden with the Swiss café Groppi's most delectable cakes, while records of Egyptian folk songs were put on the gramophone.

After tea he motored us back to the Bab-el-Luk station in Cairo for the train to Helwan, past the palm-planted gardens of Heliopolis, down the Sharia Ibrahim Pasha, past the Shepheard's Hotel, the Ezbekiya Gardens, the Opera House and Abdin Palace. The stars and pale crescent moon were now dimmed by the brilliant electric lights of the city; great white buildings towered above us, traffic hemmed us in. A button was pressed on the switchboard of the car and Arab music was heard, followed by the radio news bulletin.

February 27th, 1939

We left Helwan at eleven this morning to lunch at the Shepheard's Hotel in Cairo. So this is Shepheard's, famed for its grandeur and opulence, where the aristocratic and celebrity elite sip tea on the terrace overlooking the Nile, with the object of seeing and being seen. This pseudo-Egyptian-Arabesque-Greco-Roman architectural atrocity, with its ornately gilded modern grill room, provided a lunch that would have grieved the soul of the French restaurateur Marcel Boulestin.

Apparently Douglas Fairbanks Junior and Mary Pickford, 'better known and better loved than any other couple in the whole world', said the *Egyptian Gazette*, stayed at Shepheard's in 1929 and were interviewed by a journalist who asked what Fairbanks thought of the talkies: 'The talkies are a wonderful invention,' he replied, 'and have a great future but so far the talking has been exaggerated.' He then reportedly gave a demonstration in his room of how he leapt from the bough of a tree to a windowsill thirty feet away.

And so finally to the Pyramids. It is difficult to adjust to the reality of their almost overwhelming greatness and wonder. One longed to be alone and to think of all they stood for and the civilisation and religion of which they were the expression, and I resolved to come again. I wanted above all to come by moonlight and camp in the desert and to approach them from the western side on camel back. But instead, we returned to Cairo and took tea in the cool, cream-coloured drawing room of the archdeaconry – a Georgian house that forms part of the compound of cathedral buildings.

March 9th, 1939 – Luxor

We motored from Helwan to Cairo in time to catch the 8.20 morning train for Luxor. Wyndham skilfully pushed through the crowds and secured two corner seats in a 'harem' or ladies' compartment. Our travelling companions were Egyptians, one a beautiful young mother with her first baby – a boy. Both mother and baby were dressed in elegant Parisian garments. She was met by her husband at Assiut, and he told us, in English (the wife only spoke French), that this was the first time he had seen his son. He was obviously delighted with his offspring and boyishly shy in the presence of us women. We gladly consented to his staying in the harem compartment until they got out at Maghagha.

Here four young girls got in instead. One of them spoke English fluently. She was a college girl, reading for her degree in English, and told us her ambition was to go to England. In answer to my question as to why English was spoken so little in Cairo after over fifty years of British occupation, she explained that French had always been used for diplomacy and commerce, while English was only a cultural language; also, the French Catholics had been swift to take advantage of the Egyptian desire for modern education, and had founded innumerable schools and colleges.

As we continued our journey, following the course of the Nile, we were surprised at the number of large towns, which seemed to be much more prosperous and flourishing than those of the Nile Delta, where the landscape is dotted with clusters of dilapidated mud dwellings and poorly clad inhabitants.

Scenes at the railway stations were varied and often amusing. It was the time of year when men were returning from the Mecca pilgrimage, and large crowds came to welcome them. A native band led the deputation, tom-toms and drums were beaten, swarms of children, as everywhere, followed in the procession and venerable-looking sheiks of the town or village would fall on the neck of the returned pilgrim, in the same manner that the Bible describes the greeting of the prodigal son.

Many vendors of fruit boarded the train, and one stayed too long to barter his oranges and got carried off. The shouts of excited passengers warning him that we were now beyond the platform worked him up to such a desperate pitch that he made a dash for his escape. I was standing near the door. He implored me, in Arabic I suppose, to open it for him, which I did, fearfully expecting to see him dashed to his death. However, he landed on his feet and sweeping off his turban from his head, gave me a most graceful *salaam*.

We arrived in the late evening in Luxor, dust-covered and weary, and drove, under a starlit sky in an *arabiyeh* with tinkling bells, to the Savoy Hotel, which is situated amid palm-shaded grounds right on the banks of the Nile.

No words can describe the beauty – the broad shining river with its medley of sailing craft, steamers and aquaplanes in constant motion and the interminable stretch of the Libyan sandstone hills bordering its western shores with ever-changing lights and shades heralded by sunrise and yet more gorgeous sunsets. It is no wonder the Egyptians were sun-worshippers.

March 11th, 1939

Today we visited the temples at Karnak (Thebes). The famous temple of Queen Hatshepsut is in the process of reconstruction. She was the daughter of Pharaoh I, who had ordered the slaughter of the infant sons of the Israelites, and she it was who found and adopted the infant Moses during her summer sojourn in Upper Egypt, when she went to bathe in the Nile. All her history tells of her being a remarkable woman, who deposed her husband (or it might have been her stepson) and ruled over all Egypt for twenty-five years, when the country enjoyed great prosperity. The hatred of the menfolk of the family towards this extraordinary woman is most amusingly recorded by the fact that after her death they had her face hacked out of every carved image of her on the temple walls and pillars.

In her great temple at Karnak she had two huge obelisks erected, one of which still stands – 90 feet high, and weighing 600 tons, 'built by my majesty to the glory of Ammon Ra to stand forever and ever'. So it has stood for 3,400 years. The other obelisk fell in the great earthquake of 27 BC. Her successor hated her so violently that not only were all images of her damaged, but he even threatened to destroy the two famous obelisks, and was deterred by the priests only because they were the largest in Egypt.

March 12th, 1939

Today is the great day of our visit to the Valley of the Kings and Queens on the west bank of the Nile, the land of the setting sun. It was so fascinating that I could write interminably of all we saw, but time forbids.

On emerging from the tombs and temples there are the modern plagues of Egypt to contend with – the beggars and the flies. The beggars will reveal their sores on which the flies have festered and you must give them *baksheesh* to get rid of them. Then there are the persistent vendors, trying to impose their spurious wares on you. 'Mummy beads' indeed. I quite inadvertently hit on a marvellous ruse, which protected me from their importunity. On emerging from one of the tombs I drew my long sun veil across my nose and mouth to protect them from the dust that the crowd of beggars had stirred up, and I heard them say, in a somewhat awed whisper, 'Muslim', and instantly they dropped their eyes and ceased to speak to me. No Mohammedan man must speak to a veiled Muslim woman. I had learned the secret and it worked unfailingly.

April 4th, 1939

I am safely back at Ardvreck, which seems very strange, grey and cold after my great adventures.

Having responded to a mound of letters that awaited my return, and continuing to wade through the accumulations of letters still on my desk, I came across sundry newspaper cuttings among my papers and laughed over my curious tendency to 'write to *The Times* about it'. I realised eventually that only a grand name would carry any real weight with *The Times*, so have tended more recently to write to the 'lesser breeds' instead.

We Are At War Once More

1939–45

June 20th, 1939, The Evening Telegraph, Dundee
To Present Prizes

Presenting the prizes at the closing exhibition of Seymour Lodge Private Girls' School, Dundee, on Wednesday of next week, will be a lady who has had wide experience in educational matters.

Mrs Grattan Guinness, who is to fulfil this duty, is the widow of Dr H. Grattan Guinness, FRCS, FRAS, traveller and author. She is herself the author of a book which deals with the religious side of life in mid-Victorian days and describes how long and how difficult was the path to feminine emancipation.

Mrs Grattan Guinness has travelled extensively and she has always been keenly interested in educational work. She has lectured in colleges and schools in many countries and witnessed the inception of modern education methods both in China and Japan. Her present work is at Ardvreck, the boys' preparatory school at Crieff, now under the headmastership of Mr David Smythe of Braco House, Perth.

September 3rd, 1939

And so, this beautiful September day, we are once again at war. It seems unreal and I feel strangely divorced from it all up here amongst the peaceful hills of Crieff. How long must I stay so far away from my family? I so fear the implications for my two fine boys and their little families. John, as a schoolmaster, is, I hope, exempt from conscription. But Paul? I entrusted them to God so many years ago. Now, more than ever.

April 2nd, 1940
To the Editor, The Scotsman

Sir – Would you kindly grant space for a plea to open churches for prayer? Our King and Queen, Prime Minister, Dominion Premiers, Cabinet Ministers, Labour Leaders, church leaders and many others have stated that the present conflict in which we are engaged is a spiritual conflict, a holy war against the powers of evil. If we are convinced of this, then it follows that all our spiritual as well as our material forces must be mobilised to combat this evil.

Many persons have lost the habit of church-going, but it does not follow that they have lost their belief in prayer, and the church might well offer the opportunity for the exercise of this spiritual force.

It is almost with a feeling of embarrassment that one attempts an entry into a church other than at service hour, and, personally, I experience a sense of rebuff when I find all entrances closed and locked against me.

Could not our church authorities issue an order for all the churches throughout the country to be thrown open at this time of crisis in the world's history? The display of large posters, bearing the words 'Open for Prayer' and with some such quotation as, 'Call upon me and I will answer', might lead to dynamic results. I am, etc.

G. Grattan Guinness

July 3rd, 1940

My worst fears are realised. Paul feels he must play his part in this dreadful conflict and has signed up as a forces chaplain – even though Jean is pregnant with their second child. He insists she go back to her parents in Canada for the birth so that he can rest assured his little family is safe. But crossing the Atlantic alone in these troubled times – pregnant and with a three-year-old – doesn't bear thinking about. The newspapers are full of tales of indiscriminate submarine attacks on both merchant and passenger vessels, wreaking dreadful havoc with supplies and on our hearts. I went all the way down to London to say goodbye to them with a sinking heart, not knowing when, and even if, I might see her and little Margaret again. I won't imagine the worst. I won't think about it. I will trust.

August 28th, 1940

I have decided to say farewell to Ardvreck School. I am sixty-five, after all, and the work is becoming too arduous. The boys are delightful, but children are demanding and the long hours intolerable. It is hard to be so far from my family at such a time, and travel is becoming increasingly hazardous. So off I set into the big wide world once more, with no fixed abode and only meagre savings in the bank.

Stayed the night with my old friends Douglas and Evelyn Crick, whom I had met many years ago at St Aidan's, when he was chaplain to the Mersey Mission to Seafarers. Douglas is now Bishop of Chester and kindly invited me to come to Bishop's House to meet Paul, who was training for his work as a forces chaplain nearby. Paul came to dinner and we all had a delightful evening.

A disturbed night with sirens, and planes swooping overhead on their way to attack Liverpool. How can anyone sleep, knowing that many there won't awake in the morning? God watch over them.

Then back to High Hurstwood Vicarage and Ruth. Until I can find the means to live independently again.

September 18th, 1940

Terrible news. The ship *The City of Benares* evacuating ninety children from Britain to Canada has been torpedoed and sunk by the German submarine U-48. Seventy-seven children are dead. How close my own loved ones came to meeting such an end I shall never know. But they are safely in Canada and for that I am truly grateful, yet still grieving for all the parents, who, like my Paul, thought they were doing the best for their children.

January 1st, 1942

Dr Cosmo Lang, the Archbishop of Canterbury, has announced his resignation to take effect on March 31st. 'The times demand', he said, 'from those who have any responsibilities of leadership an ardour, a vigour, a decisiveness of mind and spirit which cannot be expected from a man who is in his seventy-eighth year and who has for thirty-three years borne the burden of the office of archbishop, for twenty years at York, and the last thirteen at Canterbury.'

Ah, I understand that weariness, even if I haven't quite his years. He ended his statement as follows: 'I cannot close without adding in all sincerity that in laying down my life's work I am overwhelmed by the thought that so few of my hopes and ideals for it have been fulfilled, that I have accomplished so little for the good of the church and the people. Because I know how much this manifold and manifest failure is due to my own faults and sins, I must need welcome the prospect of a few years when, by God's grace, I may be able to gain that communion with Him which has been so sadly broken by the incessant pressure of work, and to prepare aright for the last stage in the journey of life.'

A true, yet rather heart-rending admission. How we need a new leader with fresh vision. And may it not be that for each one of us who are on our way to, or have passed the span of the threescore years and ten, that the withdrawal from life's activities and the opportunity of making use of this closing earthly period, 'to gain that communion with Him', may prove to be the most important work of our life on earth. May it be so for Dr Lang. Lord, teach us to pray.

'We are always sowing our future, we are always reaping our past.' Dean Inge

February 4th, 1942

Stayed the night with John, Karis and their little Lindis, my first visit to the Manor House, Stoke Park, the premises for 'Long Dene', the new school they have founded in Jordans, Buckinghamshire, along rather radical, progressive lines.

John and Karis have long admired the ideas of A.S. Neill, who founded Summerhill School. He believes that the happiness of the child should be paramount, that this happiness grows from a sense of personal freedom, and that unhappiness due to repression is responsible for many of the psychological disorders of adulthood.

Unlike other boarding schools, the Long Dene community is structured to function as one large happy family. Pupils call staff by their first names, which I find rather odd. Together they do the housework, wash the dishes, empty the bins and tend the extensive gardens – a much better preparation for the real world, no doubt. Personal responsibility and mutual respect are the key words here. There are no examinations, and discipline is carried out by a sanction committee of staff and pupils, who ensure that the perpetrators of a crime make appropriate reparation. There is great emphasis on fresh air, exercise and creativity: every child plays an instrument, is a member of an orchestra, learns to dance and perform.

I think it is quite visionary and very adventurous of them, I must say. Especially at such a time.

March 24th, 1942

I am finally on the move – this time to Scarborough, to take up a post as housekeeper for the Revd James Leigh, Vicar of St Martin's. If the man is amiable and therefore manageable, and he certainly seemed so at interview, it shouldn't prove too onerous a task.

Went to Paul's new headquarters on the way there. He is now stationed at RAF Woodhall Spa in Lincolnshire, with pastoral responsibility for all those dear airmen who risk their lives in the skies every day.

April 26th, 1942

This is not a proper diary at all and many of the most important events that happen in my little circle are passed over; but I must refer to those of Easter last (4th – 7th), namely Jean's return from Canada with darling little Margaret, and baby John, now thirteen months and Canadian born, after an absence of one year and nine months. Such a brave decision. In the newspapers there Jean read of the gravity of the situation, and could not bear to be so cut off from having any news of Paul. She says she would rather be in the thick of it, as he is.

In Canada, Margaret, aged four, had apparently asked her mother why her daddy did not come to them. On being told on account of the war, she said, 'Yes, of course, they would not know what to do without Daddy, would they, Mummy?' Their crossing was without incident and 'uneventful' as all the papers put it, in a convoy of around thirty ships with a large naval escort to protect them from attack. Nonetheless each day was spent in fear of torpedoes. Each day they were borne up in prayer by a little company of us meeting in the Scarborough vicarage. And 'we believed and saw', the fulfilment of every word of Psalm 91, which was given to me from the day I had Paul's telegram to say that passages had been granted.

You shall not be afraid of the terror by night,
Nor of the arrow that flies by day,
Nor of the pestilence that walks in darkness,
Nor of the destruction that lays waste at noonday.
A thousand may fall at your side,
And ten thousand at your right hand;
But it shall not come near you . . .
Because you have made the Lord, who is my refuge,
Even the Most High, your dwelling place,
No evil shall befall you,
Nor shall any plague come near your dwelling;
For he shall give his angels charge over you,
To keep you in all your ways.

It was a wonderful Easter Day. We met in Lincoln, where Paul was to preach, and all attended an impressive service in the cathedral in the afternoon, when it was filled with men and women in khaki. To hear those men singing 'Crown Him with Many Crowns' was to feel one was truly at a coronation. And when Paul mounted the pulpit of that glorious old cathedral, it was my coronation.

In the evening I went with Paul and Jean to their lovely little temporary home in Woodhall Spa (how true it is these days that we have no continuing city), a bungalow rented from Lady Decima Moore-Guggisberg.

The actress Decima Moore was, I remember (from the days when a visit to a musical theatre was still a guilty pleasure), a much fêted soprano with the D'Oyly Carte Opera Company. The Brigadier General Sir Frederick Guggisberg, her second husband, seems to have been the catalyst for her love affair with the military. She was made a Commander of the Most Excellent Order of the British Empire for her services during the First World War, and her charity work on behalf of the veterans continued throughout her retirement. At the beginning of this war she re-established the British Leave Club in Paris, only fleeing the city hours before the Germans arrived, and attaching a notice to the doors that said 'Temporarily Closed'.

And now she has let Paul and Jean have her bungalow for these few precious weeks they have together after so long apart and before separation is imposed once more. How good is the God we adore.

On being corrected for holding her cup in her left hand, Margaret replied, 'My Daddy always holds his cup in his left hand and his cake in his right hand. We are made that way.'

August 10th, 1942

News this morning, Sunday, that Gandhi, Pandit Nehru and many Congress leaders in India have all been arrested. Who can foresee what the consequences will be? Gandhi, the religious leader of the independence movement, has called for a mass non-violent resistance campaign, but the British government has pre-empted civil disobedience by threatening to imprison all those shopkeepers who close their shops, which in this case will be taken over and run by those appointed by the government.

Gandhi is a truly remarkable man. One cannot help but admire him. We have tried to win him, suppress him, twice imprisoned him – and again, today, he goes to prison with a smile on his face. In his address to Congress yesterday he declares, 'I am a greater friend of the British now than ever I was. The reason is that at this moment they are in distress. My friendship demands that I make them aware of their mistakes. I know that they are on the brink of a ditch and are about to fall into it.'

This starts me thinking. Is it not possible that Gandhi's way – non-violence and passive resistance – is the better way? The Christian way? As Jesus said, 'He that taketh the sword shall perish with the sword.' What a heart-searching problem India is, and at such a difficult time for Britain. But then, Gandhi knows that, and he also knows that he has right on his side, and must, therefore, eventually, succeed.

September 24th, 1942

In the *Yorkshire Post* today I read the following: 'A milestone in British ecclesiastical history was reached yesterday with the inauguration of the British Council of Churches at a special service at St Paul's Cathedral. Dr Temple, the new Archbishop of Canterbury, said: 'We owe united witness as a duty to our nation and to the hope of Christian civilisation; but we owe it still more to our Lord himself . . .'

I thank God for this and all that will come out of it. At last! The dawn of the promise: 'That they may be one.'

October 10th, 1942

I was reading this week's *Church Times* in the library this morning and it reported the Archbishop as having referred to the British Council of Churches as 'the latest step in the ecumenical movement that had begun with the Edinburgh Missionary Conference of 1910'. I was particularly interested that the Archbishop saw the 1910 conference as the beginning of a worldwide movement. It was of this conference that my beloved Henry spoke in the very last conversation we had alone together in his study, as he sat in his invalid chair looking out over the beautiful city of Bath. 'I am thinking of my children and of all the work they are doing in the world; and of this great missionary conference and of all that will come out of it.'

It was as if the veil was lifted, and he already had a vision – a timeless vision – from the other side. His face shone with a heavenly light as he spoke, and I wondered at it. On the morrow, he passed over.

Margaret, silently listening to her father talking at the breakfast table, says, 'Daddy, what a chatterbox you are; you talk so much that I have quite forgotten what I wanted to say.'

October 16th, 1942

The convocations of Canterbury and York are in session; it is heartening to realise how wide awake the church now is to her responsibilities and how many drastic reforms are afoot under the inspirational leadership of the Archbishop. Dr Temple suggests that supplementary forms of service be used outside the church buildings, that is, in canteens, cinemas and factories, which implies the church's awakened sense that it must go to the people, since the people do not come to the church.

Let's hope his suggestions are heeded.

November 9th, 1942

Have been staying with John and Karis at their school in Stoke Park. Lindis, aged three and a half, showed me to my room, taking my hand up the stairs. Then she opened the empty drawers which had been cleared for my weekend visit: 'And there is a drawer if you want it. And there is another drawer if you want it,' and then, opening the bottom drawer and finding in it a pot of jam, her little eyes sparkled with delight as she said, 'And there is a pot of jam if you want it.'

At night strange to hear sound of the ack-ack fire – a distant echo of London, where the anti-aircraft batteries are taking on enemy bombers. Karis says she saw London on fire just a few months ago from an upstairs window, which frightened her rather.

The village of Stoke Poges is in an industrial area near Slough that has experienced heavy bombardment itself, and Stoke Park has no air raid shelters. In the event of a raid, the staff usher the children into the dining room, where they shelter beneath the tables. It doesn't seem a satisfactory situation at all, but when I said so to John, he was completely unperturbed and tells me if a doodlebug lands they wouldn't know anything about it anyway. Karis says he's always telling her not to worry, stays in his bed throughout the raids and sleeps through them regardless.

After I left, Lindis apparently said to her mother, 'Isn't my Granny a lovely girl?' (It is many years since I have had a compliment like that paid me!)

From the *Daily Telegraph*. General Montgomery's final words to his staff at the south-eastern command HQ before he left for Egypt were: 'Gentlemen, I read my Bible every day and I recommend you do the same.'

December 10th, 1942

I received a telegram from Paul this morning to say he was being posted abroad and must report to the London transit camp on December 22nd. He plans to come to Scarborough tomorrow night to say goodbye.

I wired him back, 'Come. Love to my darling Jean. The utmost for the Highest.'

But oh, how my heart aches for them! Another separation after their joyous reunion a mere nine months ago.

I thought of the words of a hymn Paul had written, 'In freedom's name you gladly pay the price', and I link this up with the prayer John uses in his school, 'May we strive and take our place, keenly and gladly, in the world's great struggle for the freedom of mankind.'

Thank God for two such sons! They were dedicated to God's service in infancy. They have both given their lives to this cause – the true freedom.

December 19th, 1942

On hearing from Jean that Paul had gone, I read that evening in Psalm 37:

The Lord ordereth a good man's goings . . .
The Lord shall stand by them and save them;
He shall deliver them from the ungodly and shall save them,
because they put their trust in him.

Jean and the children are living with my dear old friend VR[*] in Sanderstead near Croydon Airport. Paul arranged it before he left. It sounds to me far too close to the bombing for comfort.

January 29th, 1943

I received a telegram from Jean at 8.15 a.m. telling of Paul's arrival in North Africa. The telegram arrived in Scarborough evening of the 28th – so the voyage (supposing he sailed on January 7th) took three weeks approximately. Normally it would take three to four days. I suspect there has been fighting *en route*. The thought terrifies me.

In today's morning prayers, Psalm 140: 'O God the Lord, the strength of my salvation, Thou hast covered my head in the day of battle.'

Cover his head, cover him altogether – all through the coming days.

February 27th, 1943

Paul's first letter arrived today, and he tells of a most extraordinary event. Who should he discover on the same troop ship but his cousin, Karl Kumm Junior, Lucy's youngest son, raised in America and a chaplain to the US forces. They had never met and only discovered each other when they fell into conversation as fellow padres.

---

[*] Her full name was Violet Reynolds

It was remarkably providential – too much so to be a coincidence. Paul said to him, 'I have always wanted to meet you, to ask you whether you feel any calling to fulfil your mother's dying wish.'

Lucy, on her deathbed, had written, 'When Karl is old enough I should like him to know that all the time before he was born I had one prayer, one longing, one hunger – that he should continue Father's prophetic studies and research, for in the later years of his life he may perhaps see the restored Jewish state, and in those unutterable days, he may understand and tell.'

Karl obviously knew of his mother's wishes, but told Paul he had never felt under any obligation to fulfil them. Paul was overjoyed, for he has always felt so strongly that in this, he was the one to take up his father's mantle.

It thrills me beyond measure, of course, and not just because Henry's work will continue. If Paul is right, then surely he must be protected for the duration? And return to fulfil his calling? Or is this merely wishful thinking?

Sunday, February 28th, 1943

Felt anxious and depressed today, thinking of Paul right in the heart of the danger zone, with fierce fighting now taking place in North Tunisia.

I went as usual to 10.15 matins at St Martin's, and with the singing of the first hymn my load of care was lifted.

> *Why restless, why cast down my soul?*
> *Hope still, and thou shalt sing*
> *The praise of him who is thy God*
> *Thy heart's eternal spring.*

Then followed the 121st Psalm and it was as if the sun had come out from behind the clouds, dispelling the gloom.

The Lord is thy keeper: the Lord is thy shade upon thy right hand.
The sun shall not smite thee by day, nor the moon by night.
The Lord shall preserve thee from all evil: he shall preserve thy soul.
The Lord shall preserve thy going out and thy coming in from
*   this time forth, and even for evermore.*

March 17th, St Patrick's Day, 1943

The following telegram came from Jean this afternoon: 'In touch with War Office regarding report in cheap press that Paul is missing at Sedjenane but believed safe. Best love Jean.'

I replied, 'God keep him and calm our fears. Psalm 71 verses 1–6 given me – Mother.'

It was the Revd Leigh who gave me this psalm, which he said had been in his thoughts strongly since the verses were sung in church last Sunday morning. These words in verse 3, 'Thou hast given commandment to save me', seem to be in exact accord with all the previous messages I have had. Oh, what consolation and comfort and glorious promises. This after the subtle temptation of doubt had come to me – in the same form as to Eve: Yea, hath God said? Yes, he has said.

I have found it hard to fight against depression today, and prayed tonight that the burden might be lifted. Then my dear little Catholic maid came in at 10 o'clock and said, 'I have been to church this evening and prayed to our Holy Mother for your son, and I lit a candle. He will be all right, Madam.'

I was deeply touched. She has such a strong, simple faith.

The Daily Mirror, March 17th, 1943
They Stayed Behind

Two British army chaplains stayed behind with doctors in the front line in the Sedjenane area of Tunisia to be with British wounded during the recent German advance.

One of them is believed to be safe, but a prisoner. The second is missing.

A German officer captured by the British forces said the padre taken prisoner was the Rev H.O. Laurence who comes from Thimbleby, Horncastle, Lincolnshire.

The second padre, about whom no information is received, is the Rev P.G. Guinness, who is believed to be safe as there was little firing in the area where he was.

Sedjenane was of great strategic importance to the Allies in their rush for Tunis. But despite a brave attack by the 16th Battalion Durham Light Infantry the town had fallen to the Germans on March 4th, with many casualties.

March 24th, 1943

I asked the Revd Leigh if he'd mind if I went south for a while to be with Jean, and wired a friend asking if she could come and temporarily take my place at the Scarborough vicarage.

Jean met me at King's Cross and as we arrived at Sanderstead, little Margaret and John were with VR at the gate to welcome us.

The following day Geraldine and Howard came all the way from Southborough to lunch and tea with us, and we four had prayers together. We had to shout them into Howard's ear trumpet, as he is so desperately hard of hearing. Both are rather frail now, but such pets.

March 27th, 1943

A rather disturbing letter arrived from John today. He says he has twice seen Paul in his dreams, standing on a high hill, and twice he has been awoken from sleep by the awful noise of bursting shells. He believes that the dreams are to prepare us for the fact that Paul is dead.

I did not show this letter to Jean. It was a tremendous challenge to my faith and to all the promises I had received. But it took me to Gethsemane. 'O my Father, if it be possible, let this cup pass from me. Nevertheless, not as I will, but as thou wilt . . .'

I have no idea how to reply. Better to say nothing.

March 28th, 1943

The rector of Sanderstead, Howard Rose, rang us on the telephone to give us the marvellous news that a message from Paul had been broadcast on the English-speaking German radio programme, *Germany Calling*, and would be repeated in the evening. Our joy was beyond telling . . . all the promises fulfilled. *Te Deum laudamus*. I gave John and Karis, Ruth and Geraldine trunk calls to let them know.

Germany Calling is a Nazi propaganda programme presented every night by an Englishman nicknamed 'Lord Haw Haw' in the British press because of his drawling, upper-crust accent. I couldn't think why Paul should be on the programme and feared Howard Rose had got it wrong.

We sat glued to the wireless for the rest of the day, holding our breath, waiting and waiting for the evening broadcast. And then, oh, the wonder of it. To hear his voice. I could not keep back the tears of joy, especially at his closing personal message of love, 'to my wife and the two children . . . and my mother'.

As padre he simply appeared to name the British dead. The intention is to demoralise the British, but Jean, with great wisdom, said, 'Mother, don't you see? Paul did that knowing that we at home would far rather know the truth – that our loved ones have been killed, or have survived and are prisoners of war.'

Geraldine rang us back immediately to say she had heard every word.

April 30th, 1943

Now that the situation is a little clearer I have returned to my duties in Scarborough with the Revd Leigh. I do enjoy the chance of intelligent conversation and rather chatter on. I fear Jean may have found it more of a trial than a help.

She wrote today to say she had had the following telegram from the War Office: 'Official report received that Rev P.G. Guinness, chaplain to the forces previously reported as missing, is a prisoner of war. Letter to follow shortly. Secretary of State for War.'

May 19th, 1943

Received today from Jean the first news we have had from Paul as a POW. Thank God, he is safe, transported by boat to Brindisi, to 'what is probably the best officers' camp in Italy', he says.

I feel like shouting, 'Oh sing unto the Lord . . . for he hath done marvellous things.'

June 5th, 1943

In today's issue of the *Sunday Times* appears a letter from a recently killed soldier in North Africa to his father:

> *There is I feel, both in England and America, a tremendous surge of feeling, which for want of a better word I shall call 'goodness'. It is the heartfelt longing of all the 'middling folk' for something better – a world more worthy of their children, a world more simple in its beliefs, nearer to earth and to God. This feeling is no less powerful or significant than the Renaissance was, and will, I hope and pray, surge over the whole world in a tidal wave. That is the ideal for which we are fighting.*

October 10th, 1943

Nothing from Paul for over a month. Jean and I were sick with worry. And then, from a heavily edited letter, received yesterday, Jean discovers that he has been transported with others in a convoy of trucks across Europe to Stalag V camp in Germany. After the censor's deletions little else of interest remains, except that he tries to remain strong to sustain the morale of the men, and that they are all truly grateful for Red Cross parcels. I hope he is fed and warm and well, as our POWs are. Do the Nazis observe the Geneva Convention? Our newspapers think it unlikely. Oh please God, may this accursed war not drag on too much longer.

March 6th, 1944

But it does. There is no end in sight. And I am stuck out here in Scarborough. The Revd Leigh is a dear man and very undemanding, but my life passes me by in dreary regularity, broken only by occasional trips to Stoke Poges and a few letters from Paul, so edited there is no real news, though I pore over every word, and holding them up to the light, desperately try to read what is behind the crossings out. He is alive at least. We know little more.

June 6th, 1944

The BBC reports that thousands of Allied troops have begun landing in northern France at the start of a major offensive against the Germans. The landings were preceded by air attacks along the French coast, and the Allies have already penetrated several miles inland. In his broadcast last night, King George warned us that this would be the 'supreme test' and called on the nation to pray for the liberation of Europe.

Not much sleep for anyone. In our hearts and minds we are all there, stomachs churning, on the beaches of Normandy, in the fray with our boys. I came down at 3.30 a.m. and almost tripped over the Revd Leigh on his knees in the living room. We drank tea, and waited for the dawn and news.

It seems all is going to plan, thank God. But too soon yet to rejoice. Might it be possible that this is the beginning of the end, that Paul may soon be restored to us?

June 14th, 1944

How could I have ever hoped for a swift end to this loathsome war – now we have V-1 flying bombs that give us no warning of their coming, but simply explode before anyone can take shelter. Eighty an hour land on the south-east. Oh, how I wish my little families – Jean and the children in Sanderstead, John and Karis, the family at the school in Stoke – were tucked safely away from the risk.

June 21st, 1944

There is always a glimmer of hope amongst the ruins. The newspapers tell us that the new wonder drug, penicillin, now ready for widespread use on our wounded, is proving very effective. Who would have ever guessed that a fungus, of all things, could provide such benefits to our health? The newspapers say that blood poisoning in children, with all the terror that went with it – lancing the pus, and even amputations – could become a thing of the past. Would that I had had such a medicine to offer in my nursing days. And Paul might have been spared the long interruption in his childhood education.

August 4th, 1944

The new Education Act makes a daily Christian act of worship compulsory in every school. John and Karis had stalwartly resisted such a convention at Long Dene, despite my best attempts to share the benefits I receive of reading a daily psalm. But now, says Karis, the war has taught them that human endeavour and creativity on their own are not enough – that it's the spiritual that energises the mind and body. So she will introduce the children to the elevating power of music, while John will read inspirational texts from a wide variety of sacred traditions.

September 10th, 1944

Given my personal situation, I felt I should be of more use to the war effort. Though I am in my sixty-eighth year, I still have my marbles (well, most of them), am fit, efficient, organised and experienced. I saw in the papers that there was a job vacancy for clerical work at the Admiralty in Bath, a city that holds so many happy memories for me. I applied and was duly accepted – above much younger competition with the latest hairdos and rouged lips, who waited their turn with me in an interview room in the requisitioned, once-stylish Empire Hotel. There are advantages in no longer being a distraction to the opposite sex – though I tell myself that it was my long experience got me the job.

Seeing Bath again was deeply shocking. The Blitz of 1942, a reprisal attack by the Germans for the Allied destruction of the beautiful ancient city of Lübeck, had destroyed so much of its Regency splendour and grace. Everywhere huge mounds of bricks and glass and other debris. Derelict buildings and patched-up houses stand shakily on their foundations like wounded soldiers. There is barely a home or monument without boarded-up windows. And so many dead. Everyone in my office, where we are responsible for naval pay, has lost either a loved one or a home, which gives us an unspoken understanding as we all soldier on together. It is exacting work, but fortunately, mental arithmetic has always been a forte of mine, and I do feel more in the thick of things, knowing what excellent work is done here in the designing of warships. More I cannot say, having signed the Official Secrets Act, though now that the end appears to be in sight it is all far less cloak and dagger.

I am billeted with a dear, almost blind elderly lady on the outskirts of the city. The Admiralty pays one guinea a week for my bed, breakfast and an evening meal, a meal which is not only adequate but a miracle given my landlady's lack of eyesight. On my first night I went up to the cemetery and, mercifully, found it untouched. No disturbance to my beloved Henry, who lies peacefully beneath his shady copper beech, unaware of the tumult in the world he left behind. I feel less alone, his presence here with me in this devastated city. Still so little news of Paul, except for the occasional few words that tell us he is receiving the regular parcels we send, that life is spartan, food scarce and that he is grateful to have survived another atrociously cold winter. This is not how we treat our German POWs. The newspapers tell us they have soap, warm clothing, better food than our meagre rations permit.

February, 1945

John and Karis have moved their school, Long Dene, lock, stock and barrel, to Chiddingstone Castle in Kent.

The lease at Stoke Park Manor expired at Christmas and conditions were too cramped. They had been looking for something larger for many months, away from the bombs, but unobtainable as all substantial properties were requisitioned by the army. But now, with victory in sight and all forces deployed in the liberation, Chiddingstone, which belonged to Lord Astor, Nancy's son, and had served as a base for military forces, suddenly came onto the market (General Montgomery reviewed his troops there before taking command of the 8th Army).

It is a former medieval manor house set in thirty-five acres, with a grand Regency frontage and wonderful views over the North Downs. Several cottages in the castle grounds, some of them subdivided, make the place ideal for housing staff, and the lease of additional farmland will enable more self-sufficiency in organic food production, the fulfilment of a dream John has held in his heart for many years.

The army personnel have apparently left it in rather a dismal state ('the less said the better', says Karis). They almost burned the gracious sitting room down – a lighted cigarette probably – so everywhere is covered in soot. Small wonder the Astors wanted rid of it and offered it to John for a reasonable price, which he managed to afford only with the help of a large loan from Henry's brewing cousin, Lord Moyne, whom John knew at Oxford. It will still be a great challenge to pay it back, and to also carry out some basic repairs. My brave boy.

The removal was a major military manoeuvre, the younger children sent home for half term, the older children packing up at one end while staff at the other end quickly cleaned the filthy castle before the imminent arrival of children, furniture, equipment, books, stores, animals, etcetera! John advised parents to send their children back not only with their sugar and fats rations wrapped in greaseproof paper, but also with dungarees and boiler suits!

What a marvellous provision, however – just as John had been served with a writ for possession by the owner of Stoke Park Manor. Impeccable timing as ever.

April 28th, 1945, 9 p.m.

I have just heard on the wireless that Stalag V-A has been liberated. It was the first of several freed POW camps. Thank God!

Thank God! How we have hoped and longed for this moment. All our prayers answered.

On the day he sailed for the front – January 7th, 1943 – the psalm for that evening was the 37th. I am reading it again tonight. How wonderfully fulfilled – every bit of it, and this grand news has come just as we have heard of Himmler offering 'unconditional surrender' to the Allies. All Germany is crumbling – most of her cities and ports are in our hands. The Russians are in Berlin and the three big powers have met at Torgau on the Elbe.

> *Fret not thyself because of the ungodly,*
> *They shall soon be cut down like the grass, and wither as the*
> *green herb.*
> *Commit thy way unto the Lord; trust also in him; and he shall*
> *bring it to pass.*

I read every word over and over again, all of it realised – especially that last verse which brought me such comfort the day Paul sailed. That promise I have claimed and trusted through these long two and a quarter years.

The Lord shall stand by them, and save them: he shall deliver them from the ungodly, and save them, because they put their trust in him.

Tuesday, May 1st, 1945

At 9.30 a.m. I had a trunk call at the Admiralty from Jean in Sanderstead to say that Paul was home. He rang her the moment he set foot on British soil. After his initial greeting, he said to her, 'Darling, I'm going to put the phone down now and ring you back again in a few minutes.' He knew so well that she would be too choked to speak, and gave her a moment to collect herself.

Five minutes later, my elderly landlady rang me with the news. A near neighbour of ours, an admiral's wife, had obliged her by reading the telegram from Paul that had just been delivered to my lodgings at 33 Richmond Place. She called me at once. Imagine! The control I needed to exercise as I got this news: 'Arrived by air from Germany today travelling Worcester tonight hope return London tomorrow love Paul.'

Here in the Admiralty, where some have lost loved ones and others have loved ones still unaccounted for, I felt restraint was called for. And then received the congratulations of all the staff – with astonishing speed. My good news spread and I was surprised and touched by the many who stopped me in the corridors and the canteen to tell me how glad they were for me. They are a typically kind-hearted British crowd.

It has been a week of highlights. The Russians in Berlin. The British in Bremen and Hamburg. The surrender to Field Marshall Montgomery of all north-west Germany, Holland, Denmark, and to Field Marshall Alexander of a million men in North Italy and West Austria.

The telegram

Wednesday, May 2nd, 1945

And now I am free to say – as the papers tell everyone anyway – that it was the development of the cavity magnetron here in Britain that gave our radars a considerable advantage over German and Japanese radar from the end of 1941. It meant that maritime patrol aircraft could detect objects as small as a periscope, previously undetectable from the air, and destroy the submarine immediately, sparing us the dreadful losses of our naval convoys that we sustained earlier in the war, when Jean crossed to Canada and back. We have much to be proud of and thankful for – our unknown scientists, a few of them women, I see, as well as the boys who used their marvellous inventions.

May 5th, 1945

Jean went to meet Paul at the station today. She was shocked to see how fat he was, yet with barely the energy to lift his small, almost empty suitcase. She had to carry it for him. The War Office has told her that he is emaciated, blown up by his near-starvation rations, and that she must increase his intake slowly and carefully over a period of time so she doesn't make him ill.

When John, nearly three, saw his daddy for the first time, he shouted, 'Hello Mr Van der Pants,' and took off. The little chap has to make a relationship with an almost complete stranger. Even Margaret seems unsure of him. How hard this all must be for him. I have leave to go to Sanderstead to celebrate his birthday and can hardly wait.

May 8th, 1945

Paul's birthday – his thirty-seventh – his first as a free man since 1943. And today is VICTORY IN EUROPE DAY. At 3 p.m. the

Prime Minister announced the unconditional surrender of Germany on land, sea and air. The terms were signed at 2.41 p.m. French time yesterday and countersigned today in the little red schoolhouse which is General Eisenhower's HQ at Rheims. After signing, General Jodl said, 'With this signature the German people and the German armed forces are, for better or worse, delivered into the victors' hands.'

Wonderful news, but still the best thing about today was to hold my big son in my arms again. As always, he had to bend right down to me. I was horrified to see him so gaunt and pasty – a bloated body, with stick-like arms and legs – but Jean had warned me and I think I hid it well. He smiles a lot, delighted just to be in the bosom of his little family again. He says little of his experiences, determined to put them all behind him. Later Jean told me that he was stuffed into cattle trucks along with hundreds of other prisoners, so crushed together they could hardly move or even breathe, and taken across Europe from Italy to Stalag V-A in Ludwigsburg, a former concentration camp. The journey took nine days and no one was ever allowed out. Conditions in the trucks were almost too appalling to imagine. Some died of thirst or asphyxiation where they stood, propped up by their comrades. My poor, poor boy. No wonder he longs to forget.

The 'camp' was no more than a collection of barracks surrounded by barbed wire, where they slept on thin mattresses on wooden benches. 'Food' consisted of a watery vegetable soup and whatever arrived in Red Cross parcels – after the guards had helped themselves. The humanitarian protocols of the Geneva Convention were ignored, officers shown no respect. Cruelty was the only order of the day. In these circumstances Paul, as padre, was forced to become chief negotiator. He has seen things, such awful things, things he cannot bear to speak about. And we must let him be. Let him mend in mind and body. Time will heal.

Six-year-old Margaret, on being asked to tell us about meeting her daddy after such a long separation, said, 'Well, you know, I had forgotten my daddy's voice, but when I heard his voice, I said, I will go everywhere with my daddy.'

At Chiddingstone John gave the domestic staff the day off, and the pupils cooked the meals. They found a flag to fly from the castle tower.

Among other headlines in today's papers are: Goebbels took poison with his family. Their dead bodies have been found in an air raid shelter. The commander of the German garrison at Pilsen shoots himself after surrendering to General Patten. Runstedt weeps over surrender. (He is one of the many German generals who are POWs in our country. He said, 'It is not the Wehrmacht that is to blame. The political leaders of our country were bad.')

In Count Schwerin von Krosigk's broadcast as foreign minister in the new German government set up by Admiral Donitz (Hitler's reputed successor), I read no word of repentance for all the misery and bloodshed they have brought on the world, nor any recognition of their unprovoked and unwarrantable aggression on unarmed, unprepared and peace-loving peoples, whose countries they overran and mercilessly bombed in their first great onslaught and conquest of Western Europe and later. He speaks of 'six years of heroic struggle' and pleads for his people to make 'justice the guiding principle'. Three stars must guide us, he says, through the dark future. Three stars which have always been the essence of the genuine German nature – unity, justice and liberty.

This – after the appalling conditions found recently by the Allied armies in the vile Nazi concentration camps, evidence of the enslavement and torture of their captives from all over Europe, millions of them employed (as Paul seems to have been) in slave labour; and the awful records of their Gestapo and their mass murder of the Jewish people, whose blood now cries out from the ground for justice.

Krosigk ends by saying, 'May God not forsake us in our distress.' But it was they who had forsaken him. 'There is no God

but Hitler,' said a young Nazi fanatic the other day as he refused
to take an oath in the customary way by kissing the Bible.

Forty years ago, when Henry and I sailed in a Nordischer Lloyd
liner from Japan to Australia, one of the German officers said to
us, 'No thinking German believes in God. We are all followers of
Nietzsche.' The 'superman' theory was just beginning to develop
then, and its ultimate evolution formed Hitler's concept of the
super race.

The day ended with an excellent radio programme, *Tribute to
the King*, from his people all over the world and from representatives of all the services. (Was I partial in my opinion that the tribute of the Navy was the best of all? I felt very proud of being a
humble unit in the Senior Service.) And then the King himself gave
a very fine broadcast to all his people throughout the world to end
a memorable day.

'Let us thank God for his mercies, and in this hour of victory,
commit ourselves and our new task to the guidance of that same
strong hand.'

July 2nd, 1945, The Bath Chronicle

*Sir – Would you kindly permit space for a plea for the better
care and upkeep of Bath cemeteries? Present-day shortage of
labour is not wholly an explanation of their neglect.*

  *The situation of so many of the cemeteries is incomparable,
with superb vistas of the city and surrounding country, but
within the cemetery confines there are weeds, overgrowth and
dilapidations, where there should be beauty, order and
harmony, befitting to a garden of God.*

  *I plead that in the re-planning of Bath, the beautifying of its
cemeteries may be given consideration. Both past and future are
part of the eternal present.*

  G. Grattan Guinness
  33 Richmond Place

July 29th, 1945

My job at the Admiralty came to its natural conclusion, as of course it would, on July 10th. My immediate concern was to find somewhere to live, not easy for an elderly lady, alone, and of reduced means, my annuity worth even less than before this last war. I discovered a vacancy for a housekeeper at Drayton Court in Somerset, the very grand vicarage of the Eastments. He is the youngest son of a family who have been lords of the manor there for some centuries and are patrons of the church. It's hard to believe such appointments still happen in this day and age.

It was meant to be a trial. I have to say it is exactly that. I am not used to moving in these exalted circles, in being treated as 'staff'. The Eastments strike me as superficial rather than spiritual – the church, and the exceptionally large endowments it adds to the vicar's personal coffers, merely a means to their busy social life.

On Thursday last (26th) I listened in my room to the astonishing election results. After Churchill's marvellous premiership and war leadership, we could not credit that the country would throw him out.

On reflection, however, it is possibly the best thing that could happen; for with a majority of over 152 it is the greatest challenge and chance the Labour Party could have had.

Any government has an unenviable task ahead, both at home and abroad. There will be unprecedented problems to face, and it is doubtful if Churchill, now he has turned seventy, could have stood up to the strain. Better his sun should set in a halo of glory than a holocaust of adversity and, perhaps, failure. Let the younger party and generation (two thirds of the party are under thirty) now shoulder the responsibilities.

August 6th, 1945

The atomic bomb is heralded as the greatest invention of all time. Today it is the greatest weapon of destruction. It has obliterated the town of Hiroshima and is said to be the certain end of the Japanese war. Its blast is 2,000 times greater than any RAF explosive bomb.

By strange irony an Austrian Jewish woman, Lise Meitner, expelled by Hitler, is stated to be the mathematician whose research work provided the starting point for its development. It is interesting to recall Madame Curie's part in the discovery of uranium, and now this new development in which yet another woman has played so great a part.

The predictions of the future use of this wonderful discovery open up possibilities of unimaginable wonders when atomic power will be applied constructively. 'The universal stuff of the universe at our command.'

August 17th, 1945

Left Drayton Court today. The little venture has not been a great success and so I am now in Sanderstead with Paul and Jean while I wait to discover where I should go next. Paul has taken on the job as priest-in-charge of the little church there. He is currently editing some writing he began in the prison camp – weaving the four Gospels into one story.

Christmas Day, 1945

'Hold fast by the spirit that refuses to admit defeat; by the faith that never falters; by the hope that cannot be quenched. Let us have no fear of the future, but think of it as an opportunity and an adventure.' So says the King.

Just before Christmas Paul left for Geneva for a four-month assignment, editing *World Communiqué*, the YMCA's bi-monthly international magazine, highlighting its work with the many displaced persons and refugees the war has left behind in its wake like so much flotsam and jetsam on the beach. It is very hard for the little family to have to spend Christmas without him, but Jean is as stoical as ever.

On January 9th I move to Amersham, in response to an advert to look after the Misses Gee, two dear little old Buckinghamshire ladies.

My Nomadic And Transitory Life
1946–54

January, 1946

I visit my little family at Chiddingstone Castle when I can get away for a weekend. I do so love being with them. The girls are growing up fast. I sat four-year-old Chloe on the floor and brushed her lovely hair – a hundred times, as I did to mine when I was a girl. The sweet little thing almost fell asleep.

I fear my constant prattle irritates my dear daughters-in-law and grandchildren, who find it hard to follow an adult interchange of ideas at such a young age. But there is so much I want to tell them, and so little opportunity. The Misses Gee show little interest in conversation, which is a great pity.

May 13th, 1946

In April I was informed that the Misses Gee had no further need of my ministrations, and I was at a loss to know where to go, Paul having just moved his family out to Geneva when his 'assignment' with the YMCA became a permanent post. So I did what I always do, took myself to Ruth and Arthur's. They have finally retired to Eastbourne after fifty years' work in the church at home and abroad, and have settled into their own house on Calverley Road.

All their sentimental past which a large vicarage can accommodate is now crammed into a small suburban semi. From the outside no one would ever believe that the inside is Uganda in miniature. The narrow passage from the door to the living room

Ruth and Arthur

is lined with African spears, the living room crammed with glass cabinets displaying elephant tusks, African masks, shields and other memorabilia, including a tiger skin one of the chiefs had given Ruth for teaching him to read and write. Every shelf is covered with African knick-knacks, and in the corners, more weapons. I have to negotiate my way carefully to the fireplace for fear I may be impaled on the way.

I was becoming heartily weary of being a homeless nomad, when something happened which I had always longed for. I was offered a sunny bed-sitting-room in 'The Abbey', 15 Carew Road, just around the corner from Arthur and Ruth. My new landlady, a widow named Mrs Florence Liebenrood, is a friend of theirs through her long support for their work in Uganda. She is the daughter of Sir Charles Tritton, former MP for Norwood, and once Vice President of the Church Missionary Society. Her husband John was raised at Prospect House, a large Regency manor in extensive parkland, which now belongs to the Reading Corporation. She lives very modestly at 'The Abbey', and is a dear soul, well read and interesting, and so we get on extremely well.

September 16th, 1946

So this is what 1946 has brought me – my new God-given abode in Eastbourne.

I am amused to notice that this year is one of those multiples of seven. Seven has been a special number all through my life, bringing me good things. I was born in 1876, the seventh child, married (without any planning) on the seventh day of the seventh month, for seven years, and scores of little happy incidents and successes came in periods related to the number seven. When I think back to my childhood and of how I laughed at my Grandfather Holmes for saying all the mysteries of the Bible could be unlocked by the holy number seven!

This is also my seventieth year and it has brought me this present blessing – a lovely room in a home-like house, with its dear hostess's lifelong Christian associations – and with the Guinness family specifically. She once stayed at Cliff College in Derbyshire. Her kindness has fulfilled to the uttermost God's promise to the fatherless and the widow.

My next septennial year will be 1953. I wonder what that will bring? Maybe life's last great adventure? The trans-terrestrial flight? How wonderful!

November 17th, 1946

After reading the special number of *The Record* on the rebuilding of Coventry I had a very deep sense, all through the sleepless night, of the great spiritual import of this epoch.

Henry foresaw it – an 'approaching end of the age' – and although he saw it in the theological, or rather eschatological terms of his century, yet many of his conclusions went far beyond his interpretations of his own times. He anticipated 1945 as a significant terminal year, heralding the end of the great imperial dynasties. And so it proved. Not only the end of World War II, but the beginning of the United Nations and all that may come of it. But, deeper still, that inauguration of a new outlook among the churches, of which Coventry Cathedral, with its ministry of reconciliation, is one of the many manifestations; but above and beyond that, a great awakening amongst individuals as to the spiritual import of this new age.

January 21st, 1947

I have my cosy little bedsit and am more content than I have been for many a year. Once a week I dine with Ruth and her children and grandchildren. My increasingly failing hearing rather cuts me off from the general conversation, and the children do so laugh when I make an inappropriate response.

We listen to the nine o'clock news on the radio and then have prayers, Arthur in his big chair on one side of the fireplace next to the bookcase, so that he can reach the Bibles and prayer books. The young kneel, but I fear if I got down I should never get up again. How Ruth manages it with the arthritis in her hip, I fail to comprehend.

February 13th, 1947

Our country is passing through another great crisis, due to post-war conditions, primarily, but greatly accentuated by a continuous spell of very cold weather and heavy snow that has prevented the transport of coal and threatened all the electricity and gas supplies throughout the country. Two million workers are now unemployed as a result and we are all back on wartime lighting restrictions, and worse – as I do not think we then had candles in place of electric light in all the shops.

The Admiralty and War Office have been called on to help with transport and daily conferences of a Joint Committee under Prime Minister Attlee's chairmanship are being held at 10 Downing Street. Many train services are cancelled. Publications of all periodicals are forbidden, dog racing banned, and many orders under our old wartime defence regulations have been reinstated. It is truly a case of 'as you were', but a little more so. Cigarettes and beer, it is said, will be finished in two weeks. We now touch the rock-bottom of our material prosperity.

May, 1947

THE SCHOOLS' HANDBOOK

Long Dene School, Chiddingstone Castle, Kent
Incorporated as a non-profit-making Limited Company

Directors:
J.C. Guinness BA and Karis Guinness R.G.H. Job, BSc

This community with a present membership of 30 adults and 90 children is engaging in a double task. Its first concern is the fullest possible education of all its members; but closely related to this is its experiment in the creating of a way of life based on the association of families into a larger unit, co-operative in the work of administration, teaching, domestic management, production and husbandry.

Self-disciplined and self-reliant, the older children learn in small groups, highly qualified tuition being combined with exceptional facilities for music, arts and crafts.

Food reform and vegetarian menus include a plentiful supply of milk, fruit and eggs, salads and honey.

At Long Dene spiritual connection, which John refers to as 'nature mysticism' – a return to the simple life of nature – is essential for a balanced growth of body, mind and spirit. The children spend most of their time out of doors, learning organic gardening, farming, woodwork and building, and when indoors, music, eurythmics and other creative outlets. John and Karis believe that education must encourage self-responsibility and mutual respect. Unlike most public schools, no caning. Discipline consists of cleaning out the pig sty, or repairing the windows they have broken.

Many of the educational establishments I have worked for would find their methods unconventional, to say the least. But John and Karis's philosophy is much kinder to the child. Nonetheless, my own work in various educational establishments makes me wonder whether the children will be adequately prepared for Oxbridge. And if not, will their parents mind?

September, 1947

I have been sewing – making six tiny dolls for sweet little Chloe, who has been admitted to hospital with anaemia. Food rationing barely provides enough minerals for a growing child. Such a worry for John and Karis, especially when they have an entire community of children to care for.

I have embroidered each of the dolls' dresses in different colours, a labour of love but a pleasure to do. I hope they will amuse her. I do so love giving presents. Not much else I can do for my little family these days.

Thursday, October 30th, 1947

The Daily Mail
The Gospel as a Thriller

The Bishop of Chelmsford looks at a new book people will find difficult to put down – the work of a POW padre.

A great many well-known and even famous books were written in prison, Bunyan's *Pilgrim's Progress*, Oscar Wilde's *De Profundis*, Hitler's *Mein Kampf* to name but a few.

We have another example in Paul Guinness' *The Christ of All Nations*, a most remarkable and striking performance which will attract widespread attention.

The author was for several years a prisoner of war, first in Italy and then in Germany, where, with 80,000 compatriots, he arrived after a nine-day journey in cattle trucks, without proper food or sanitation.

The prisoners were allowed to take with them only the barest necessities, but some of them were careful to take their New Testaments.

Working throughout the winter of 1943 in a freezing, deserted shed, the only place where solitude could be found in a camp of 2,000 men, the author set about his task.

His materials were a pencil and a few torn scraps of paper. Of reference books he had none. But he has produced a book of outstanding interest, the main purpose of which is to present the Gospel story, as told by the four evangelists, in one connected whole, by a process of reconstruction and chronological arrangement.

This reconstruction of the great story has nothing of the nerveless and anaemic piety which so often passes for religion in these days. The Christ stands out as the Supreme Hero, leading a handful of simple people in a campaign against incredible odds.

It is a vivid and admirable performance which seizes and holds the imagination in a most remarkable fashion. People who might never feel the inclination to read the Gospels in the familiar form will find it difficult to put this book down. It is not an overstatement to say that Guinness has transformed the Gospel narratives into a religious thriller which holds the attention from cover to cover. It is very surprising that no one has thought of doing this kind of thing in this particular way long before now.[13]

I am so proud of Paul – his achievement of far greater import than my poor attempt at writing. His dreadful wartime experiences have not been in vain. The Bishop is right – it is a marvellous read.

THE GOSPEL AS A THRILLER
Produced in a prison camp

A GREAT many well - known and even famous books were written in prison. Sir Walter Raleigh's "History of the World," Bunyan's "Pilgrim's Progress," Oscar Wilde's "De Profundis," Hitler's "Mein Kampf" are a few which immediately occur to the mind.

We have another example in Paul Guinness's "The Christ of All Nations,'" a most remarkable and striking performance which will attract widespread attention.

The author was for several years a prisoner of war, first in Italy, and, after the collapse of Italy, in Germany, where, with 80,000 compatriots, he arrived after a nine-day journey in cattle-trucks.

Born in a shed

THE prisoners were allowed to take with them only the barest necessities, but some of them were careful to take their New Testaments.

The BISHOP OF CHELMSFORD

looks at a new book "people will find difficult to put down" —the work of a PoW padre

story has nothing of the nerveless and anemic piety which so often passes for religion in these days. The Christ stands out as the Supreme Hero leading a handful of simple people in a campaign against incredible odds.

It is a vivid and admirable performance which seizes and holds the imagination in a most remarkable fashion. People who might never feel the inclination to read the Gospels in the familiar form will find it difficult to put this book down.

Numerous harmonies of the

no reference of any kind to the first 30 years of Christ's life. They are fragmentary narratives of incidents and instruction put together with no continuity and little chronological sequence.

The purpose of the authors was achieved by collecting those sayings of Christ and by vivid word-sketches of outstanding events which they had either heard or seen themselves or which had been passed on to them by word of mouth by eye-witnesses.

Nurtured in truth

INCIDENTALLY, that is striking evidence of the genuineness of the record, for no inventor of a fictitious character would adopt such a haphazard method.

The writers of the Gospels were concerned to tell only what they knew, or what was recorded by recognised authorities, of the central figure of Christ.

But their transparent honesty and ignorance of editorial method have provided the material for such a rearrangement of the Gospels as Guinness has given us.

He has taken the New Testament records and as far as possible put all that the Four Evangelists have given us into an ordered sequence.

November 20th, 1947

The wedding of our Princess Elizabeth to the Duke of Edinburgh in this time of such austerity and gloom is, as the *Sunday Times* said at the weekend, 'a rainbow's promise, framed in a dark and cloudy sky, that the ancient polity of England which has endured for a thousand years shall continue to endure'.

Listening to our young princess on the wireless on her twenty-first birthday, I could not but reflect on how enduring and living a thing this human tradition of our English monarchy has become, despite the rather large hiccough caused by her uncle.

But this modest, gentle, unassuming English girl spoke to us with the same accents of love and faith as her great namesake and predecessor. 'I declare before you all that my whole life, whether it be long or short, shall be devoted to your service and to the service of our great imperial family to which we all belong. I shall not have the strength to carry out this resolution alone unless you join in it with me.'

It is in this spirit that we, her father's people, join in wishing her all the happiness and strength that a true marriage can bring, and God's grace for the task before her.

May 14th, 1948

The State of Israel has formally been declared by David Ben-Gurion, the Executive Head of the World Zionist Organisation, coming into effect on termination of the British Mandate at midnight today. Did I ever think to see this day in the exact year Henry had foretold, based on his studies of the prophetic books?

Geraldine Taylor, at the ripe old age of eighty-six and living since Howard's sad demise with her nephew, the Revd Gordon, summed up my feelings exactly when she declared, 'Lord, now lettest thou thy servant depart in peace.'

My generation is being gathered homeward one by one. First Percy Hurditch, our late eldest brother Percy's only child – barely reaching his thirtieth birthday. And now dear Wyn – Percy Wyndham Guinness, Henry's nephew. I recall such happy memories of the dear old rectory in Rathdrum, where the boys and I spent such happy times immediately after Henry's death, with Wyn, his nephew, a fine young man, just a few years before his heroic actions during the First War. He was retired from the army within only a fortnight of a full colonelcy.

And then four months spent with him and dear Flo in Helwan in 1939. And a delightful long weekend when they came to see us in August last year at Eastbourne, their first visit after the long war years in Egypt. We had such a lovely family reunion at a beach picnic on the Saturday with John and Karis and their two girls, and Paul (on a visit to England from his post in Geneva).

Wyn died as he would have wished, working to the end. He and Flo were having a much needed rest up in the hills of Cyprus. A few English people in the hotel asked if they could have a little service, which he gladly arranged. He passed over to the other side shortly after the service and was laid to rest in Kyrenia.

February 13th, 1949

I am constantly coming across the word 'existentialism', both in books and magazines. Yet when asked by a lady in Belsaye last week what I thought it meant, I really couldn't give an exact definition. Now I read in today's *Sunday Times*, 'There are no rules: the Greek ethic, the Mosaic decalogue, Christian tradition, are thrown aside . . . life is a becoming, but as to what it is becoming, they keep an open mind.' I take it that the central point of existentialism is the necessity and freedom of choice. This seems to me the same challenge as Moses set before his people. 'Choose ye this day whom ye will serve.'

February 15th, 1949

The first session of the newly elected Israeli Assembly was opened today by the President, Dr Chaim Weizmann. He said, 'It is with a deep sense of this holy moment that I am opening the first parliament in the eternal capital of Jerusalem. Israel offers the hand of friendship to all peace-loving countries.'

In connection with this historic event, one should read all that has led up to its fulfilment in Dr Weizmann's autobiography. Yet when I say all, I must go back to Moses, to Abraham, Isaac and the Old Testament prophets, and then to AD 70 and the banishment of the Jewish people to the Diaspora. Then look forward to what St Paul writes in his letter to the Romans of all that is yet to be fulfilled.

My Paul, with his father's calling to 'understand and tell', as his step-aunt Lucy called it, is in correspondence with Dr Weizmann about just these matters.

March 27th, 1949

Amused to read the actor, film star, director, manager Sir Laurence Olivier described as a gale of activity. What a phrase! My Paul is also a 'gale of activity' and always has been. I only hope he won't blow himself out. Thank God he has within him the power of an endless life.

June 8th, 1949

We are once more in life and death. Paul and Jean over in Geneva were blessed there with a son on May 22nd – Peter.

Then, on June 6th, our beloved Geraldine, the last surviving child of Henry's first marriage, 'departed in peace' as she was ready to do. To most people she was the writer Mrs Howard Taylor. Her life of her father-in-law, the great pioneer missionary Hudson Taylor, sold in the hundreds of thousands. As did her biographies of the Chinese Pastor Hsi, and of the martyred John and Betty Stam.

She was also known for her great gift of public speaking, holding her own on the platform of many conferences alongside some of the foremost male preachers. No one and nothing fazed her – the sweetness of her smile, disguising a formidable Niagara-like force within, could turn granite into putty. She was a tremendous role model for younger women, and a great mentor to Paul, for whom she opened numerous doors when he was a raw young preacher fresh out of theological college. I shall never forget her kindness in adding to my own annuity the legacy left to her by her father because my boys needed it more. We shall never see her like again.

October 3rd, 1949

The golden wedding day of Jean's parents, Mr and Mrs Elliot, and she has flown over from Geneva to Boston, USA to be with her family for the celebrations at Stowe, Vermont, where they have a quiet holiday home.

I sent them my congratulations in the following lines, hurriedly composed:

Fifty golden years –
How soon they speed,
Smiles mingled with tears,
Plenitude and need
Highest hopes and fears;
Yet still we plead
For life – The compass steers
Our barque square-rigged,
Bound for eternal shores.

Jean returned by plane, flying at an altitude of twenty-one thousand feet, above the Atlantic gales and tempestuous seas. What a marvel air transport is. Paul, meanwhile, was twenty-one hours on a boat on the English Channel from Dunkirk to Dover, usually a two-hour journey, as he came from Geneva to meet her.

It was a great joy for me to see them both, even for so short a visit, after such a long parting – over two years.

October 6th, 1949

Dr Emily Daymond, my neighbour, who lived in one of the flats next door, has passed away. Dr Daymond was the first woman in the country to hold a doctorate in music. It was earned in 1901, but took another twenty years before Oxford granted her the privilege of owning the degree she had won. Meanwhile, she taught piano and harmony at the Royal College of Music, then became secretary to Sir Hubert Parry, whose student she had been and whom she admired enormously, collaborating with him in a number of his compositions.

She had become a dear friend since my move to The Abbey. I used to pop in on her, and she would play to me on her precious grand piano. She told me she often got in touch with Parry, now long deceased. He was apparently an atheist in his lifetime, but a spiritualist like her after his death, and in his recent communications with her, had asked her to make that known!

January 3rd, 1950

Flo – my exact contemporary in years – has gone, and barely a year after her brother Wyn. The last link of my generation with my beloved Henry's family has finally been broken and leaves me with a great sense of loss.

I think of her as I first knew her in the Rathdrum Rectory in 1910 – a village rector's daughter, simple, kindly, unsophisticated. How good she was with the boys. What happy days we spent together.

The First World War that gave her brother the DSO cost her any last hope of finding a suitable husband, and there followed many years of devoted nursing care for her aged parents.

After their death her life's horizon widened. First she worked at the Sandes Soldiers' Homes in Ireland and India, an organisation of some thirty or so Christian centres attached to army barracks, devoted to the recreation and general welfare of the military. Then, after her brother Wyn became a widower, she joined him in Egypt, supporting his work as chaplain to the English churches there. During the Second World War, with thousands of troops stationed in Egypt, he and Flo were in the thick of active service.

When Wyn died, Flo lost her home, her work, her reason for living, and went into a nursing home at 3 Parklands in Surbiton. But even there, the astonishing thing was the large number of friends who visited daily – not just from nearby, but many she had known in Egypt. Letters came to her from all over the world – Egypt, Abyssinia, South Africa, India. When I visited her the nurses said to me, 'Miss Guinness has a birthday every day.'

She was called home just before Christmas, December 9th, but Christmas greetings still came pouring in and her cousin Pearl and I have been dealing with them ever since. The replies all strike a similar note. I quote, as an example, one from an ex-serviceman who was stationed in Egypt during the war.

May I offer you my very real sympathy in your great loss. I have suffered a little too, because to me Miss Guinness and her brother were the personification of what God wishes us all to be. I knew both of them while I was in Cairo during the war and their vicarage in Ma'adi became for me a second home. I know there will be thousands who will be the poorer for the loss of that lovely friendship she extended to everyone. I know I am one. I can only pray that her example will always be with me on my way through this life.

Yet another wrote:

Racked by illness and constant pain, yet there was something about her that defied definition in words. Her spirit carried her through situation after situation, any one of which ought to have killed her. I have seen her at a Christmas party, a perfect hostess, giving herself unstintingly to each guest and yet, as I touched her hand I knew she had a high fever. Till midnight she acted her part and no one knew of the effort, so completely did she forget herself, but the next day she was in bed, paying for what she had given so lavishly.

On the morning she passed over (before I knew of it) I was reading the psalm for the day in my prayer book – Psalm 45, and for reasons I know not, became deeply conscious of her. It was almost as if her presence was in the room as I read, 'She shall be brought unto the King . . . with joy and gladness . . . and shall enter into the King's palace.' It was thus no surprise when, that afternoon, I received the telegram to say she had peacefully passed away at 3 a.m. that very morning.

So many of my contemporaries are passing on that I begin to feel the pull is now stronger on the Other Side. Oh, to be spared a waiting time of uselessness. To be called home the moment active service is past.

I have just read a very apposite quote by the priest and poet

George Macdonald: 'If I can put one touch of a rosy sunset into the life of any man or woman of my care, I shall feel that I have worked with God.'

April 3rd, 1950

I note with interest some words of the Archbishop of Canterbury at a conference on mental health and the family. He apparently impressed on the company that in every field of study there is an extreme danger of using a multitude of words to express very little. It was due to two causes: the dreadful pressure of work – the more tired one was, the more words one was likely to use; and the introduction of the typewriter and the secretary.

Long before the Archbishop expressed his opinion, I had often observed that excessive loquacity was indicative of physical fatigue or nervous exhaustion. I have suffered from this curious condition myself, but now I live alone and not in the crowds of previous years, I am being cured – by solitude and quietness. Sadly, that makes me far more susceptible to the fault in others. And I long to give them a holiday too.

June 12th, 1950

I wrote to the Nestlé company suggesting that their milk tins might be made with a deeper ridge to enable one to use the modern key type of tin opener in place of the old-fashioned ox-headed one that left a horrible jagged edge to the lid when cut open and involved the probably septic or germ-infected blade coming into contact with the milk.

Their reply (typically English for a French company – for the English market, I presume), after thanking me for my kindly interest, said that they had appreciated the difficulty, but their particular packing 'has a vested goodwill extending over 70 years, and there is always a section of the public who are inclined to be sceptical if not suspicious when an old friend appears in a new guise'.

Honestly! The germ of our country's decline is to be found in just this attitude of mind. Change nothing. It applies to everything, from religion (prayer book reform rejected by the House of Commons) to education, the Admiralty and every department of our civic life – this 'vested goodwill' extending over centuries and hindering reform.

Hence it is that world leadership has passed to America.

July 23rd, 1950

Borrowed a friend's car and motored to Chiddingstone Castle. It was a delight to see my family and the school community flourishing. After lunch we witnessed the Juniors' end of term play, *The Sleeping Beauty*, in which Chloe (aged eight) took the named part and Anthea (aged two and a quarter) was among the fairies. She stood still sucking her thumb and admired all the wonderful stage setting, quite unmindful of the audience, and at the close, when the curtain began to fall, she rushed out through the backstage door. This was her first appearance, and disappearance, before the footlights. John wrote the play and Karis composed the music. The dresses and the stage setting were beautiful – the children's own handiwork.

The children call me 'Little Granny', as Gene, their maternal granny, and now a teacher at the school, is somewhat larger than I – which wouldn't be difficult.

Some of the rooms at the castle still haven't been painted – not enough funds, and when it rains everyone rushes for bowls to catch the water that leaks through the top landing ceiling. Still, it is such a happy community – and that is more important.

November 11th, 1950

What a strange faculty is memory. In our advancing years it becomes so weakened that even important and impressive news and events are quickly forgotten, and it is increasingly difficult to retain the memory of one's reading. How extraordinary in contrast is the vivid memory one has of the most trivial and foolish happenings of youth. Often there floats up into my mind some ridiculous piece of doggerel that Henry wrote for me, most of them totally unprintable. (All these memories centre around one's love life – the 'libido' of the psychologists!) Enough said.

December 2nd, 1950

My seventy-fourth birthday! I began the delights on the 1st with a roast chicken luncheon and a glass of sherry at No. 11, as I call Arthur and Ruth's little home, where love dwells.

Then, to my joy, John gave me a telephone call that evening to say that he and Karis would motor over from Chiddingstone to have lunch with me on my birthday. Not very easy to provide a lunch for three on the last day of the last week of the rations period, when there is nothing more to draw upon. However, I managed to provide a three-course luncheon and our hunger was satisfied with chicken soup, sausages and bacon, tomatoes, celery and potatoes and a Christmas pudding and coffee. They came laden with gifts, including three dozen of the renowned Long Dene new-laid eggs and some beautifully cultivated chrysanthemums, and a charming piece of Dartington pottery. The morning post brought me six cards and letters of good wishes.

January 28th, 1951

What a week of tragic events. Terrible avalanches in Switzerland, the Austrian Tyrol and Italy resulting in hundreds of deaths. In New Guinea the eruption of Mount Lamington which has wiped out half the population. Here, over a thousand deaths from influenza and ten from smallpox. And then the disquieting reports of our disagreement with America over the China and Korean situation, and America insisting that China be called an aggressor. Attlee, our Prime Minister, tells us we must face 'serious sacrifices' for the rearmament programme now that Marshall Aid[14] has ceased. So the meat ration is to be reduced again to 8d a week – what an anticlimax.

I am wondering what kind of a world I hand on to my grandchildren. Not what I might have wished, that's for sure. But there is nothing new under the sun, and I must trust each generation will be given the strength to face whatever struggles it must – as we were.

May 4th, 1951

The Festival of Britain was inaugurated today by the King from the steps of St Paul's after the service in the cathedral. Another service at the Royal Festival Hall in the evening, at which Archbishop Fisher preached again, commenced with the singing of the hymn 'All People that on Earth Do Dwell', accompanied by the orchestra and choirs conducted by Sir Adrian Boult and Sir Malcolm Sargent.

As I listened, even over the wireless the inspiration and glory came through.

July 2nd, 1951

Mrs Liebenrood informed me this morning that she is giving over this house to a missionary society. It is a staggering blow. Of course, I shall have to find another home. I prayed to be delivered from all anxiety and fear, turned to the psalm for today (Psalm 9) and read, 'The Lord will be a defence, even a refuge, in the due time of trouble. And they that know thy name will put their trust in Thee, for Thou, Lord, has never failed them that seek Thee.'

Whenever I feel downcast about my future, I turn to the Psalms and am impressed by the frequent recurrence of references to God's never-failing providence, and the exhortation to patience. Am I failing in making such constant efforts to find a home? Should one just be still and do nothing? Perplexing, this.

August 19th, 1951

In my daily reading today from *Year of Grace*, this from St John of the Cross: 'Keep your heart at peace; let nothing in this world disturb it: all things have an end. To endure all things with an equable and peaceful mind not only brings many blessings to the soul, but also enables us, in the midst of our own difficulties, to have a clear judgement about them, and to minister a fitting remedy for them.'

August 20th, 1951

Received this morning four delightful letters from my family on holiday, camping for a month in a bombed-out villa at Boulouris on the Côte d'Azur, each one giving a graphic description of the joy of meeting after all these years. Karis and Jean haven't seen each other since the end of the war, before Anthea or Peter were born.

It is all so lovely, so exhilarating, to think of them all together in such perfect surroundings, that I became infected with their enjoyment and lived again in memory the days of long ago spent in my beloved France and Switzerland, knowing I shall probably never go there again.

November 3rd, 1951

From my new address – 7 Southcliffe Avenue, Eastbourne.

On the last page of this current diary I must put on record the wonderful fulfilment of all the promises I received in connection with my having to give up my home at The Abbey after five years, and the strange last experience I had there.

On Friday, October 26th, I was feeling particularly downcast and depressed over the difficulty of finding accommodation (after having visited or corresponded with forty-three places or people), when I turned on the wireless at 8 a.m., ostensibly to hear the results of the election, but instead, a very beautiful and cultured voice twice repeated, 'The Lord will help thee.'

They were the last words of the broadcast in the *Lift Up Your Heart* series and it was as if someone was in my room, speaking those words directly to me. I was filled with a new sense of peace and joy.

A week later I was here, in my new home, a private guesthouse. 'Thou, Lord, hast never failed them that seek Thee.'

January 2nd, 1952

I start my new diary with immense joy at the news from Long Dene, expressed in John's 'Parents Letter' telling of their decision to start building the 'power house' as he calls it – first, in a literal 'upper room' in the castle, and later on, as the means are forth-coming, a separate chapel. Many parents have sent gifts for the refurbishment of this upper room and they now have sufficient hymn books for fifteen and prayer books for everyone. Arthur, the wood carver and carpentry teacher, has been making a very beau-tiful cherrywood cross for the table, and my small payment has been used to fund it. Nothing could have given me greater pleas-ure than that gift of a cross, with all its beautiful symbolism and associations.

John has been a seeker after truth for so many years. I am so glad he has discovered a more mystical expression of his faith that satisfies him so thoroughly. Unfortunately, however, some of the staff (convinced atheists, he says) are very unhappy with these developments. His assemblies have always been very eclectic, reflecting all religious traditions and spiritualities, but now, in appearing to submit to government legislation that makes a more Christian act of worship compulsory, the school, they say, will lose its radical edge.

I feel sure that in time they will see the wisdom of his actions.

February 1st, 1952

A private confession following an unhappy incident last week at No. 11 (my name for Ruth and Arthur's home), when my anger was raised on hearing that Larema had sent her mother a large box of mending to be done – knowing that Ruth has cataracts in both eyes. Ruth, naturally, hotly defended her daughter, so I wrote to her to say:

> *Darling, I cannot go to Communion on Sunday without asking your forgiveness (which I know you will give) for what I said the other day. What I could never want to do is 'come between you and your children'. I love you, and them, too much for that. My reactions are solely due to all I know of what you*

have done for them and given to them for nearly half a century.
But my resolve is never to express myself again, realising as I
now do, that you have your reward in living that beautiful
prayer:

> *'Teach us to give, and not to count the cost,*
> *To fight, and not to heed the wounds,*
> *To toil and not to look for rest,*
> *To labour, and not to seek a reward.'*

My stupid mouth moves before it engages with my brain. But
Ruth came up this evening with a lovely bunch of snowdrops.
There cannot be anything between us for long. We are too close
for that.

Wednesday, February 6th, 1952

It was announced from Sandringham at 10.45 a.m. today that the
King, who retired to rest last night in his usual health, passed
peacefully away in his sleep early this morning.

The Duke of Edinburgh broke the news to the Princess Elizabeth
in Kenya. The young couple had only left Clarence House eight
days ago for their visits to Nairobi, Ceylon, Australia and New
Zealand. How hard for her. He was only in his fifty-sixth year,
and she adored him, they say. And now she must fly home and as
Queen maintain a brave face before the world, while inside her
heart is breaking.

What an onerous task she has for one so young, and so newly a
mother.

February 25th, 1952

Sir Charles Oman, the Oxford historian, says that to find oneself cited in the *Dictionary of National Biography* is 'equivalent to immortality'. So it is very satisfying to find my name in one of the volumes! But this honour solely as the second wife of the immortal Henry Grattan Guinness, 'by whom he had two sons' (Second Supplement, Vol. II, pp. 175–176).

I recollect that the warden of Wadham said to John, when he was admitted as an undergraduate in 1924, that he would never refuse to accept one whose father's name was in the *DNB* – so it has its advantages.

March 4th, 1952

The foundational thesis of the League of Nations after the last war was that disarmament was the only hope for world peace. Now we have NATO (North Atlantic Treaty Organisation), and their principle is rearmament in order to procure peace. So each country that joins is producing armaments up to the hilt.

In the past thirty-four years we have seen the full swing of the pendulum and who can foretell what may now happen? Last year Parliament voted £1,400,000 for the defence programme. And of course, when I say that all the NATO countries are rearming, that also means Russia and China arm likewise, while the Korean conflict is in full swing. So how can spending so much money on arms contribute to peace?

March 16th, 1952

I went this afternoon to a Chopin recital by Irene Scharrer at the Winter Gardens – a very fine performance. As a Victorian I am a great lover of Chopin's music. The next generation swung over to

Wagner, but two world wars have killed off that craze fortunately. Our grandchildren are being raised on Benjamin Britten and Michael Tippett – but I am still enamoured with the eighteenth- and nineteenth-century composers.

During the interval my mind ran over all the great musicians I have heard in my time – Paderewski (my own personal perfor- mance, when I visited his home in Switzerland), Pachmann (who was so mad that he had to have two attendants with him when he played at the Albert Hall), Moseiwitsch, Myra Hess, Kreisler, the great Suggia on the cello, Adelina Patti, Dame Nellie Melba, Clara Butt, Tetrazzini, Chaliapin, Sir Henry Wood, Sir Adrian Boult, Sir Thomas Beecham, Barbirolli. I have been blessed indeed to be treated to such perfection.

July 7th, 1952

My accommodation at a private hotel has proved too much for my means and I am therefore housekeeper once more in a shared flat with an elderly gentleman called Mr Gunther. Caring for the needs of men of any age can be onerous, but in ripe old age their demands are endless. I do hope I have the patience and stamina for it. It is disappointing to lose my inde- pendence at this stage of life, but I must do my best to lay something by for my boys.

March 22nd, 1953

Another of those septennial years. I had written in my diary of 1946 that I wondered what this next such year would bring. It brought me a return to The Abbey on January 9th after a mere seven months with Mr Gunther. A veritable release.

When weeks and months elapse without my having made a single entry in my little diary, it becomes almost impossible (especially for a seventy-seven-year-old lady, whose memory is only one of her many failing powers) to recall events of the past three months. Probably, the best thing to record is what so many others have said of this year – that it is 'A Year of Destiny'. The many signs that it is and will be are reflected in every country throughout the world, and are commented on in the press and on all those important public occasions when speeches are made by leading public men.

For us in England it is the coronation of our dear Queen, and for the United States, the election of President Eisenhower, who had the largest popular vote ever received by a presidential candidate.

I feel inclined to add a very personal note on what this year has meant to me so far – unbelievably, a return to The Abbey once again, which I left so sadly two years ago for very different, but rather unsatisfactory accommodation – one a guesthouse, the other a shared flat just down the road. Finally, Mrs Liebenrood's arrangement with the missionary society fell through.

So, after seven months at 7 Southcliffe Avenue, then seven months at 56 Carew Rd, in my seventy-seventh year, I have returned. And today, my appointed reading for Passion Sunday is, 'And he shall shew you a large upper room, furnished . . .' which is exactly what I have.

March 3rd, 1953

Mrs Liebenrood confided in me today that she is deeply worried about her son John. He was an Anglican clergyman, vicar of Christ Church, Bromley, for eight years, but felt pressurised to leave the ministry altogether as, to her profound dismay, his theological views have become somewhat 'unorthodox'. He has found work difficult to come by, and she wonders, from what I have said of the progressive nature of Long

Dene, whether John might not have a vacancy that may prove helpful to them both. I promised I would discuss it with him.

March 24th, 1953

At 11.15 this morning a bulletin was posted outside Marlborough House: 'While sleeping peacefully, Queen Mary died at 10.20 a.m.'

How old it makes me seem that during my lifetime three kings and three queens have died – Queen Victoria, King Edward VII, Queen Alexandra, King George V, King George VI and now our beloved Queen Mary. I was amongst the throngs in The Strand, seated in a chemist's window, to see her on her wedding day. I was also a spectator at her silver wedding in 1918, and then at their Silver Jubilee in 1935. And now, from the quiet comfort of my room at The Abbey, I read of her passing and all of the wonderful tributes paid from every quarter of the globe. I always remember a remark she once made to the Dean of Westminster at the time of her great sorrow over her son's abdication, 'There is only one way to meet these things and that is to go straight on.'

April 14th, 1953

John Liebenrood has joined the staff at Long Dene. There were no vacancies, but John, with his usual liberality of spirit, has taken him on, as bee-keeper!

They got along famously when they met, kindred spirits in their view that the spiritual needs of the child are far too narrowly served by the church, and so the newly appointed bee-keeper and former clergyman will take over much of the leadership of the 'power house', teaching young people the art of contemplation. John hopes his broad, contemporary approach will silence the few voices that still mumble and rumble about a daily service.

June 3rd, 1953

The great Day has come and gone. I cannot attempt to write about what has been written and said so ably by all the press and participators in the great and glorious ceremony; this will all pass into history. To those of us who could not take a visible part with the crowds of London came the wonders of the wireless, and to those who had the new apparatus: television. It was a triumph on the part of the British Broadcasting Company. Forty-three languages were used in the broadcasts to Europe and the overseas service.

On the eve of the coronation there were two happenings of significance. On Monday night, over the nine o'clock news broadcast, it was said that a double rainbow had shone in great splendour (it is a very ancient belief that this is a good portent), which arched the sky, spanning the space between the Abbey and Buckingham Palace. But the greatest news that came to the Queen was that Mount Everest had been conquered and the summit reached by the British expedition. The story of this triumph by E.P. Hillary and the sherpa Tenzing Norgay, achieved on May 29th, appeared in *The Times* on June 2nd.

The thought occurred to me that in the reign of Queen Victoria we conquered India in the great days of our material prosperity and imperial expansion; it was conquered by our military power and held until India's Day of Independence. Then we lost India, but today we have gained the highest mountain in the world. This is no visible gain, as gain is understood in the marketplace, says *The Times*, but 'these men of valour and resolution are representatives and champions of humanity itself. Their victory is a victory for the human spirit.'

What a gift to lay at the feet of our Queen on the eve of her coronation.

June 4th, 1953

Ruth and I went by coach to London to see the decorations, leaving Eastbourne at 2.15 and returning at 11 p.m. A most enjoyable experience, and great fun seeing the crowds of London and all the gay banners and streamers.

June 7th, 1953

Record-breaking accounts of the speed with which the coronation films are flown to the USA and other parts of the world are being given in the press every day. The first coronation pictures to Australia broke the record for a London to Sydney flight – 53 hours 28 minutes.

The newsreels were being shown in Sydney, Brisbane and Melbourne on Friday evening, a mere three days after the coronation.

June 16th, 1953

Margaret Bondfield, the Labour MP and the first woman to reach Cabinet status, has died today. She was someone I admired. Her strong nonconformist faith and ethic came from her parents, as well as her belief in the dignity of work and the equality of women. Her contact with philanthropists and preachers opened her eyes to the spiritual imperative of social action. Ramsay MacDonald made her Minister of Labour in 1929. She never married, saying she had no vocation to wifehood or motherhood, and that they would have interfered with her career. And to think, I managed both.

July 11th, 1953

It appears John and Karis are now facing grave difficulties at Long Dene. They didn't want to tell me lest I should worry, but finally felt I should know that their hold on the school has become precarious.

According to their letter, a whole host of problems has beset them all at once. First, a full-blown mutiny. Opposition to John's daily 'act of worship' has finally cost him the unity that was the bedrock of the community. John Liebenrood's presence has been a provocative rather than calming influence, his immense popularity with the children deeply resented by the staff. Around a dozen or so are claiming that his guided meditations are a form of brain-washing and therefore morally suspect. They have presented John with a petition, demanding he hand over leadership to the vice principal immediately.

Second, they are in disagreement with his decision to take on some very troubled children which the local authorities have been unable to place. But great changes to the educational system, too numerous for me to mention, have led to an increasing demand for higher academic achievement and better equipment and materials, which John simply cannot afford. Thus the customary applications from doctors, lawyers and even an ambassador or two for their intelligent, artistic offspring had tailed off, leaving John no choice.

In addition, the sponsors of the organic farm have, for financial reasons, decided to withdraw their support, leaving the school without their milk supply and much of their food. The school is run on a shoestring anyway, Karis and John never taking full salaries for themselves.

John says he and Karis decided to resign, then had second thoughts. Why should they, when it was their school? So they have made up their minds to battle on for another year, and with their usual generosity of spirit have allowed their disaffected, unrepentant staff to stay on until they find suitable alternative employment. I'm not sure of the wisdom of such benevolence and fear this may not end well.

Oh, how angry it all makes me. One feels one's children's pain so much more than one's own. And I have nothing to offer by way of advice or consolation. But this much I must say – that in all life's experiences, both tragic or joyous, disheartening and sorrow-making, and even almost overwhelming anxieties, I have always found comfort, consolation and relief when I pray, or turn to my Bible or prayer book, not opening them in a haphazard way, but simply reading the psalms or scriptures appointed for the day.

So today's psalm might have been written with a view to all that is currently happening within my little family. It ends with these words:

> *The Lord sitteth above the water-flood, and*
> *The Lord remaineth King for ever.*
> *The Lord shall give strength unto his people,*
> *The Lord shall give his people the blessing of peace.*

I have sent them both this encouraging quote from Daphne du Maurier's *Mary Anne*, which I am currently reading: 'Never be apprehensive. Never dread the future. A hopeful heart wins three quarters of the battle . . .'

October 25th, 1953

What a time for the increase of women's power and influence in the world: a woman on the throne of Britain and head of the Commonwealth of Nations; a queen on the throne of Holland; a woman (Mrs Pandit, sister of Nehru) President of United Nations; two women USA ambassadors, one to Italy, one to Switzerland, and, we must add, the woman who charmed everyone in the coronation procession, Queen Salote of Tonga, a powerful influence for good in those little islands in the Pacific. And so many more names I could add – even astronomers like Mrs Cecilia Payne-Gaposchkin, a British-born Cambridge graduate, currently Phillips Astronomer at Harvard University.

November 10th, 1953

And now, three international women riders win the main events against the world's male contenders in the New York National Horse Show, including Miss Pat Smythe of the British team. This has never happened before in the seventy-year history of the show.

Among writers, I would mention two outstanding women of great spiritual power (both young) – Simone Weil, who died in 1952, and Elizabeth Myers, who died in 1947. Born in poverty in Ireland to a drunken father, Myers, at the age of thirty, married Littleton Powys, one of the most distinguished schoolmasters of his day. He was over seventy and they enjoyed a mere three and a half years of perfect marital bliss before she died of tuberculosis. I don't need to say how well I understand that kind of passion, even with such an age disparity – even if others do not.

The President of the World Council of Churches is an Indian Christian, Miss Sarah Chakko, Principal of the Isabella Thoburn College in Lucknow, the only woman ever to hold such a position.

It is indeed a new world for women, full of opportunity and challenge. I envy them just a little, but am glad to have lived to see the day.

December 29th, 1953

Splendid news from the USA today that my step-grandson, Henry Kumm, Lucy's eldest son, has been made Director of Research for the Polio Foundation there. Lucy foresaw so clearly, though he was still a small child when she died, that her eldest son would excel in the medical world, and she would have been so proud today.

And I am so proud of my own two boys and of all they have achieved: Paul informing the world of the urgent, ongoing need for post-war reconciliation and refugee work; and John at Long Dene, which has served so many children so well these past years, and where the situation remains critical. He puts on a brave face, but I know my boy is hurting inside and my heart goes out to him.

January 30th, 1954

John says it was not such a good idea to keep on the rebellious staff after all as they are now poisoning the older children with their criticisms, spoiling the happy, open atmosphere that he and Karis have worked so hard to create. He wonders what the children will tell their parents and how it will affect applications for next year.

John Liebenrood has handed in his notice in an attempt to calm troubled waters. Would it were the defiant staff instead. On my many visits they all seemed so accommodating, so pleasant, yet how two-faced and unprofessional they have turned out to be. If only I had the chance to speak my mind.

May 24th, 1954

The three-month Billy Graham Mission at Haringey, North London, ended on Saturday, May 22nd. Despite the rain and cold wind, the Empire Stadium at Wembley was packed to overflowing for the evening meeting; 120,000 people (and at the afternoon meeting at White City, 60,000).

In the royal box were the Lord Mayor of London and Lady Bowater, Mr W.T. Boston, the Sword Bearer, Lord and Lady Luke, Viscount Lambton, Sir John Weir, the Archbishop of Canterbury (Mrs Graham sat next to Mrs Fisher), and a number of MPs and industrialists. In his short address Billy Graham said, 'The past twelve weeks have been the most wonderful and thrilling weeks I have ever known in my life . . .'

As he stood on the podium, in my mind's eye I could not help but see Henry standing there – but in 1859. I was not born then, of course, but I caught the excitement it must have been for my parents in the audience, and for Henry, preaching to such a crowd.

On Sunday Billy Graham went to Oxford to preach at St Aldate's at a service for undergraduates. The church was packed an hour before the service began. Students stood six deep in the aisles. Crowds waited in the streets to hear the relay of the service. Afterwards, over 200 remained behind in response to Mr Graham's call to become a follower of Christ.

Apropos of the criticisms his missions raise, an editorial in *The Christian* says, 'We are reminded of D.L. Moody's reply to his critics, that he preferred his way of doing it to their way of not doing it.'

June 5th, 1954

I am so bitterly disappointed. John writes to say he and Karis feel they have no choice but to give up Long Dene School. A large number of children have been removed, and there are simply not enough applications to make another year financially viable. I suppose it was to be expected – but what a blow for them, after all their efforts and so much sacrifice.

They are, he says, very, very weary, and so no great plans for the future, except to stay on and try their hand at organic farming.

Chloe has a place at Moira House School here in Eastbourne. What a joy for me to have one of my grandchildren nearby for visits. She is such a bright, loving soul and has always written me the most touching letters. I tell her she is a Virginia Woolf in the making. But after the freedoms of Long Dene, what on earth will she make of a traditional boarding school?

August 1st, 1954

The first day of sunshine and warmth for many weeks. Ruth and I went along the front this afternoon and enjoyed seeing the thousands of holidaymakers revelling in sea bathing, swarming on the beach and filling all the deckchairs. Almost the first summer's day we have had this year.

On the seafront at Eastbourne with Ruth

A newly published book called *African Bush Adventures* by J.A. Hunter and Dan Mannix quotes an interview with Ruth about her adventures in Uganda.

'How did you get up from the coast?' I asked Mrs Fisher. 'Rode on my bicycle,' said Mrs Fisher promptly. 'We followed the elephant trails up from Mombasa and they're quite smooth, you know' . . . To me, there was something very appealing in the idea of seven young Victorian ladies, dressed in the costumes of the times, riding bicycles eight hundred miles through jungles, deserts and mountain passes. I asked for details. 'Victorian girls weren't nearly as delicate as people think,' Mrs Fisher explained.

October 16th – 18th, 1954

A lovely weekend with the family gathering on Saturday for lunch at the Sussex Lounge: Arthur and Ruth, John, Karis and their children, Paul (over from Geneva).

John and Karis appear more reposed, greatly relieved to have given up their school work after fourteen years of it, despite the uncertain future they face, but of course, my children will try to protect me from their anxieties. As if a mother cannot see them etched in their faces.

Paul tells me he isn't surprised at the situation. John was never good at managing money. Furthermore, Paul's John was at the school for a year and academic standards were not achieved. Jean is having to coach him now.

As I suspected, Chloe is finding a more formal education quite an eye-opener, but these are early days.

December 2nd, 1954

My seventy-eighth birthday and my deepest joy is in having such wonderful sons, who have written me such beautiful letters; also their children, and my beloved Ruth, and sister Gertrude – literally showers of blessing, exceeding in abundance the torrential rains that are flooding our country just now.

My portion in today's Bible Reading Plan was Isaiah 41:8–14, and so very apt in the circumstances and my current temptation to worry.

I am with thee; be not dismayed,
for I am thy God: I will strengthen thee,
Yea, I will help thee,
yea, I will uphold thee with the right hand of my righteousness.

December 31st, 1954

For the first time since I came to Eastbourne in 1946, I did not spend Christmas Day with Arthur and Ruth in their little home at No. 11. They had their own children with them, and I felt John and Karis needed me more, so went to Chiddingstone for the weekend. It was a joyous time, as it always is when one is in the heart of one's own family.

There were seventeen of us in all in Tye Hall, their staff home in the castle grounds, for Christmas Day and Sunday evening dinners. But we enjoyed breakfasts alone with our own little circle and had prolonged enjoyment over all the Christmas gifts with which the tables were laden.

It was my first visit to the castle since the school was given up at the end of the summer term, and pigs and poultry have taken the place of 'problem children'. John and Karis seem very optimistic about their new venture.

Two delightful incidents during my four days with them will always remain in my memory. The first: Karis at the piano, baby Anthea, aged six and three quarters, playing her little violin with wonderful expression and good movement of her bow, Chloe with her cello and Lindis joining them on her flute. It was a lovely picture to see their poise and expressions, all so engrossed in the music, and such a spontaneous little performance, just before we sat down to dinner.

The second incident was just before I left and was having an early lunch, alone in their dining room, a loud knock on the door and there stood the farmer Nicholson in his working overall, with his ruddy cheeks and brown eyes, telling me he 'had just come to shake hands with John's mother' as his wife had told him she had met me yesterday, and after an exchange of a few remarks he ended with this about John: 'Oh, he's a grand man to work with.'

With this I end my journal for 1952–54. I will start a new one for the forthcoming year, especially as it may be a new episode in my pilgrimage through life. This last week of the year brings the news that yet again The Abbey may be given up. The doctor came to see 'the Abbess', now eighty years of age, and says she should give up this big house, and undoubtedly it is too much for her, especially as she has no domestic help whatsoever and does not wish to have any.

I was almost overwhelmed with this news, but (as is my usual custom), after she told me this, I turned to the psalms for the day in my prayer book and read Psalm 146:

> *The Lord helpeth them that are fallen,*
> *The Lord careth for the righteous . . .*
> *The Lord careth for the strangers,*
> *He defendeth the fatherless and widow.*

The latter line refers to myself and my two boys, as I have proved the past forty-four years, since the death of my beloved Henry.

153.

End of the Year 1954

For the first time since I came to Eastbourne in 1946 I did not spend Christmas day with in Arthur & Ruth's little home — no 11 Calverley Road. They had Bryan, Irené & their three boys there; so I went to Chiddingstone for the week-end, with John, Karis & their three darling girls — It was a joyous time, as it always is when one is in the heart of one's own family.

It was more than a _family_ party, as there were 17 people in all for Christmas day & Sunday evening dinners — But we enjoyed breakfasts alone with our own little circle & had prolonged enjoyment over all the Christmas gifts with which the tables were laden. It was my first visit to the Castle since the School was given up (at end of the Summer term 1954) and Pigs & Poultry have taken the place of the "Problem Children" which had begun to be in the majority among the pupils — There were many other issues

Grace's diary entry

I am now reading a recently published book by Sir W.K. Hancock, former Chair of History at Oxford, who has become so widely known as mediator to Uganda, preventing the country from being thrown into civil war with his wise handling of the government's senseless act in deposing the Kabaka kings of Buganda.

He is the son of an Australian clergyman, and his description of his mother so exactly describes my beloved sister Ruth that I must put it on record:

> Throughout my father's working life for nearly fifty years, it was she who had shielded and sustained him. Amidst all her public duties (Mother's Union, Sunday School, entertaining parishioners and visiting clergy etc.) she cooked and cleaned and sewed and chopped; it was her planning and work that eked out the scanty housekeeping money. Her working day began when she rose to get breakfast for the seven of us, and went on into the evening, when we children sat around the lamp with our lesson books, Mother at the end of the table, whirling the handle of her sewing machine, as she made our new shirts or remade the trousers of an older boy to fit a younger one . . . Father himself could hardly have known how much of her vitality she was expending on service to him, to us and to the parish . . . Both he and she took it for granted that the demands of his calling came first: he must have his mornings free for study and preparing his sermons, his afternoon free for parochial visiting, his evenings free for meetings – which meant she never had any free time for rest and recreation, except perhaps as a rare, unexpected luxury.

This is Ruth exactly.

And then, at other moments, he reminded me of my beloved Paul. 'I found myself incapable of giving the best of myself to one task without giving less than my best to another.' And then he says elsewhere, 'Not that I had any inhibitions about calling on important persons.'

And neither does Paul. He dreams big dreams, not for himself but for the fulfilment of the destiny of Israel and the church, and to that end will request an interview with anyone – from the writer Sholem Asch, to the great philosopher, Martin Buber, and usually gets his way.

So many wonderful library books to read. Some I must buy, otherwise I may forget many things I should like to remember, like this poem by Rainer Maria Rilke, quoted by Graham Greene in *The Heart of the Matter*:

> *We are all falling. This hand's falling too – all have this falling*
> *sickness none withstands.*
> *And yet there's always One whose gentle hands this universal*
> *falling cannot fall through.*

'If the outlook is bad, try the uplook.' This was said to Miss Charlotte Elliott one day when depressed by her chronic invalidism and sense of uselessness. She tried the uplook and a great peace filled her mind, replacing her many doubts and conflicts, so much so that she wrote the hymn 'Just As I Am, Without One Plea' – a blessing to millions and said by D.L. Moody to have done the greatest good to the greatest number of people.

March 26th, 1955

Awful! No newspapers due to a strike by maintenance workers. I feel so cut off. In fact, Ruth and I were so fed up with it we have ordered *The Scotsman* from Edinburgh, as the Scots have not joined the industrial action.

April 19th, 1955

In today's *Scotsman* the death of Professor Albert Einstein is announced, the greatest scientist of the century. His remarkable life story and scientific achievements will become international history. I cannot attempt even a brief summary.

Ruth's Stanley has just published his first novel, under the pseudonym Michael Scarrott. *Ambassador of Loss* is about as far from his usual religious poetry and writings as anything is possible to be. It is a kind of love story – between boys. Of course, I know and have seen these things at public school, but am glad nonetheless, for Ruth's sake, that the pseudonym protects his family and also Bryanston School where he was chaplain. He claims in the frontispiece that the incidents 'are based on actual experiences of schoolboys, from widely different schools, who have given me their confidence and encouraged me to write this book'.

It is primarily a plea for the comprehension of the emotional life of adolescents sent by uncaring parents to boarding institutions that starve them of affection. I find it all rather disturbing, and try to think, were the boys in my care ever denied my love?

The frontispiece says, 'Many of the wrong attitudes described here are, let us hope, dated, so the story has been put into the England of the 30s, but the urgency of the need to learn how to love one another is greater than ever.' There are echoes here of my John's understanding of the breadth of education a child needs, never addressed by a government curriculum, or experienced in most public schools. Attitudes change and develop over the years, I suppose, including my own, and all I can say is that I did my best at the time.

Stanley was one of a Christ Church College literary set in the late 1920s in Oxford, with the poet W.H. Auden and the writer Christopher Isherwood amongst his closest friends.[15] I wonder how far their influence is felt here?

April 21st, 1955

All newspapers resume publication today after twenty-six days. It has been a colossal loss to the country, for this period has included such important matters as Sir Winston Churchill's resignation, the forming of a new government by Sir Anthony Eden, the announcement of a general election, the budget, the Austrian agreement with Russia and the French ratification of the United Nations Convention on the human rights and status of refugees – highly significant for Paul's work at the YMCA.

The Times, wisely, issued a special strike supplement covering the chief events during this period. Twenty thousand maintenance men are now out of work, no thanks to the seven hundred who went on strike, and thousands of newspaper vendors, wholesalers and their employees have lost all or part of their livelihood. Stores, publishers, theatres, business and other advertisers also have suffered serious repercussions. The stoppage cost the newspapers themselves millions of pounds, pushing up the prices. The *Sunday Times* leader states, 'The public has been warned of the ease with which a handful of communists can play on labour solidarity to stop a great national industry and defeat the freedom of the press.'

July 10th, 1955

Today's papers print an important statement signed by eight eminent scientists, four of whom are Nobel Prize winners, warning the world that a war with nuclear weapons could end with the extermination of the entire human race. The declaration was released by the atheist philosopher and mathematician Bertrand Russell, saying the problem is the most serious ever to confront the human race. Thank God that the scientists are now realising the horror of the terrible misuse of their discoveries should they be applied to all-out war.

July 24th, 1955

Jean has sent me a detailed account from the *Journal de Genève* of the conference of the 'Big Four'. Britain, America, France and Russia met in Geneva a few days ago. With the papers claiming that the spies Burgess and Maclean urged Russia to adopt a conciliatory policy towards the West in the hope that the Allies would relax their guard, this didn't seem a very positive augury for a positive peaceful outcome.

Nonetheless, it was impressive and hopeful, which one would expect after last Sunday's special prayers in all the churches for peace and goodwill amongst all men, reflecting the world longing that 'war shall be no more', as Isaiah the Jewish prophet said over 700 years BC.

Today's Sunday press comes out with optimistic headlines: 'The announcement of a full agreement will be hailed with heart-felt relief by the ordinary people of all the nations, who long for real peace. It is true that much of the agreement is dependent on further discussion but that was foreseen by even the most optimistic . . .'

Then follow special articles by leading men on all the details. Such a lot of male pomposity and hot air. I refrain from comment, except to say – would that one piece at least had been written by a woman. We know so much better what makes for peace.

July 31st, 1955

The end of July – and of a perfect day. Paul here for twenty-one hours from London and Chiddingstone, and before that, Paris; and now, back to Paris this evening at 6 p.m. to be met by his Margaret, who is in Paris doing some little preparatory jobs in connection with the Centennial Conference of the World's Committee of the YMCA, to which she is one of the girl delegates. Jean joins them next week as one of the hostesses to the wives of the delegates – 10,000 of them, and visitors from seventy different countries.

September 23rd, 1955

John and Chloe arrived this afternoon and had tea with me before he took her back to Moira House School, the first term in her second year there. I am so excited to have her back, as we had some lovely days out together last year and such interesting conversations.

He returned to me after and we had a long talk together. The farming experiment at Chiddingstone has not been a success. He barely earns enough to feed his family, let alone pay off his debts, so alternative accommodation and employment must be found and the castle sold.

I cannot help but feel deeply depressed, and despite my normal recourse to my daily reading and prayer book, I am still unable to rid my mind of the anxiety.

Strangely I found comfort instead in re-reading the late King's broadcast on the first Christmas Day of the war (December 25th, 1939)

> I feel that we may all find a message of encouragement in the lines, which in my closing words, I would like to say to you: 'I said to the man who stood at the gate of the year, "Give me a light that I may tread safely into the unknown," and he replied: "Go out into the darkness and put your hand into the hand of God. That shall be to you better than a light and safer than a known way."' May that Almighty hand guide and uphold us.[16]

And it did – through all those dark and terrible years.

October 14th, 1955

John and Karis came to tea on their way back to Chiddingstone, after taking Chloe out to lunch. The farm and castle have finally sold for £6,000, far less than they are worth, to a man called Denys Eyre Bower, who has bought the property to house his collections of fine art and antiques. It is enough to pay off all their debts and will keep them until they find work. They must vacate the premises immediately, and wonderfully, the well-known mystic Anglo-Catholic healer Dorothy Kerin, whose visionary work John had gone to see, has offered them a house on her Groombridge estate until the future is revealed.

This evening's psalm was so responsive to my mood:

> *My flesh and my heart faileth,*
> *but God is the strength of my heart, and my portion for*
> *ever . . .*
> *It is good for me to hold fast to God, to put my trust in the*
> *Lord God . . .*
> *for God is my king of old.*

November 17th, 1955

Our dear old Arthur – Ruth's husband for fifty-three years – has joined the 'innumerable company'.

On November 3rd, he passed over peacefully, without any pain or suffering. I had had lunch with them as usual that day, and he ate a hearty meal. I left them immediately after, as Ruth wanted to write to Stanley. She tells me Arthur took his siesta and afternoon tea, then said he did not feel very well and thought he should go to bed.

Ruth helped him upstairs and to undress, and as he lay down his eyes closed. The doctor, whom she had telephoned to come, told her gently that there was no more he could do, and stood by as Ruth took Arthur's hand and said, 'We will have our evening prayer together, Darling, as usual.' It was the traditional Anglican evening prayer they always said at bedtime, except that they had substituted the word 'wondrous', for 'troublous' (life) in the liturgy as they felt it more appropriate.

'Support us, O Lord, all the day long of this wondrous life, until the shades lengthen, and the evening comes, the busy world is hushed, the fever of life is over, and our work done. Then, Lord, in thy mercy, grant us safe lodging, a holy rest, and peace at the last, through Jesus Christ our Lord.'

And as she finished those words, his pulse ceased.

She called me and I at once went back down to be with her and stayed until Geraldine arrived from Harrogate at 7.15. The rest of the family came on the following days and were of the greatest help to their beloved mother.

Letters and telegrams and airmail have poured in, and the whole town has mourned his loss. His passing was broadcast throughout the Uganda Protectorate in both English and Luganda, and it was also broadcast on the World News programme in South Africa (Shelagh wrote to tell us from Rhodesia*). Fortunately, she had received the cablegram the day before, so was spared the shock of hearing the news over the radio.

Everything connected with his passing was wonderful, even the almost immediate decision that Ruth would go to Corsham, Wiltshire, to live with her son Bryan in his large house. He has a room especially for her which can accommodate a few pieces of her favourite furniture and a small number of her Ugandan trinkets.

January 25th – 30th, 1956

Stayed five days with Ruth at the little house, so soon to be given up. Probably my last stay there as she leaves for Rhodesia on February 15th, and upon her return Bryan will be there to help with the move.

We both felt we had come to the parting of the ways. I certainly should not want to stay on in Eastbourne after she leaves. My only motive in coming here ten years ago was to be near her.

We were both impressed as we read in the personal column of today's *Times*: 'Go in peace: before the Lord is your way wherein ye go' (Judges 18:6).

* Now Zimbabwe

February 15th, 1956

It is a desolation to be without my beloved sister. I had a lovely farewell note from her in which she wrote:

> *Partings towards the end of life are almost too hard to bear. The present and the past are the only life we know, and to break the tendrils that we have clung to so long leaves us feeling so alone. You have been so precious to me, and so loyal and loving, that I feel we shall yet come close to each other again.*

I truly hope we may.

'Merely to live, or even to live long is not the thing that matters. What matters is that you live fully, usefully and happily.' (Lord Horder)

The Lady Of Bathampton Manor
1956–63

March 31st, 1956

And so, back to Bath once again for the third time – the first time with Henry and our two babes, the second when I worked at the War Office, and now to Bathampton Manor, a Bath Council of Social Services property, purchased in 1947 for £6,075 from Lady Frances Gurney as a retirement home for 'genteel ladies in need'.

It was at Ruth's suggestion that I come to Bath to be near Henry's grave so that I could cut down on funeral costs when it was time to join him and leave what little money I might have left to John and Paul. It seemed a very good idea, particularly as Ruth would not be far away, living with Bryan and Irene and their three boys in his rambling house in Corsham. Irene teaches in a prep school, and Ruth feels she could be useful looking after the children if Irene has to work late.

I came here on March 20th, rather unexpectedly and earlier than I planned, but it is among the many 'exceeding abundancies' of my life. My years at The Abbey with Mrs Liebenrood ended and I am adapting myself (I hope?) to community life once again. In a community, especially one of about twenty septuagenarians and octogenarians, we have to adapt ourselves to the personality of others and subordinate our own egotism. Not easy in my eightieth year. Truth is, though it pains me to admit it, Bathampton Manor is actually a rather superior place of residence for old girls like me to be put out to graze like pit ponies.

I have a cosy little room up in the roof and everything I could ever need. It is a joyous prospect that I shall soon see my beloved Ruth again on her return from Rhodèsia. It was strange that in her little farewell note on leaving Eastbourne she said she had a feeling we would not be parted for long, and this has come true. We are both nearing the end of life's journey, and it is good to be near each other, even if not actually living together, as we said in our youth we would do. That was in the long-ago days before either of us were married, and we both expected to be spinsters.

April 17th, 1956

In Mr Macmillan's budget today he has introduced something called Premium Bonds to encourage people to start saving again after the war. Shall I have a go? I never seem to win any prizes. And at my age what would I do with a win? Paint the town red? An elderly delinquent loose in Bath! No wonder the papers have called it 'Saving with a thrill', but the church condemns it as a form of gambling, so perhaps, after all, I should desist.

May 11th, 1956

In every branch of life the increasing influence of women is more and more marked. I read in today's *Times* that the Presbyterian Church has appointed its first woman minister. Miss Gordon is an MA, BD, BSc of Aberdeen University, and was for ten years a missionary in Manchuria and India, and afterwards, a science teacher in a Glasgow secondary school. She says she thinks there may be some difficulty in finding a congregation that will accept her – but she will wait and see. All power to her elbow, say I. Good for her.

June 18th, 1956

A letter from John:

> *I went to Dorset last week for an interview with the Assistant
> County Education Officer. No, sorry, this isn't news about a
> job! But he was very helpful in telling me about the snags in
> getting headmasterships under the local authorities, and the
> biggest of these is that my experience to date will probably not
> count for Burnham Scale, so it means looking more in the direc-
> tion of the independent schools again. However, I have
> answered quite a number of hopeful advertisements recently, so
> something should come of all this activity.*
>
> *Paul and I had a wonderful lunch together at the Waverley on
> Thursday, when he was able to tell me the essence of his world
> news. We had a tremendous talk about it all, of course, and I
> was able to tell him too about some of my recent reading and
> thinking, which supplemented his. We went together to the
> YMCA headquarters, met the chief of their education depart-
> ment (to whom I gave details of my experience etc.), and then
> Paul and I went on to the BBC, where I left him to make the
> recording for his broadcast. His world tour of twenty countries
> for the YMCA has been a unique experience, and I don't
> wonder the Bishop of Chichester listened to him for two
> hours![17]*

June 18th, 1956

And now a woman – Golda Meir – appointed Israel's Secretary
for Foreign Affairs. It is impossible to continue recording the
increasing influence of women in public life – there are now too
many to mention.

Grace

September 10th, 1956

An overnight telegram delivered by the first post, from John: 'Leamington appointment at Barnardo's confirmed. Love from family. John.'

He is to run a Dr Barnardo's home for 120 young orphans at 'Oakfield', Binswood Avenue, Leamington Spa. His father's friendship with Dr Barnardo all those years ago, when Barnardo studied under Henry and Henry introduced him to Lord Shaftesbury, his future patron, gained John some mileage at the interview, I gather.

How fortuitous and extraordinary these little twists of fate are. And so, all the promises have been fulfilled, and my (foolish!) anxieties allayed. I can only say, 'Lord, increase our faith.'

September 30th, 1956

The wettest summer for five years. Certainly more than local effects. Many of us have remarked on the possibility of aeroplanes causing the excessive rainfall all over the world. But now scientists are suggesting it might be due to particles from the atomic explosion fallout entering the clouds. What else might atomic disaster bring?

October 4th, 1956

A week of tragic news! The Suez crisis, Nasser, the Egyptian counterpart of Hitler and Mussolini, refusing all appeals for the international control of the Canal, in defiance of international agreement. Now, in quick succession comes the news of Israel's attack on Egypt and Britain's invasion of the Sinai Peninsula.

America and most of the Commonwealth countries are against the action we have taken, but Anthony Eden, the Prime Minister, justifies it on the ground of the urgency of warlike action to prevent future world disasters.

The Prime Minister cannot fail to see Russia's sympathy with Nasser's ambition for the headship of Africa, and his determination to extinguish the Jewish nation. What turmoil our world is in. Where are all the hopes for peace we had a mere ten years ago?

There are those who think my Paul bears a strong resemblance to the handsome Mr Eden. In fact, he has been mistaken for the Prime Minister several times. This is no longer as amusing as it once was! Paul has shaven off his moustache.

November 13th, 1956

And now the Hungarian uprising, viciously suppressed by the Soviet Union, exerting its hold over its empire; 2,500 at least are dead, 200,000 Hungarians fled as refugees. Jean writes that Paul is working day and night to try and raise funding for their care.

December 2nd, 1956

My eightieth birthday, this first Sunday in Advent. I stayed on to Communion at our local church (St Nicholas, Bathampton), then during the week celebrated the occasion by walking into Bath from Bathampton, around two miles along the canal footpath, with Miss Bell, one of the septuagenarian residents at the manor. We lunched in the town and then wandered through some of the interesting byways of Bath, and came across Bishop Butler's beautiful old house in Kingsmead Square, which I remember visiting with Henry in 1909. How strange that the last stages of my life should be filled with such bittersweet memories. Henry's image never fades from my mind, and being in Bath makes it more vivid than ever.

I read this in the St Martin-in-the-Fields parish magazine and wrote to the editor asking if he knew who the author was, but he did not know.

Let me grow lovely growing old;
So many old things do:
Laces and ivory and gold,
And silks need not be new,
And there is beauty in old trees,
Old streets a glamour hold,
Why may not I, as well as these,
Grow lovely, growing old.[18]

I also hope I may never lose my sense of humour. I had a good laugh tonight at this story told me by one of the Manor old folks: a small boy coming home from school excitedly told his mother that the devil was dead. The mother's contradiction was met with, 'He is dead, Mother. I saw his funeral and I know it was him because I overheard a gentleman say, "The old devil is dead at last."'

Christmas Day, 1956

A really festive time, despite the fact that for me it was the first for many years spent apart from any members of my family, but the eight septuagenarians and octogenarians who had not gone away managed to enjoy the feast and have fun, while our warden and her colleague, who, alas, are leaving here after Christmas, gave us a marvellous time. The table decorations were beautiful and the fat English turkey with all the extras perfect, followed by the usual plum pudding, mince pies and dessert, with the essential sherry and port.

We all went to our little village church in the morning and took Holy Communion with 'all the company of heaven', though my thoughts were with our dear family on earth – Beatrice, as I am, amongst old people in Kent; Ruth with her Stanley in Oxford, revelling in the Christmas Eve celebrations at Magdalen College, where Stanley preached; brother Phil in Sydney; John and Karis with their three girls in their new work in Leamington; Paul, Jean and their John and Peter in Geneva, Paul taking the Christmas service in the Vevey English church; while Margaret, now in the USA, studying at Earlham College, is spending the day with the Sibleys of Rochester – old friends from Geneva.

But amidst all the joys and festivities there was an undercurrent of sorrow and concern over world events, the envy, hatred and malice behind the Egyptian crisis and the horrors of Russia's actions in Hungary, even the reactions of the USA to our actions in Suez, all producing deep concern as to the future of the entire world. We can only say that 'God is in his heaven' as Browning did, but not as he added, 'And all is right with the world' – rather that all is wrong with the world! But we must remember Christ's words to his disciples in the days of Rome's power: 'Fear not, I have overcome the world.'

Fancy dress fun at Bathampton Manor

January 13th, 1957

World news in general is terribly depressing . . . unrest fills every page of today's *Times*.

And now a great political upheaval on top of everything else. Sir Anthony Eden has resigned as Prime Minister on the grounds of ill health, and the Queen, on the advice of Lord Salisbury, has appointed Harold Macmillan as his successor. The choice is a very popular one, however, both in England and the USA.

January 19th, 1957

Our sister Ruth had a note from our new Prime Minister – an astonishing fact that he could even acknowledge her letter the week he became Prime Minister, when he must have had hundreds of letters to deal with, in addition to all his ministerial duties. She had written:

> *After listening to your broadcast last night, despite the avalanche of letters that poured in upon you, I felt I must write to thank you for the firm, clear and decisive statement you gave us. With the strong cabinet led by two Scots – yourself and Mr John Maclay, we must all feel strengthened and inspired by your leadership.*
>
> *We are turning over a new page in world history. Class and race barriers are being broken down. Our Empire has become a Commonwealth of Nations and a quite new concept of statesmanship.*
>
> *May I be allowed to make a suggestion – that the Lords and Commons of our parliament might be changed into the 'House of Commonwealth', and the 'House of Britain'.*
>
> *An annual or tri-annual conference of Commonwealth prime ministers affects little. The time has come when all nations of our Commonwealth should have a place and a voice*

*in our government. My husband and I spent many years in
Uganda, and my six children have all lived in India and Africa.
I mention this so that you may see we have broad and deep
interest in the Commonwealth and hope the words imperialism
and colonialism will ultimately be merged in a wider federation
of self-elected governors with members serving in a
Commonwealth parliament at Westminster.*

Yours faithfully
Ruth B. Fisher,
author of On the Borders of Pygmyland
and Folklore of Uganda

The Prime Minister thanked her most warmly for her kind message – in his own handwriting.

March 6th, 1957

Today sees the celebrations marking the turning of the African Gold Coast colony into an independent Commonwealth state called Ghana – the first in Africa. A significant event in Africa's future history.

April 19th, 1957

A letter from Ruth this morning from the House of Rest at 10 Finchley Road in London. She says there are fifteen nationalities staying there – a veritable United Nations of Japanese, Chinese, Indians, Egyptians, Germans, Swedes, Finlanders, Borneo, Scotch and Irish, Americans and Australians.

Among those from Egypt were the headmaster and his wife of the school in Cairo (whom I met when I wintered there with Wyndham and Flo at Helwan). He, with many others, including the Bishop and his wife, were all interned in the English cathedral, then ultimately deported from the country with nothing except the money for their fares. Everything confiscated by Nasser.

Ruth then went on to tell of her visits to our old home, 164 Alexandra Road in St John's Wood, and how several of the larger houses had been destroyed in the Blitz. The leases of many of the older houses fall out this year so they had not been repaired, but our old home was an exception.

> *A dear lady was gardening at the front and she took me all over the garden with lovely flowers in full spring beauty; the breakfast room with the French doors were open and I felt a child again running in and out.*

She then went on to describe her visit to the Hampstead cemetery to see the Hurditch family graves.

> *I could only hear the words, 'Why seek ye the living among the dead? They are not here, but risen.' It has all been a wonderful last-likely adventure, even to the step climb-up to our old high school, where we had our first excitement of mass education. Remember 'Big Ben', the headmistress, whom you used to mimic, and the old maths teacher who caused you such grief? Where did our lives go?*

June 17th – July 1st, 1957

My first holiday from the Manor. First, a week with our niece Kathleen in her lovely little cottage in Castlemorton, Worcestershire with motor runs in the Malvern Hills, and then my first visit to my own dear family, John, Karis and the children in their new sphere of work in Leamington Spa, and a joy to be present at their first 'Barnardo's Day Garden Fête' – a lovely day and a great success.

The Lady Of Bathampton Manor

Grow old along with me!
The best is yet to be,
The last of life, for which the first was made:
Our times are in His hand
Who saith 'A whole I planned,
Youth shows but half; trust God: see all, nor be afraid!'

May 1st, 1957

I love this piece of doggerel written by a delightful man visitor to
the Manor to see his cousin, Constance Carter (our musician and
owner of a grand piano and cello, which delight us when she plays).

Ladies of the Manor

Bath has old ladies by the score,
Just let me deal with three or four:
First dear old Constance, Cousin C
A mellow music-maker, she
Lives at the manor, topping place,
Adorns it with her charm and grace.
And talking of Grace, there's Guinness too
A graceful Grace to me and you,
And even if she's over eighty
She's quite a peach and very matey
With Christian Hacker, racked with pain,
Who laughs and jokes with might and main.
Just say 'Guinness is good for Hacker'
And watch those Christian brows grow blacker.
When Tinker Bell calls all to sup
We come and eat the good things up.
And Cookie Smith, now bless her heart

---

* From the poem 'Rabbi Ben Ezra' by Robert Browning

She always gives me extra tart
Till Christian Hacker, more's the shame,
Went purple when that pudding came,
As purple as the fruit it bore,
Then loudly she demanded more.
Dear Mrs May with tact so good
Makes all behave the way she should,
Like Mrs Cunnington so tough,
Who never seems to have enough.
She's never slack and never shirking
Her motto: 'Girls should go on working.'
Then some play cards, like all three Gs
And Constance tickles up the keys.
Till ABC to XYZ
The old girls totter off to bed.

Her motto: 'Girls should keep on working'.
Then some play cards, like, all three G's
And Constance tickles up her keys.
Till ABC to XYZ
The Old Girls totter off to bed.

THE MANOR.
X - My little room in the roof —

Ladies of the Manor

October 31st, 1957

Our warden, Mrs May, has left us today for a similar post in London. Among other reasons she feels too far away from old associations and does not like country life. This is the second change of warden since I came here in March 1956 and very unsettling. I scribbled the following doggerel and slipped it under her door this morning. She has been so kind to me, accompanying me several times to the Eye Hospital, but particularly during the five weeks of my fractured leg accident.

> *Our kind Mrs May*
> *Is going away,*
> *Oh! what can we say?*
> *For we're filled with dismay –*
> *But we wish God bless*
> *Despite our distress –*
> *(Then she cheered us with wine*
> *So we must not repine!)*
> *Though we're losing a mother*
> *We trust God will send us*
> *Just such Another.*

December 2nd, 1957

My eighty-first birthday and a joyous one with my Paul and Jean who came to Bathampton to celebrate it with me. Paul had come from extensive travel (by air mostly) in the USA and Canada, meeting Jean from Geneva in Paris, attending a UNO luncheon there, and preaching at the cathedral in the morning, then by plane to London and train to Bath and Bathampton, where we met the next morning and spent a joyous day, mainly at the Fernley Hotel, where I rested most of the afternoon owing to my recently broken leg.

All Paul had to tell me of his opportunities and contacts in his recent four months were an inspiration.

And then came the shock. He has given six months' notice at the YMCA, feeling his work there is done. He seemed so contented just two weeks ago. What I particularly cannot understand, and said so, is why he should do so without first having an alternative in view. But he tells me not to worry, that he will go and see his old patron and friend, Bishop Bell of Chichester, and ask him to find him a parish. Six months should be more than enough time.

I was distracted from our conversation by a woman in the new Italian-style shoes – stilettos, they are called, after a kind of Italian dagger. She tottered in on what must have been at least eight inches, looking for all the world as if she were on stilts. Really, these new female fashions are totally impractical, limiting a woman's freedom as they do. I said so to Paul and Jean. Paul laughed, but Jean shushed me and told me not to tut so loudly.

But honestly, if I had worn such shoes in my youth, I should not have managed to work. And would probably have broken my leg much sooner.

December 3rd, 1957

And then, in today's post, John writes to say that much as he enjoys working with difficult children, he and Karis miss using their teaching skills.

So both my boys are seeking fresh employment and a new future. A worrying time, and then for reasons I can't comprehend, I haphazardly glanced through my much-loved nephew George's letters to his parents, Ruth and Arthur, when he set off for India and which I edited many years ago. This closing extract, written shortly before he died in the polo accident, came to me with great force, almost as if he were speaking to me:

I have tried to give you all of me . . . read and understand.
Remember that what you could do or give, you have done and
given – to the utmost. For the rest, you must allow perfect free-
dom and have faith . . .

Thank you, dear George. I needed those comforting thoughts of
yours just now.

December 31st, 1957

Our eldest sister – dear old Bee, the eldest of our seven, died today
at Marlands, Barn's Green in Horsham, aged ninety-one and
three quarters. I had not seen her for so many years that I cannot
say I will miss her. Yet the many memories of her as she was in our
younger days, presiding so forcefully over 'Little Africa' in our
childhood home, trying bravely to run Wilton House without
staff when she had so little experience of domesticity, fill my mind
and make me both smile and fill up with tears.

Bishop Bell has nothing for Paul – despite giving my son two
hours of his time as he did just a few months ago. However impressed
he might have been then, the Bishop is on the point of retirement
and nothing in his diocese is currently available or suitable. Paul has
been out of the country for so long he has no other important epis-
copal contacts, so just as my brother-in-law Arthur discovered all
those years ago, it is going to prove very hard to find a living.

April 14th – 15th, 1958

The budget. Income tax reduced by 9d in the £, that is from 8/6d to
7/9d. I can remember when I was a small child my father telling Mother
in apprehensive tones that the budget had risen to 6d in the pound.

A visit from Canon Gordon Guinness, who was Paul's training
vicar before the war. I do love having visitors, and it is fun to catch

up on the family news – and then I am quizzed on the well-being of my eternal soul. Every now and then, Gordon or Desmond, Harry's youngest sons, both Anglican clergymen in the firmly evangelical mould, turn up and try to 'convert' me. They appear to think me wishy-washy in my beliefs because I now feel comfortable in the bosom of middle Anglicanism. I give them no reassurances, just for the fun of it, as their consternation is so entertaining.

May 9th – 23rd, 1958

A lovely fortnight with my beloved Ruth at Skegness, and our visit to see John, Karis and the children in the little holiday home they have acquired nearby. They now live at South Collingham Hall in Newark, Nottinghamshire, where John runs a home and school for children waiting to be found foster care. Karis is using her musical skills to soothe them, and both they and the children they care for appear to be thriving.

July 5th and 6th, 1958

A wonderful weekend! Paul came to Bathampton Saturday evening (5th) – a great surprise to get his trunk call from London telling me he was on the way. I did not even know he was back in England. He brought great news of the offer from the Bishop of Manchester of the living of Christ Church, Ashton-under-Lyne, Lancashire. The Bishop – the Rt Revd Dr William Derrick Lindsey Greer, had written to Paul, 'it needs a man with plenty of energy and experience'. Paul certainly has that!

Curiously enough he received the letter from the Bishop the very day his ten years' work with the International YMCA terminated. A wonderful ten years' experience that has entailed worldwide travel and contact with many nationalities. I do wonder, after such excitement, how he and the family will find parish life in Ashton-under-Lyne, after Geneva? A rambling old vicarage in a smoky, industrial Lancashire town is somewhat far removed from their lovely lakeside flat.

September 22nd, 1958

Upon their arrival back in England, they spent the weekend in Bath with me, a wonderful time marred only by Paul going down with this awful Asian influenza on the Saturday, resulting in a postponement of one day of their journey north. We are having a veritable epidemic, which, fortunately, I have been spared, but the entire family succumbed the following week – and they were staying in temporary accommodation with church members as the old seventeen-room vicarage has been left in a state and is not ready for them. So now they have discovered the joys of an outside toilet. I remember it so well in Ruth and Arthur's parish in Leeds – the shared toilet in an alleyway behind the rows of terraced dwellings. But that was forty years ago. Why has progress still not arrived in the north? The war has set it back years, no doubt. But it is scandalous. I shall write to the papers about it.

Not a happy start to their new life.

Paul was installed as vicar of Christ Church, Ashton-under-Lyne on September 18th. 'The service was an inspiring experience . . . deeply moving,' he wrote. But Paul manages to find most things in life deeply inspirational and moving. Let's hope that includes Ashton-under-Lyne.

October 24th, 1958

My darling and precious sister Ruth is passing through the valley of the shadow of death.

With Paul at Christ Church vicarage

I had not heard from her recently and wrote to her on Friday 17th to say I was anxious, and still no reply. Then I got a telephone message from Bryan to say he was coming to see me at 5 p.m. on Wednesday, October 22nd. He told me then that both heart and other troubles had developed and he telephoned again later that evening that he had decided to go to Blackheath (to Venn House, the CMS home where she has been happily living for over a year now).

He came again this evening and tells me that when he got there he found most of the family had gathered and she was happy with them all around her, expectant of her imminent departure. After he had gone I went into our music room as usual at 6 p.m. to hear Constance Carter play, and during her playing I had a wonderful sense of contact with my beloved sister and a sense of peace. I asked Constance to write down for me the pieces she had played. They were Schumann's *Sonata Op. 118*, and a Beethoven *Sonata*

Op. 49. Not in the whirlwind but in the 'still small voice' of heavenly music.

November 9th, 1958

I have just had a telephone message to say Ruth appears to be fading, and all her family are going to the hospital where she is under observation. In her last letter of November 3rd, she wrote:

> *I hope this is my last move – but . . . I cannot write more now, only thank our Father for all His love. Such happy memories of our Skegness holiday. My weight was then 8 stone 6, but now only 6 stone 4.*

November 13th, 1958

It seems the dear old girl has rallied – despite all our expectations. She will go to Larema's on Saturday 15th, where a nurse has been engaged to look after her. She tells me the doctors told Stanley she is suffering from arterial sclerosis and adds, 'How lovely it will be to reach my final home when the busy world is hushed.'

December 30th, 1958

The Times announces today that the renowned Bible teacher Dr W. Graham Scroggie, DD, has died aged eighty-one. He was a very old friend, whose parents were also well known to our family. When I told his sister I had decided to take up nursing as my career, she had exclaimed, 'Oh, Graham wants to marry you instead!'

So, as it happens, did Edgar Plummer, who afterwards became Sir Edgar P. Who knew in those days what these unprepossessing young men would become? But by special providence, I was reserved for HGG!

January 21st, 1959

As I feared, my little family in the north is finding it hard to settle in Ashton-under-Lyne. Jean finds it 'grim', she says. Not a tree or flower in the endless rows of back-to-back terraced streets. And their large vicarage is almost impossible to heat. Margaret has decided to go back to Switzerland. Peter, aged nine, has been playing truant from school. Even my irrepressible Paul is somewhat cowed by the greyness of it all, the endless demands of such a large parish, with its many funerals, leaving him neither the time nor energy for his work on Jewish–Christian dialogue. How I wish they could be spared, but as Ruth and Arthur discovered, it is not we who choose our destiny.

November 14th, 1959

I have lost my last two dear sisters this week. Gertrude (Evill), and this evening Bryan Fisher came over from Corsham to tell me that their beloved mother and my most precious sister Ruth passed over to the other side today. Her last message before losing full consciousness, three weeks ago, was: 'Don't let my parting be sad: I shall be at the start of an exciting new adventure.' So characteristic. The same dauntless spirit that prompted her to climb the Mountains of the Moon in Uganda at the source of the White Nile.

In one of my beloved Henry's poems he wrote, 'This remains when all besides has perished with the past: He loved us from the first of time, He loves us to the last.'

Her memorial service will be held at High Hurstwood Church.

November 17th, 1959

The Times
Mrs R.B. Fisher

Ruth B. Fisher, who died on Saturday, was one of the great Victorians. Born at Marylebone in 1875, she was the sixth child of a leading evangelical missioner, C. Russell Hurditch, and helped him in the organization of mass meetings in the Exeter Hall and all over England.

In 1900 she went out to Uganda to work for the Church Missionary Society and there married the pioneer missionary, the Rev A.B. Fisher. She worked for 15 years in Toro, Hoima and Gulu. She learnt five of the languages of the country and helped to get some of them into writing and to work out a system of grammar.

Kings, Prime Ministers and Bishops have come from her schools. One of her first pupils was Hana Kageye, the widow of a senior chief in the kingdom of Toro and therefore of high social status. In 1902 Hana travelled to the neighbouring kingdom of Ankole, teaching the Christian faith and reading to the women at the royal court. She caused a sensation by being the first woman in Ankole to wear spectacles. The first converts to be baptized there in the June of that year were Hana's pupils.

Ruth Fisher wrote two books: a vivid account of the first few years of her experiences, *On the Borders of Pygmy Land*, and an account of the traditions and early history of the country, gathered from the local witch doctors, with the help of the Kings of Toro and Bunyoro. Among many admirers of her work was Sir Henry M. Stanley, the renowned explorer, who stood godfather to her second son.

There followed years of hard labour as mother of six children and 'unpaid' curate in parishes in Leeds, South

London and Sussex. She was always a powerful speaker, and one of her many notable speeches was on the occasion of the CMS Uganda Jubilee meeting in the Albert Hall in 1927, when she spoke after Lord Lugard. Almost the last letter she was able to read, from the Archbishop of Canterbury, reminded her that she had preached for him at Repton School, the first and perhaps only woman to have done so.

She kept her courage, unconventionality, and vigour of mind to the end, offering herself at 82 as a suitable guinea pig for a sputnik. This courage and a radiant Christian faith she brought to thousands, who will indeed 'rise up and call her blessed'.

In his sermon at Gertrude's funeral, Revd F. Lampen, a former curate of the Evills, seemed to think that her greatest contribution to society was as a splendid organiser. 'As the vicar's wife in Edmonton, she was ready to do more than she was asked or called upon to do, chairing societies and running endless meetings.' Hardly the most exciting of epitaphs, but very Gertrude: a typical woman of her time.

All my dear ones are leaving me, one by one. Till I alone am left. I wonder how much longer I shall have? Whatever, I shall make the most of it.

May 6th, 1960

The wedding of Princess Margaret to Anthony Armstrong-Jones. From Bathampton Manor we old ladies watched the wonderful television representation of the whole pageant, from the departures from Buckingham Palace, the arrivals at Westminster Abbey.

Any comments on her choice are uncalled for. '*Chacun à son gout*', as the French say. She gave up her first choice, Captain Peter Townsend, because he was a divorcee, which always struck me as rather hard luck. Perhaps, after the débacle with her uncle, she was making a point about duty and sacrifice. But that was so long ago, and now, in her case, we wonder, what did it really matter?

July 16th, 1960

Owing to the difficulty of finding appropriate education for their two younger girls, Chloe and Anthea, John and Karis have been obliged to move yet again, to a secondary school in Sandridgebury near Watford (500 boys), where John has an appointment as a French master.

December 2nd, 1960

I am eighty-four today. 'There was a prophetess, Anna, the daughter of Phanuel of the tribe of Asher. She was very old; she had lived with her husband seven years after her marriage, and was then a widow until she was 84.' Why had I never noticed this before? Seven years married, as I was to Henry. A widow ever after. Perhaps she married an older man too, and felt she could not replace him. 'She never left the Temple, but worshipped night and day, fasting and praying.' And so recognised the Christ child when she saw him, and spoke of him to all who were looking forward to the redemption of Jerusalem. As I do here. Perhaps we all have a biblical character we resemble, and relive, to a certain measure, their calling.

This quote in *The Times*, attributed to a young poet called Sylvia Plath, caught my eye today: 'Apparently, the most difficult feat for a Cambridge male is to accept a woman not merely as feeling, not merely as thinking, but as managing a complex, vital interweaving of both.'

December 31st – January 2nd, 1961

John came to see me at Bathampton Manor this weekend. Such a joy to have him. He tells me the job at the secondary modern in Watford doesn't really suit him. The children are difficult and can barely speak proper English, let alone learn French. His colleagues are unfriendly, smoke incessantly, and are rude and rough with the children. This is not the kind of environment my gentle boy is used to at all, but he accepts it calmly and quietly, reminding me so much of his father – not in looks, rather in little characteristic ways.

On Sunday we went to Bath Abbey, and afterwards lunched at the Fernley Hotel. A woman walked into the restaurant in what was little more than her knickers. These so-called 'skirts' are, I gather, no cheaper than the longer, more practical variety. 'How does she get about, do a day's work, or keep warm?' I asked John, but he merely smiled and put a finger to his lips. I am too loud, Jean always tells me when she is out with me. I have lived long enough to be an embarrassment to my children.

Monday morning we spent in Bath, having elevenses at Carwardine's. I do so love it there – the smart waitresses in their lovely uniforms, the delicious cakes, but most of all, that pungent aroma of roasting coffee beans.

He bought me a most useful electric fitting which enables me to have the fire and kettle on at the same time. Such a comfort – in my little room in the roof.

March 12th, 1961

'A successful person must have the strength of a horse, the hide of an elephant, the eye of a hawk, the wisdom of a serpent, the harmlessness of a dove . . . indeed, he must be a miniature zoo.' (Revd Henry Halsey, Vicar of St Stephen's, Chatham, in the *Sunday Times*)

April 10th, 1961

Praise be, John has moved once more – this time to Aylesford House School, a boys' prep school just outside St Albans. He sent me a most interesting bundle of illustrated prospectuses. The headmaster is T.K. Thompson. He and his wife are old friends of John and Karis's, and the house, formerly belonging to the Earl Spencer of Althorpe, with a large acreage, appears to be run along the same radical lines as Long Dene. The boys are very distinctive in the town. They wear pink blazers and caps – a little . . . namby pamby perhaps?

This new work, I am glad to say, seems much more to John's liking and interest.

June 19th, 1961

Just back from a visit to Aylesford House. Put my pearls (the ones Henry gave me) under Chloe's mattress for safety, and have come home without them. Such is one's memory in old age. I have told Chloe to keep them. They are not valuable, except to me, for Henry gave them to me. But perhaps this is a sign – time to divest myself of these sentimental trinkets and pass them on to the family.

I am getting rather tired. Writing in my diary is becoming more of a chore than a pleasure, especially as one's eyesight starts to fail. I shall restrict myself to recording merely the 'big' events in my life.

November 23rd, 1961

A more upbeat letter from Paul today than I have had in a while, telling me he has had a telephone call from London inviting him to share in next Sunday evening's ITV programme entitled *Sunday*

Break (somewhere between 6.15 p.m. and 7.00). It is a programme on the Jewish people and Jewish–Christian relations, which has found a place in this television programme because of next week's 'Brotherhood Week'. Paul was invited to contribute because of his involvement in the Manchester Council of Christians and Jews.

Unfortunately we were not able to get it on Bath television as the Bath operators were all on strike. But I heard from my niece, Eileen, in London, who saw it (as did many others), and she thought he was wonderful. My son, on television, and I missed it! How selfish these strikers are.

April, 1962

It has all been rather wonderful and nerve-racking, and I have been so touched by the enthusiasm and support of my friends here at Bathampton Manor, who have entered into my excitement as if it were their own little family.

John and Karis and the three girls appeared on TV too – in one of those talent shows on television called *New Faces*, playing some madrigal pipes John designed himself. They are traditional bamboo pipes, rather like recorders, but easier to finger, allowing five-year-olds to play Mozart. The winner out of the ten contestants is awarded a contract.

We were shown the little family playing together with some of the pupils at Aylesford House, then they played in the studio, and then John was interviewed about the pipes' design.

Well, we old dears crossed our fingers, prayed, and cheered them on – but they came second, which means they do not get a grant to develop the pipes. A little disappointing – but I was so proud of them all the same. And they now have their pictures in the papers.

August 11th, 1962

Four glorious days – Paul and Jean and their youngest, Peter, came to Bathampton (staying at the Weir Tea Gardens). It is such a joy to see any of one's own family – especially either of my precious sons. They left today, motoring to London, where they go by aeroplane to Majorca for their annual summer holiday.

Parting becomes harder as the years go by, never knowing on each occasion if we are saying our last goodbyes.

January, 1963

And now I have – said what must be my last goodbye – to my eldest son and his precious little family.

I went to stay with them one last time at Aylesford House, and realised how hard it had been for him to become a master again, having run his own school – though he never complained.

Lindis, who has been working in California for the past four years, had enthused repeatedly in her letters about the sunshine and exotic fruits like avocados there, and begged them to go and join her. And then, a possible opening for the pipes presented itself.

The TV programme appears to have been a watershed. They feel there is nothing for them in this country, and that America may be the land of opportunity. So thanks to a loan for the tickets from Lindis, they are to move out there. Perhaps it will at last give them the financial independence John longs for. I pray it may be so.

I don't know when or even whether I shall ever see them again on this earth. But how can I hold on to them, keep them near when they all have their own path to follow, and mine is coming to an end?

In their little old car, on the way to the Sunday service at Anthea's school, he called me 'Mummy'. So strange after all these years. It almost broke my heart. I think the same thought was going through his head – that this would be our last farewell.

July 7th, 1963

Sixty years ago today I walked down the aisle into Henry's waiting arms – and remained there for seven short years. My wedding day. Was it really so long ago? It seems like yesterday. I relive almost continually those seven perfect years we had together – more real to me now than the minor events of these last days and weeks.

Oh Henry, I see you so clearly today. There's a closeness that has been so elusive in these intervening years. I feel your presence and my heart leaps with joy. Fifty-three years is such a very long time to be without you. I have missed you so, my Darling. And now I am so very, very tired. Come for me soon, won't you?

Oh – I hear you now, whispering back to me those precious words you wrote just for me:

> *Sleep, darling, sleep, the shades are falling,*
> *The midnight chimes are softly calling;*
> *The winds and waves have gone to rest,*
> *Sleep, darling, on thy husband's breast;*
> *While angels still their watches keep,*
> *Sleep darling, on my bosom sleep.*
>
> *Sleep, darling, sleep, the stars are shining,*
> *The flowers are in their rest reclining;*
> *The stream of time in silence flows,*
> *No sound shall break thy sweet repose;*
> *The angels round their watches keep,*
> *Sleep, darling, on my bosom sleep.*

Epilogue

Here the diaries end.

In 1966, the staff at Bathampton Manor informed the family that Grace's memory was failing and that they could no longer provide the kind of care she needed.

Meanwhile, in the USA John had found a businessman apparently willing to invest in the pipes, with a factory prepared to produce them. The project proved merely a tax dodge, however, and their production put on hold. Once again, they found themselves without work or income. But in the end, the owner of the factory was so impressed by John's graciousness that he manufactured just enough pipes for John and Karis's personal use. This was their lifeline. They wrote their own teach-yourself and music books, and taught the pipes as part of the University of California Los Angeles extension programme. They also formed a small private music school of their own. Though they managed to make ends meet, even buying a small house on Amalfi Drive overlooking the Pacific Ocean, finances were too tight for them ever to return to the UK. Grace was right. She never saw John and his family again.

Paul and Jean took her back to Manchester, where Paul was now Ecumenical Officer for the Diocese, initially to live with them, but after a month they realised that she required the constant nursing care of a dedicated nursing home. They found the perfect place in the lovely surroundings of the Peak District, not too far from them. Whenever they visited she knew them, and was always gracious, considerate and grateful to them for coming. Thinking she was still in Bath she would say, 'Goodness, you've come all this way to see me. How kind.'

She died only a few months later, in 1967 – another of her special years with the number seven in it; a strange irony, though she, of course, was not to know it.

To the very end she would sit in her chair, upright and dignified, her white curls swept up into a topknot, fingering the cameo Henry had given her, which was fastened to the front of a ruffled collar that framed a face still bearing the faint traces of its former beauty. She read Henry's poems and letters to herself over and over again, and as she did so her face would light up and she would once more become the young woman passionately in love with the only man who ever visited her in her dreams. In the seven years they had together, Henry had provided her with enough romance and passion to last the remainder of her ninety years.

In her eyes he had never left her. 'Even now,' he once wrote, 'softly fall the whispers of the departed, as they stand in the cloudless light on the other side of death's dark portal, saying, "We wait for you here – we love you still."'

Notes

1. 'The survival of the fittest' is a reference to the radical new theories of Charles Darwin, who became the *bête noire* of much of the evangelical movement for challenging its views on creation. Impossible not to see Grace's wry humour here.

2. At the turn of the nineteenth century the King's printers in England, Scotland and Ireland, and the universities of Oxford and Cambridge, had a monopoly on production of the Bible. Samuel Bagster, the publisher, determined to meet the need for an accessible, inexpensive version, discovered that Bibles with printed notes were exempt from this restriction. So in 1816 he produced a Bible with over 60,000 parallel references, most selected and all verified by himself. It became hugely popular with evangelicals for well over a century.

3. For many anecdotes about Ruth and Arthur I am indebted to Margaret Surie for her memoirs of her grandmother entitled *Grandmother's Tracks*, which she published for her family under the name of Margaret Fisher. It is available online from Lulu.com.

4. Arthur H. Habershon, head teacher of White Rock Preparatory School for Young Gentlemen, and honorary superintendent of the St Leonards Railway Mission on Portland Street (a church dedicated to the moral, physical and social welfare of railway employees), was, according to the many references to him in the *Hastings and St Leonards Observer*, 'a well-known evangelist and temperance worker', 'a prominent and popular personality', and even 'a Hastings favourite'. A local celebrity, he and his wife Edith were on countless committees and he preached regularly to congregations of over a thousand, occasionally accompanied by 'Miss B. Hurditch on her zither'.

    After their move to London in 1900, the Habershons began to move in a rather exalted evangelical circle that included the Lords Radstock and Kinnaird.

5. Arthur Kinnaird, 11th Baron Kinnaird, was football's first superstar, the best player of his day. He played in nine FA Cup Finals (a record to this day) and was President of the Football Association for thirty-three years. Under his leadership football became Britain's favourite national sport. He was also a Cambridge University tennis blue, university fives and swimming champion, and played competitive cricket past his fiftieth birthday.

Like Lords Radstock and Shaftesbury he was an evangelical Christian and consummate philanthropist, giving away most of his banking fortune to social causes near to his heart. Lord Kinnaird chaired many national bodies and missions such as the YMCA, and was Lord High Commissioner to the General Assembly of the Church of Scotland. He lost two sons in the First World War which led to the title becoming defunct.

6. In an interview regarding his world tour, published upon his return in February 1909. The *Daily News* was a national daily newspaper founded by Charles Dickens, and owned from 1901 by George Cadbury, the chocolate manufacturer.

7. Courtesy of The University of Liverpool Special Collections and Archives.

8. In his biography, *Reminiscences of Sport and War* (Eyre and Spottiswood, London, 1939, pp. 229–30).

9. Stanley Fisher had a room on the same floor as the poet Wystan Auden. They used to have long arguments into the night on religious matters, as Stanley endeavoured to restore Auden to the Anglican fold, when his mother's Anglo-Catholic ritualism had left him disillusioned. Stanley, it appears, succeeded.

10. Harry and Annie Guinness's eldest daughter Gene had married Ian Mackenzie, the son of their oldest friends. The marriage was a disaster from the start and they separated soon after Karis was born, to the shock of both sets of parents and their social circle, where marriage breakdown simply did not happen. After years of travel abroad and constant womanising, Ian appeared at Brickwall when John was there recuperating, to ask for a divorce. Gene, who had become a Roman Catholic, stood at the top of the stairs, shouting at him that she would never sign the divorce papers and accusing him of giving her syphilis. Ian never got his divorce.

11. Sylvia Pankhurst was a rebellious, left-wing suffragette, who went her own way and became a founder member of the Communist Party. During the First World War and in the 1920s she wrote and lectured widely on the interests of women caught in the poverty trap. Grace and Ruth were no doubt sympathetic to her views. In 1927, at the age of 45, she had given birth to a son and was shunned by her mother, Emmeline Pankhurst, for refusing to marry the father, her long-term partner. By the 1930s Sylvia was committed to promoting peace, fighting fascism, assisting Jewish refugees and supporting Spanish republicans.

12. It is unimpaired. Peter, my husband, has seen to that, and has added the names of his own parents, Paul (buried in Ibiza) and Jean (whose ashes lie there), to the monument.

13. *The Gospel as a Thriller* by The Bishop of Chelmsford. Used by the permission of the *Daily Mail*.

14. The Marshall Plan was an American initiative to help Europe back on its feet after World War II. The United States gave $13 billion (worth

approximately $130 billion today) in economic support to help rebuild European economies.

15. It was Stanley who reintroduced W.H. Auden to Christopher Isherwood, in 1925. Isherwood had been his elder brother George's fag at Repton. A fag was a junior boy who acted as servant to a senior boy at a British public school and was often mistreated or abused by him. Isherwood, however, later portrayed George Fisher as the unusually kindly Ponds in his autobiography *Lions and Shadows*. Auden and Isherwood had a fairly public on-off relationship for several years. *Ambassador of Loss* was illustrated by B.H. Surie, a pupil at Bryanston School, who was sent to Stanley Fisher, the chaplain, for swearing. Stanley nurtured Surie's artistic talents, and Surie later married Stanley's daughter, Margaret, whom he met in the chaplain's home.

16. The King quoted from 'God Knows' by Minnie Louise Haskins, part of a collection called *The Desert*, published in 1908. Princess Elizabeth gave a copy to her father, George VI, which he used in his Christmas broadcast.

17. George Bell, Bishop of Chichester, was probably the most high-profile bishop in the country, having challenged the government during the war over its policy of blanket area bombing. In 1944, when Archbishop of Canterbury William Temple died after only two years in that post, Bell was considered a leading possibility to succeed him, but bishops were chosen ultimately by the Prime Minister, and Winston Churchill strongly disapproved of Bell's speeches against his policy. Bell, who was a friend of Dietrich Bonhoeffer, was a natural patron for Paul's work of reconciliation at the YMCA.

18. Karle Wilson Baker, 1878–1960, Texas's most celebrated female poet in the first half of the twentieth century. Every effort has been made to find out who holds the copyright, but I have been unable to do so.

Acknowledgements

Many, many thanks to Chloe Wordsworth and Anthea Guinness for all their lovely childhood memories of 'Little Granny', Long Dene School, and their parents' subsequent wanderings.

Also to Jo Giles, Margaret Surie's daughter, for information about *Grandmother's Tracks*, the story of her great grandmother, Ruth Fisher, and for the photographs of Charles Hurditch and Arthur and Ruth.

To Ian Metcalfe at Hodder & Stoughton for encouraging me to hunt for the missing pieces to Grace's life, and to Hodder's enthusiastic editorial team.

To Julian Farnham, ably assisted by his wife Suzanna, whose proof reading is second to none. What would I have done without the gift of your time?

To Gilly King, History and Heritage Advisor at the University of Roehampton, for information on Whitelands College.

And to Kate Hawke, Library Assistant, Special Collections and Archives, University of Liverpool Library for information about St Aidan's College and for her discovery of *The Weaker Sex* by 'G.G.G' – much to her surprise.

I am so grateful too to those who, as I have been writing, have allowed me to bend their ears with endless tales of my husband's unusual grandmother, and have given me the gift of their forbearance, enthusiasm and encouragement, with or without seeing the text – Margaret Humbert-Droz, John Guinness, and Pauline Jackson.

And to my family, who always bear the brunt of my writing excitement, not to mention the frustrations and the pain!

Especially Peter, who unfailingly listens, advises, explains, and finds the right word. And goes without my company, not to mention my cooking, for long chunks of his now retirement. And, of course, for making me part of a remarkable family that has provided me with such an endless fund of fascination and inspiration.